Islam in the Digital Age

Critical Studies on Islam
Series Editors: Azza Karam and Ziauddin Sardar

Islam is a complex, ambiguous term. Conventionally it has been used to describe religion, history, culture, civilisation and worldview of Muslims. But it is also impregnated with stereotypes and postmodern notions of identity and boundaries. The diversity of Muslim peoples, cultures, and interpretations, with their baggage of colonial history and postcolonial present, has transformed Islam into a powerful global force.

This unique series presents a far-reaching, critical perspective on Islam. It analyses the diversity and complexity of Islam through the eyes of people who live by it. Provocative and thoughtful works by established as well as younger scholars will examine Islamic movements, the multilayered questions of Muslim identity, the transnational trends of political Islam, the spectre of ethnic conflict, the political economy of Muslim societies and the impact of Islam and Muslims on the West.

The series is built around two fundamental questions. How are Muslims living, thinking and breathing Islam? And how are they rethinking and reformulating it and shaping and reshaping the global agendas and discourses?

As Critical Studies on Islam seeks to bridge the gap between academia and decision making environments, it will be of particular value to policy makers, politicians, journalists and activists, as well as academics.

Azza Karam is the Director of the Women's Programme at the World Conference on Religion and Peace, New York. She has published extensively on development, conflict, gender and democratisation issues. She is also author of *Islamism, State and Women* and co-author of *Islam in a non-Polarized Society*.

Ziauddin Sardar is a well-known writer, broadcaster and cultural critic. A Visiting Professor of Postcolonial Studies at City University, London, he is considered a pioneering writer on Islam. He is the author of several books for Pluto Press, most recently *Postmodernism and the Other*.

Critical Studies on Islam

Series Editors: Azza Karam (Director of the Women's Programme at the World Conference on Religion and Peace, New York) and Ziauddin Sardar (Visiting Professor of Postcolonial Studies at City University, London)

Also available:

Iraqi Invasion of Kuwait
Religion, Identity and Otherness in the Analysis of War and Conflict
Hamdi A. Hassan

Transnational Political Islam
Globalization, Ideology and Power
Edited by Azza Karam

Hizbu'llah
Politics and Religion
Amal Saad-Ghorayeb

Islam in the Digital Age

E-Jihad, Online Fatwas and Cyber Islamic Environments

Gary R. Bunt

Pluto Press

LONDON • STERLING, VIRGINIA

First published 2003 by Pluto Press
345 Archway Road, London N6 5AA
and 22883 Quicksilver Drive, Sterling, VA 20166-2012, USA

www.plutobooks.com

British Library Cataloguing in Publication Data
A catalogue record for this book is available from
the British Library

ISBN 0 7453 2099 6 hardback
ISBN 0 7453 2098 8 paperback

Library of Congress Cataloging in Publication Data
Bunt, Gary R.
    Islam in the digital age : e-jihad, online fatwas and cyber Islamic
environments / Gary R. Bunt.
        p. cm.
Includes bibliographical references.
    ISBN 0–7453–2099–6 — ISBN 0–7453–2098–8 (pbk.)
    1. Islam—Computer network resources. 2. Jihad. 3. Fatwas. I. Title.
    BP40.5 .B86 2003
    297'.0285—dc21   2003004706

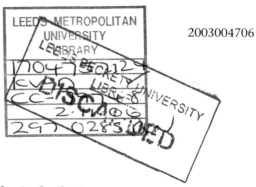

10   9   8   7   6   5   4   3   2   1

Designed and produced for Pluto Press by
Chase Publishing Services, Fortescue, Sidmouth, EX10 9QG, England
Typeset from disk by Stanford DTP Services, Towcester, England
Printed and bound in the European Union by
Antony Rowe, Chippenham and Eastbourne, England

For Yvonne, Kane and Tony

Contents

Acknowledgements

The completion of this book would not have been possible without the help of a number of people.

The support of many colleagues and students at the University of Wales, Lampeter, has been welcomed. Neal Robinson read through early draft material and provided valuable comments. I am grateful to the organisers of various events for providing opportunities for aspects of this research to be presented, including conferences and workshops at, or organised by staff at, the University of Antwerp, University of Copenhagen, University of Leeds, Duke University, London School of Economics, Université Lumière Lyon 2, University of Surrey and University of Sussex. I have appreciated dialogues with the Muslim Networks Consortium, in particular miriam cooke and Bruce B. Lawrence at Duke University. The support of PRS-LTSN in enabling me to facilitate a paper and colloquium on *Teaching Islam after 9–11* in 2002 is acknowledged. Many people have discussed aspects of this research with me (on- and off-line), and I have welcomed their comments. Thanks also to the editors and the team at Pluto Press.

Finally, my wife Yvonne provided indefatigable and sympathetic encouragement during the research and writing of *Islam in the Digital Age*. Kane Richard gave his unique form of editorial input. Other members of my family, particularly my parents Betty and Derek, and Tony, as always provided support and assistance.

Despite the valuable input of the above, the contents and shortcomings of this book remain wholly the writer's responsibility.

Gary R. Bunt
Lampeter

1 Introduction

The writer's computer crashed completely whilst this chapter was being drafted. Some might interpret this as a sign of critical Divine Providence, although it was in fact a computer virus, something of an occupational hazard (the writer's firewall has since been updated). Internet and e-mail access became impossible. The writer, insulated in his office in west Wales, had lost contact with friends, colleagues and the sources of information usually consulted on a daily basis.

Given his research area, he considered what would happen if 'Islam', Muslims and Islamic organisations lost their computer access: the Qur'an and other Islamic sources would not be lost forever. It would *not* be like the consequences of a battle after the death of Muhammad in 632, when so many individuals who had memorised the Qur'an were killed that concerns were raised about the preservation of the sacred text, and according to tradition a decision was made to produce a 'definitive' collection of the various texts: without the Internet, Islam as a religion may not lose anything that is intrinsic or central to beliefs. There would still be a *hajj* pilgrimage, although it might be organised differently without computers. There would still be prayers, although the calculation of timings might in some contexts revert to traditional methods. There would still be *zakah*, the annual tithe on Muslims, although some authorities would have problems without their accounting software. Scholars would still talk to one another and questions would still be asked, but the answers would be less immediate for some, and anonymity would be less ensured. In effect, Islam does not need computers; in many parts of the 'Muslim world', Islam is practised without computer interfaces or the use of a mouse, and the Internet may remain a rumour or a luxury in the hands of an elite.

So, why write about Islam and the Internet? Well, although Islam as a religion would function effectively, a substantial minority of Muslims and Islamic organisations would be bereft of their significant propagation and networking tool, unable to dialogue, research and disseminate their message to followers or to interested (Muslim and other) observers. Some would be bound by the shackles of state

1

censorship, unable to access other forms of media, and restricted in the forms of local and global contact and dialogue facilitated through the Internet. Sermons would continue to be circulated, perhaps in print, by fax or cassette, but their immediacy would be lost. Decisions on points of interpretation and reactions to current events would become restricted in their diffusion. Individuals whose international status has been enhanced through the medium, even though they are unrecognised or seen as pariahs by some local authorities, would return to their restricted local networks and a relative obscurity. Some observers would suggest that such a development would not necessarily be a bad one, and indeed they would encourage the creation of barriers to knowledge and dissemination around such individuals and organisations.

In the post-11 September 2001 climate, overt and covert efforts have been made to facilitate such restrictions – although there is also a consciousness that the Internet is in fact a window (forgive the term) into aspects of the 'Muslim world' and consciousness, which other forms of intelligence-gathering are unable to acquire. Whilst activism and Islamic activities (the two are not synonymous) were significant features of the Internet before September 2001, since that time they have acquired a new urgency and immediacy. The prolif-eration of Islamic websites, chat rooms, e-mail lists and other related media activity – including expressions of beliefs and the articulation of agendas – was a phenomenon heralding a maturity of Cyber Islamic Environments.

This is not to suggest that there was a lack of sophistication before that time; indeed, the extensive application of the Internet as a means of projecting Muslim authority and disseminating religious opinions represents a long-term and technologically adept integration of religious symbolism and traditional notions of power, wrapped up in a 56k modem and sent in digital packets on uncharted and twisted routes across the world. Measuring such activities and their impact is problematic; one scale might be to ask local imams and mosque leaders whether they would 'miss' the Internet. Some might feel more secure without it: how many in their community no longer came to them for advice, preferring a Google search or a visit to an online scholar? Others might wonder where Friday's sermon might come from as they drew upon the media for inspiration, downloaded a pre-written sermon from an affiliated superior authority elsewhere in the world, or searched an online Qur'an or hadith database for a tricky, half-remembered quotation. Some activists, seeking to synchronise the contents of sermons or discussions with their colleagues networked across the globe, would have to resort to more conventional channels of communication. Again, we may be talking about a minority, albeit a disproportionately influential one. The majority would retain their traditional, non-electronic connection with religious opinion and authority. Some scholars would suggest that this is not a bad thing: too many questions can distort beliefs. An analogy might be the physicians challenged by patients brandishing Internet opinions about treatments and diagnoses, wishing that these sources would suddenly disappear. Casual searching on the web will reveal a variety of opinions and dialogues about Islam to an interested Muslim, whilst her library shelf may contain only a copy of a Qur'an (that in itself would be seen as 'sufficient' by many!).

The tendency to set off alarm bells about the Internet is not just associated with Islam, although a number of authorities and individuals have sought to challenge or negate its influence. For external observers, the combination of the Internet and Islam with such terms as jihad or *fatwa* may be seen as a provocative or sensationalising strategy. However, this detracts from the fact that it is these two areas that have seen a most significant integration of electronic activity with religion. By discussing these themes, it may also be possible to defuse the alarmist tendencies and realistically posit a rational analysis and discussion that does not incorporate fear of the Internet or fear of Islam.

Finding appropriate models to follow in this journey can be difficult: the writer has always been struck by two very different, but significant, writers about Islam and Muslims, Ibn Battuta and Edward W. Lane. In idle moments, he has speculated how they might have reacted to time spent in Cyber Islamic Environments.

Ibn Battuta was a great explorer and recorder of the Muslim world in the fourteenth century (Common Era), venturing into regions that had been obscured by distance and history, traversing dangerous roads and ultimately writing about what he saw. A scholar of Islamic law, Ibn Battuta's book *al-Rihla* became the key guide for future travellers over the centuries and was translated into many languages. Would he have produced a guide to cyberspace or dismissed it as an irrelevance? Could it have given him an understanding of the diversity of Muslim expression, and to what extent would it have been an equivalent to its real-world manifestation?

Edward W. Lane, by contrast, lived in nineteenth-century Cairo, recording the manners and activities of Egyptians – including their religious understandings and belief patterns – and was significant in introducing many facets of Islam to his English-speaking audience for the first time, in a rational and non-sensationalistic manner, as well as recording their utterances and developing detailed Arabic–English dictionaries. This translation of statement and experience was a key to Islam for later scholars.[1] Again, the writer's contemplation of Lane's possible reaction to cyberspace engages him: would he have 'lurked' in a chat room, attempting to blend into his surroundings as he did on occasion in Cairo? How would he have recorded and chosen the sites, and how would the diffuse conceptual frameworks have manifested themselves on the page?

Both authors are no doubt rotating in their celestial havens at the thought of being integrated into such a discussion, and despite some aspirations, it is not the intention of this writer to endeavour to emulate such esteemed and influential individuals. The point of this diversion is to highlight the point that those 'traditional' Islamic landscapes and environments in contemporary contexts must be recorded and analysed, but if a holistic contemporary understanding of Islam is sought, then part of that interpretative process has to include (even as a small proportion of an overall picture) a discussion about the Internet. This present book is a modest contribution, or a single pixel, in a substantial, high-resolution screen of knowledge.

DEFINING CYBER ISLAMIC ENVIRONMENTS

Cyber Islamic Environments have the potential to transform aspects of religious understanding and expression within Muslim contexts, and the power to enable elements within Muslim populations in minority and majority arenas to dialogue (not necessarily amicably) with each other. In conjunction with traditional forms of knowledge and media about Islam, access to (and perhaps ownership of) the Internet has become a significant element of propagation and identity for Muslim individuals and organisations. The changes may be subtle rather than overt. A complex spectrum of access, dialogue, networking and application of the media associated with Cyber Islamic Environments emerges. Like the Internet itself, this spectrum is not one that can easily be classified or systemised, and does not fit neat categorisation models.

A broad range of Muslim expressions can be located online. This writer has discussed elsewhere the religious and political factors influencing the development of Internet access within Muslim contexts.[2] In particular, the pronouncements by 'authorities' on the Islamic legitimacy (or not) of the Internet have combined with political strategies, often articulated utilising religious 'values' and concepts, which have sought to engineer specific forms of what are described by this writer as Cyber Islamic Environments, an umbrella term which can refer to a variety of contexts, perspectives and applications of the media by those who define themselves as Muslims. These may contain elements of specific Muslim worldviews and notions of exclusivity, combined with regional and cultural understandings of the media and its validity. These pronouncements have often been tempered with a realism, which recognises a need to have a voice in cyberspace in order to propagate values and views within the information marketplace.

The development of online *khutbahs*, or sermons, either transmitted 'live' or recorded and uploaded onto websites, has extended the audiences for several imams. Specific interpretations of Islam, justifying political and religious actions, can also be located online and are frequently updated. They can contain news, chat and networking opportunities that go beyond the traditional ideological and religious frames of reference of many organisations. Frequently, these are networked to other platforms operating similar sites on related issues.

The writer has received responses from some readers, who have reservations about the term Cyber Islamic Environments 'inappropriately' relating to some 'Islamic' perspectives, or for the writer not criticising the application of the Internet by some 'Muslim platforms'. It is stressed here that the intention again is to 'delineate the Islamic Internet landscape'.[3] This is seen as a significant task in its own right, given the dramatic changes that have taken place within cyberspace and the real world since *Virtually Islamic* was published in 2000. Rather than simply updating that volume, this book intends to explore some of the key issues it raised in a greater depth, with the benefit of having discussed these elements with a variety of interested parties, both on- and off-line, and having continued to publish reactions and analyses in the interim period.

The evolution of using the Internet as an 'Islamic tool' has been observed in a relatively compressed historical period, and it may be only with the passage of time for an appropriate perspective for the full picture to be realised. One significant issue and problem for future research in this area is that little has been archived or recorded to date, and that sites emerge and disappear with regularity. The archiving issue is a critical one for studying Cyber Islamic Environments; this writer has made a modest effort to archive sites he writes about, although clearly it is not possible to visit every site on a regular basis, given that there are so many activities to observe in cyberspace. This is reflected in the book, which cannot offer a *scientific* analysis of web traffic, visitors, page updates and usage of sites, but can offer a commentary on significant changes in relation to content and ideas expressed on the Internet, and developments which are significant religiously, socially and politically.

The term 'Internet' in this book refers to the connected network of computers and other electronic communications tools, through which diverse forms of electronic communications and media can be facilitated. The 'web', or World Wide Web (WWW), can be defined as:

> A global Web of interconnected pages which (ideally) can be read with any computer with a Web browser and Internet connection. More technically and specifically, the WWW is the global Web of interlinked files which can be located using the HTTP protocol.[4]

The focus of the present volume is on Islam and the World Wide Web, although that term can seamlessly flow into other elements of the medium. The term 'cyberspace' is utilised when discussing the Internet, being the electronic, amorphous territory navigated or surfed through the use of a browser (such as Internet Explorer, Netscape or Opera) across the Internet.

The origins of the writer's interest in the subject are associated with approaches to Islamic knowledge and expression, and how methods of communication have adjusted and influenced forms of dialogue and self-understanding, in local, regional and global contexts. This has some linkage with cyber-cultural studies, although the writer's approach is based more deliberately in the area of phenomenology and the study of religions: symbolism, authority, diversity, experience and expression are key 'filters' for the writer when observing Cyber Islamic Environments. Other writers may select different avenues and methodologies to explore these elements of cyberspace, contributing to a developing field. The appropriate intellectual tools and rarefied conceptual frameworks may emerge within such studies. However, the current book seeks to describe and discuss essential features and observations, perhaps contributing to future analytical arguments that have had the luxury of historical perspective and resources in order to facilitate them.

One issue that surprised the writer is that the subject held a wider appeal than the Religious Studies and Islamic Studies framework it emerged from, but that there were also occasional conflicting (and unrealistic) methodological expectations from those in other disciplines. The present volume holds those expectations in mind, but still aims at the informed, general reader with an interest in Islam and the Internet. It should be stressed early on that a *complete* analysis of Cyber Islamic Environments is a task beyond the single writer and his resources, especially given the radical expansion in the number of websites, e-mail lists, chat rooms and other forms of electronic communication; there is a substantial increase in languages other than English being applied on the Internet, and this is reflected in the discussion where possible. It is hoped that future research can be encouraged, to embrace languages that cannot fully be represented in this volume. The writer has started to network with interested academics and commentators worldwide, in an effort to encourage such research and resources, with a view to publishing findings in a future volume.

Despite the relatively low levels of access and availability of the Internet in many Muslim contexts, the medium has been drawn upon by governments, organisations and individuals, both as a means of articulating views to domestic audiences, as well as networking and propagating views for international readership. Some sites are focused entirely on small cultural, political or religious groups, rather than general audiences. Unique forms of access to readers can be acquired, thus transcending conventional communication networks and opening up new opportunities for dialogue and dissemination. Whilst English has been seen as a primary Internet language and has been applied extensively, the Muslim Internet arena has been affected by the substantial growth in online Arabic language materials, together with the development of extensive resources in other languages. Questions may be asked as to levels of readership or how these materials influence societies and individuals.

The emphasis in this volume is on observation of the phenomena associated with two key aspects of Cyber Islamic Environments, surround the notions of jihad and *fatwas*. There was some contact with individuals associated with some of the websites, but the nature of others (combined with their writers' personal security concerns, and perhaps this writer's too) did not engender an appropriate climate for wideranging e-mail interviews. The post-11 September climate was not one in which such activities could take place, and this remains an ambition for a future volume rather than a realistic outcome for the present book.

ACCESSING CYBER ISLAMIC ENVIRONMENTS

Technology for surfing the World Wide Web will become cheaper, and the availability of alternative interfaces may offer improved access both in and outside urbanised areas in the Muslim world(s). Such access is related to the availability of telephone lines (at present), and several Muslim majority nations plan to improve services.[5] The extent to which this will open up the web for underrepresented groups in Muslim contexts is open to question. It will, for example, be interesting to observe the impact (if any) on Muslim women and their self-expression online. The UN Development Fund for Women (UNIFEM) noted that the Internet had increased activism opportunities for Muslim women, but that only 4 per cent of Internet users in the Arab world were women.[6] The gender digital divide in Muslim contexts is a significant area for future research and observation. There is clearly a 'market' for content aimed specifically at Muslim women on the Internet: a notable example is the Pakistani scholar Farhat Hashmi placing her sermons and commentaries of the Qur'an online in her al-Huda website, including lectures made during a tour of Dubai in Ramadan 1423 AH (2002 CE).[7] Questions might have to be raised of how 'different' such a site's content is from the 'traditional' male equivalent's site.

The growing availability of Arabic browsers and page creation tools will lead to a rapid expansion of sites, including those with Islamic identities. It has been estimated that Internet penetration in the 'Arab world', for example, will increase from 3.5 million in 2001 to 30 million people in 2005.[8] The growth in demand for computer hardware in the Middle East has been measured as against the global trend, with a market growth rate of 20 per cent (excluding the United Arab Emirates, at 28 per cent).[9] Although this may still be a relatively marginal figure in comparison with the population of the region, it illustrates a growing availability of and interest in computers. This pattern may be reflected in other areas and linguistic groups. The expansion of technological knowledge *may* increase the diversity of Islamic content online and improve the presentation quality of sites.

Whilst there may at present be a 'digital divide' between a minority of Internet users and others, the medium is sufficiently relevant for it to be the focus of concern, particularly in relation to how political and religious concepts are discussed, depicted and 'exported' to a (potential) global audience. Internet access, discussed in the *United Nations Human Development Report 2001*, indicates low levels and availability within non-'western' contexts.[10] Such statistics are problematic on a number of levels, in particular when discussing Cyber Islamic Environments, in that there is no specific source relating directly to 'Muslim' levels of access. If the descriptor 'Muslim' is applied within the context of those nation states with Muslim majority populations, then the following statistics provide indicators of the levels of access available in the year 2000 (the most recent analysis at the time of writing): Turkey had 2.5 Internet hosts per 1,000 of the population, Malaysia 2.4, Lebanon 2.3, Oman 1.4, Kyrgyzstan 1.1, Kazakhstan 0.6, Saudi Arabia and Turkmenistan had 0.3, Jordan, Senegal and Indonesia 0.2, Albania, Egypt, Morocco, Pakistan, Tajikistan and Syria 0.1; Bangladesh and Sudan 0.0; while Yemen, Iran, Tunisia, Algeria, Uzbekistan and Libya were unclassified (for a variety of reasons). There was no reference to Bosnia. Palestine was not listed, although Israel had an index of 43.2; the highest Arab Muslim level of Internet hosts was the United Arab Emirates, with 20.9 hosts per 1,000 people. By comparison, the highest rates of Internet hosts per 1,000 people were registered in Finland (200.2), followed by Norway (193.6), the United States (179.1), New Zealand (146.7) and the Netherlands (136.0).[11] The population of 'Arab states' as Internet users was estimated at 0.6 per cent (compared with a world percentage of 6.7 per cent, and a US use level of 54.3 per cent).[12] Elsewhere, in 1999 it was estimated that 3–4 per cent of Turkish people and less than 0.5 per cent of the Pakistan population were Internet users.[13]

The report suggests that the 'digital divide' is not only between nations, but within them, and that there can be broad discrepancies between and within regions.[14] Diversity of usage and patterns of access are influenced by a number of regional and cultural factors. The cost of using the Internet is an obvious factor influencing these levels, but may not be the only one. Mohamed A. El-Nawawy, in a discussion about the use of the Internet in Egypt, suggests a number of possible deterrents to the growth in the medium's usage, and that it is 'lower than its arithmetic and logical pro-rata share' compared with other Arab states. However, he does

not believe that infrastructure, individual income, language or
cultures are necessarily primary deterrents:

> The primary deterrent for Internet users' growth in Egypt is an
> individual awareness and education factor.[15]

Another important factor is the importance of 'the relationship
between the government, the ISPs [Internet Service Providers], and
the telecommunications service providers' in the development of
Internet services.[16]

Even if individuals have access to the Internet (particularly in terms
of many of the sites discussed in this book, whose content often
emerges from 'western' Muslim authors), questions emerge relating
to the constituency of readers. There are a number of unanswered
questions, such as how those individuals who may describe
themselves as 'Muslim' actually use the Internet. Do they visit Cyber
Islamic Environments, and, if so, with what levels of frequency?

Indicators may be gleaned from the observations in this book, but
substantial questions of this type require highly resourced scientific
fieldwork, together with levels of access and confidence in the
constituent communities of readers and users that may be difficult
or impossible to obtain. The anonymity of the Internet raises issues
in this regard, with readers cloaking their own identities and also
their locations (for example, through 'anonymiser' software). Despite
these factors, what *can* be seen is that something significant and
unique is occurring in cyberspace in relation to Islam and Muslims,
and that the medium has been drawn upon by substantial numbers
(albeit from certain cultural, political, religious and demographic
perspectives) in order to articulate and discuss issues which are
deemed 'Islamic' in nature.

Clearly, there are other diversions for Muslims in cyberspace, and
indeed a rapidly increasing choice of Islamic materials is on offer
too. Islamic pages that simply reproduce what is available to hear
within a local mosque may not be particularly relevant to an
urbanised surfer. However, exposure to new ideas and concepts, or
even radical notions of Islamic identity and articulation, would seem
to have a place online. Pages that have dynamic designs, applying
intelligent use of HTML (hypertext mark-up language), XML and
other page-making tools, can offer provocative interactive 'Islamic'
experiences that are deemed 'attractive' by their readership. The 'most
visited' Islamic sites often provide online experiences comparable

with the major players on the World Wide Web, drawing on the principles of intelligent intuitive design and ease of navigation in order to convey their message.

Some Islamic sites are at the cutting edge of technological application, and governments, organisations and individuals have invested substantial time and capital in acquiring the skills and technologies required to present themselves on the web to their greatest advantage. Some sites may have professional staff, although dedicated volunteers produce others. There is demonstration of substantial knowledge in the technology, with a minority of players also becoming adept at encryption, evasion, disruption and 'hacking'-related activities. It is not suggested here that these are necessarily the same individuals who are creating the 'most visited' Islamic sites, and indeed there are different skills and agendas at work through the medium, as will be demonstrated in this book.

Muslim political expression online forms part of the dialogue about Islamic identities. Some ideologues make little distinction between 'religion' and 'politics' in Islam. The Internet has not superseded traditional forms of political expression, but is a means through which conventional boundaries and barriers can be transcended. Opposition voices creating websites outside the direct influence of governments have propagated their perspectives through channels that are difficult to censor or block. The investment by some governments in filtering and censoring technologies led to an increase in the ingenuity of opposition platforms. The hacking and cracking of systems have been integrated into some forms of political activism, at both individual and group levels, notably by pro-Palestinian supporters (themselves from a variety of backgrounds and with different levels of technological abilities) attacking what they perceive as targets representative or supportive of Israel. This issue is discussed in depth in Chapter 3.

Questions may emerge as to whether these activists and/or sites are 'Islamic' or 'Muslim' in nature, and how they are identified, interpreted and challenged by a diverse global readership.[17] The skill of their designers in enhancing an organisation's online profile, for example through effective use of web design tools or multi-media, can even exaggerate the importance or profile of an organisation. Conversely, a poor site may have a negative impact on an organisation's profile – perhaps with other implications, such as reduced influence and attendant funding (especially where organisations have opportunities for readers to donate to their causes).

The notion of an 'online e-jihad', if the term jihad is defined within its militaristic sense, may suggest that using the sword of HTML can be more effective for some organisations than the use of a Kalashnikov. This online jihad activity could be low-level hacking or cracking by affiliates or supporters (formal or informal) of an organisation or perspective; it could be major disruptive activities, such as attacking Internet infrastructures or compromising major servers; it could also be through the rapid dissemination of propaganda. A good example of the latter was in 2000: the shooting of a young boy, Muhammad al-Durra, by the Israeli Defence Forces quickly appeared on the World Wide Web. Traumatic film of the youth's death was immediately highlighted on major Islamic e-mailing lists and featured on many websites, having a 'shelf-life' beyond its original place in broadcast news schedules.[18] This augmented other media coverage and enabled organisations to place their own interpretation and analysis of the film. The film, and images from it, maintained a currency and continue to feature on a variety of sites supportive of the Palestinian cause (not all operating from an 'Islamic' perspective).

The issue of Internet censorship has become contentious in relation to the expression of Islam. Some 'Muslim' majority governments seek limitations on access, whilst some Islamic platforms seek to circumvent censorship of their own materials (whilst occasionally protesting about the content of other areas of the Internet). The non-governmental organisation Human Rights Watch reported on the ways this has been done within Middle Eastern and North African contexts, and how some regional authorities had attempted to control access, content and utility of the Internet.[19] The report made a number of recommendations, including demands for the international rights of freedom of expression, facilitation of affordable access to the Internet, the control of censoring mechanisms, reducing ISP liability for page content, availability of page encryption for individual users, rights to privacy unimpaired by government surveillance, and the right to communicate and surf anonymously.[20] There is limited evidence to suggest that there has been any advance in these 'rights' within Muslim contexts, and indeed it is possible that whilst access levels have increased, so have the mechanisms or potential applications to control access and use of the Internet.

The projection of 'religious authority' via the Internet may be associated with governmental perspectives on religion or from sources not necessarily fixed within a geographical or cultural-linguistic framework. Muslim organisations or 'authorities' may not identify themselves with national geopolitical borders or frames of reference. 'Authorities' themselves may not be recognised within national geopolitical borders, and at times can even be ostracised. Some countries prefer to have 'official' religious websites.

Websites associated with diverse notions of Islamic authority have been dominated by English-language content, although the 2001–2 period saw a profusion of new Arabic and other language content. Whether this represents a challenge to the influence of the pronouncements originating from minority contexts is open to question, especially given the fluidity of site identities and interconnectivity between organisations and individuals. Having said that, areas and organisations, which were not traditional centres of scholarship or Muslim authority, entered the information marketplace with the advent of the Internet, and perhaps are themselves influencing traditional regions of Islamic learning. *Virtually Islamic* explored how this presented a number of challenges to traditional authority: the 'qualifications' of a scholar can be fluid, with ownership of an *ijazza* (degree from an Islamic university) not necessarily being a prerequisite for being an online authority.

The area of authority has also been one of interest to Islamic interests and centres with an interest in *da'wa*, particularly Saudi Arabia. The Internet offers individual or minority views an opportunity to present themselves to a wide audience internationally, if they have access to the appropriate technology; sermons can be broadcast in 'live' or recorded formats, or transcribed and circulated by e-mail, discussion rooms and the web. What makes a website 'authoritative' and 'Islamic' is a key question to consider, particularly for readers who may not be familiar with the nuances and various shades of meaning that exist between diverse Muslim interests.[21] This issue is approached in Chapter 7's discussion on online *fatwas*.

ANALYSING CYBER ISLAMIC ENVIRONMENTS

Acquiring knowledge about the relevance of the Internet in Muslim frameworks requires the methodological integration of traditional Islamic Studies-related disciplinary approaches with new techniques required to analyse cyberspace. Academics and writers have been formulating approaches to the subjects associated with Islam in cyberspace. These illustrate some of the diverse disciplinary approaches relating to Muslims, Islam and the Internet.

The anthropologist Jon Anderson wrote about the impact of the Internet on 'transnational communities', particularly Arabs, and has discussed the influence of the 'media explosion' on Islamic discourse.[22] In 1997, he evaluated the impact of the Internet on Iraqis, and suggested that '[T]he Internet facilitates but does not determine a process of rethinking Islam's social reach, which is already underway.'[23] It may now be necessary to re-evaluate this construct, especially given the new forms of discourse, electronic dissemination and information-gathering that have emerged. Anderson's themes are related to issues developed by (and which he has worked in conjunction with) Dale Eickelman. Particularly relevant is Eickelman's analysis of media, such as that contained in his collaborative work with Anderson, and separately with James Piscatori, which have considered the impact of various forms of media on diverse Muslim settings and historical frameworks.[24] Other important research associated with Islam and cyberspace includes work by the Arab Information Project, Georgetown, which produced a website linking to a series of detailed and technologically centred regional case studies on Internet development in the Middle East. Some of these are class assignments for students at the University of Georgetown, whilst there are also hyperlinks to other materials, including academic papers by subject specialists from outside the institution.[25] The impact of the Internet on Arab societies has also been a theme contained in the work of Jon Alterman. He has introduced commentaries associated with the impact of the Internet on Arab diaspora societies, including Muslims. Factors such as the increased information flow, the impact on state censorship and how US interests can engage with the Arab media in order to influence public opinion have been covered in his work.[26]

In terms of academic studies of Islam and the Internet, since the publication of *Virtually Islamic*, the writer has become aware of ongoing research which has been published or presented and which has made a substantial contribution to the field(s). Peter Mandaville has explored aspects of Islam and cyberspace from the angle of globalisation, and is concerned with the ways in which the technology allows 'greater numbers of people to take Islam into their own hands, opening new spaces for debate and critical dialogue'. He also sees the technology (in its many forms) as offering a means through which 'it also furnishes Islam with a mirror to hold up to itself and an opportunity to gaze upon its many diverse faces'.[27] Mandaville discussed the issue of control in relation to a 'virtual *ummah*', or Muslim community, and what he described as a 'shared normative framework … whose discursive norms derive from an Islamic framework'.[28] These are significant issues, which were also approached in *Virtually Islamic* and this writer's other work.[29] Questions emerge as to how those discursive norms have now evolved in reaction to new media developments and a changing world order, especially as the Internet becomes less of a 'novelty' and more of a cohesive and coherent element binding dispersed individuals and communities together.

Amongst other work in the field, to which this book seeks to make a contribution, Peter Wolcott and Seymour E. Goodman of Stanford University provided sophisticated comparative technical analysis on applications of the Internet in Pakistan and Turkey, although much of the technical content is beyond the remit of this current work.[30] Yves Gonzalez-Qijano has provided an analysis of the Internet in the Lebanon.[31] Rizwan Mawani researched identity issues associated with Ismaili webspace.[32] Lenie Brouwer explored the role of e-mail in engendering Muslim identities in minority European contexts.[33] Debbie Wheeler conducted fieldwork on the impact of the Internet in the Middle East, including a study of its role on Kuwait, and the readiness of Egypt to 'embrace' the Internet age.[34] Matthias Brückner discussed aspects of online *fatwas* in relation to the consumption of alcohol, and evaluated the role of *muftis* on the Internet.[35] Rüdiger Lohlker wrote about the Qur'an and its representation in cyberspace.[36] Henner Kirchner has provided overviews of 'digital jihad' and 'cyber-interfada'.[37] Jonah Blank referred to the application of the Internet in his research on Dawoodi Bohra Shi'a communities.[38] A University of Birmingham project explored how diverse communications tools, including the Internet, have been used to develop and maintain cohesion within a dispersed Sufi order.[39]

Naturally, it is not just scholars of Islam and the Internet who can inform discussions about the media and its application. The influences of writers such as Marshall McLuhan, Howard Rheingold and Manuel Castells – early pioneers of discussions and theories about networks, computers and communities – combine as subtexts to this volume with those of Edward Said, in particular his writings about understandings of Orientalism, and Islam and the media.[40] General works about Islam and the media have also been important, although in existing publications their (understandable) focus on global mass media generally pre-dates the influence of the Internet.[41]

These and other sources are useful in reaching an understanding of Cyber Islamic Environments, and for improving our initial 'snapshot'. The outputs of these and other scholars make a formative contribution to this developing field. It is important to emphasise that studies of Islam and cyberspace must transcend the so-called 'Arab world' and be representative of a broad range of Muslim sources and Islamic interests, drawing on different beliefs and academic interests. Particularly important are the pronouncements generated from within a minority context; the Internet has alerted the 'wider Muslim world' to minority groups and their ideologues, and generated interest and affiliations which have evolved at a rapid rate through the digital medium. Some of these groups have created a 'safety zone' in which to operate, which would not necessarily be viable in their geographical place of ideological and/or ancestral origin. Following the events of 11 September 2001, some of these avenues of expression and activity have been closed or become more discreet.

This book has been designed so that it can be read separately and independently from *Virtually Islamic* and the writer's other work in the field. It does not have to be read sequentially (rather like hypertext). *Virtually Islamic* introduced some formative influences, discussions and factors that are not repeated within this volume. There is a shift in emphasis in this book from *Virtually Islamic*, which was more of an overview, and indeed many of the issues have changed in a rapidly compressed historical period. Changes in the technical and Islamic equation have naturally adjusted the writer's outlook in the period between books. Ideally, *Virtually Islamic* and this present book will complement one another to provide a detailed picture of Cyber Islamic Environments and their evolution.

RESEARCHING CYBER ISLAMIC ENVIRONMENTS

This book, as technical experts will quickly ascertain, is *not* a *technical* guide to hacking, cracking, viruses, firewalls and/or Internet security in relation to Cyber Islamic Environments. There are several methodological and technical issues that are relevant to the research, which should be mentioned here. Several references to Whois (and related services) are made: Whois is one of several online services that can provide details of an Internet domain's ownership, together with technical data from which a computer's location and operating system can be ascertained. Whilst these data can be manipulated, they are incorporated where feasible into the discussion when reference is required to a site's owner or location of 'origin'.[42]

One significant factor that this research has revealed is that there is no single archive of material relating to Cyber Islamic Environments. It is not possible to visit all previous incarnations of a site, as few site managers preserve their old pages. This raises problems, if a researcher is attempting to track down a site from a particular date and time. The writer has kept records of the majority of sites he visited: these take the form of screen shots, printouts and saved HTML pages. Clearly, it is not possible to preserve everything, given the number of sites in cyberspace, but it is intended to create in the future a more rigid and structured archive for researchers to use. It may be that security agencies have held copies of certain sites along with their monitoring of e-mail traffic, but these resources were not available to the writer (who has no connection with such services), and indeed he is aware that many agencies did not keep full records themselves. There are a number of ways in which old page impressions can be located, although the techniques are not necessarily reliable or scientific: the search engine Google keeps a cached copy of pages it has recorded, so if a researcher has specific details, on occasions the cache can provide an impression of 'missing pages' and sites.

There is no single archive of Islam and the Internet; ideally, there would be a searchable interface and sequential copies of significant sites. Research into Islam and cyberspace has identified the need for the development of systems for recording and analysing online digital content, relating to Cyber Islamic Environments. The dramatic and substantial shifts in content during compressed time periods cannot always be recorded or observed in a scientific and systematic way by academics – and there is no single resource or institution that undertakes this task. The bulk of online material is one inhibiting factor, frequently encountered by this writer. The result is that, at a critical time in the development of 'digital Islam', coupled with the radical shifts in Muslim networks responding in various ways to post-9-11 contexts, there is no formal archive source of Islamic websites.

Critical data in a variety of languages and formats have been lost for subsequent study. In order for a coherent understanding of digital Islam, it is proposed that in the future discussions and research are undertaken with a view to establishing a methodological approach for recording these sites, especially those in relation to Islam, the Internet and the West. These would include the identification of appropriate software for automatic recording, and research into the development of an appropriate interface through which these data could be located and classified. The data would be kept in a digital content archive and be accessible to researchers.[43] Whilst there are media archives for television, radio, film and newspapers in relation to Islam, for example, there is no archive relating to Islam on the Internet.

Fortunately, there are resources available which have a limited selection of recorded Cyber Islamic Environments available. The success of such preservation is dependent on the type of site being archived. An increasingly useful source is the Internet Archive Wayback Machine, organised by Alexa, which started archiving the Internet in 1996; its database does contain records (in the form of digital copies) of some of the sites that have otherwise disappeared.[44] For example, through this resource, the writer was able to locate 88 versions of the Azzam.com site (discussed in Chapter 4), including a sequence of post 9-11 daily versions of the site (16 September–17 December 2001 inclusive). Azzam was frequently closed, hacked, disrupted or relocated online, so this makes the archive helpful for researchers; it also provides a useful resource for supporters of the site's objectives, which perhaps raises an ethical issue for archivists. It was noted by the writer that some pro-Osama bin Laden material was not included in the archive, such as the al-Neda site, which was allegedly 'taken over' by an American message board discussing the implications of 9-11. (It was interesting to see that many of the al-Qaeda-related pages were 'missing' from the archive.)[45] Al-Neda supporters subsequently hacked into other sites, and placed their content 'discreetly' into folders to provide alternative routes of access to information, albeit for a limited time.[46]

'Hacked' sites were preserved on other archive sites, such as Alldas.de and Attrition.org, although these were overwhelmed by the sheer amount of activity.[47] Outside the actual sites discussed in this book, news of such activity was derived from a number of specialist and other sources, including Moreover, SANS Institute, Wired, al-Jazeera, al-Bawaba, The Register, mi2g and general news services with Technology pages.[48] Groups with specific political, religious and social agendas, such as the Israeli International Policy Institute for Counter Terrorism, the Middle East Media Research Institute (MEMRI), the Jewish Internet Association and latterly (in terms of the writing process for this book) the Anti-Defamation League, the Jewish Federation of Southern Illinois, Southeast Missouri

& Western Kentucky (Simoky Fed), also became sources of data for this project, although as with any source, caution was applied in relation to the implicit value judgements contained in these sites.[49]

A network of personal contacts, many of which require anonymity, also provided information. Formal interviews with those involved in disruptive online activities were impossible. Individual web administrators were contacted during the preparation of this book. However, especially in the post 9-11 context, the writer noted a reluctance (with a few exceptions) to engage in discussions relating to this research. In future work, it is anticipated that users and creators of Cyber Islamic Environments will be interviewed. This present work consists primarily of the writer's personal observations and analysis.

BOOK STRUCTURE

Two significant applications of the Internet are considered in this volume: 'electronic jihad' and online *fatwas*.

Chapters 2–5, focus on 'electronic jihad', in its various embodiments and understandings; Chapter 2, '"The Digital Sword"? and Defining "E-Jihad"', includes an introduction to perspectives associated with the term 'jihad'; Chapter 3, 'Hacktivism, Hacking and Cracking in the Name of Islam', explores the integration of e-jihad into online activism, and the ways in which forms of jihad have appeared in relation to computer-mediated communication. These include hacktivism, cracking and other major and minor forms of online disruption. Reference is also made to forms of encryption.

Chapters 4, 5 and 6 provide a discussion of Cyber Islamic reactions to 9-11 in the forms of: 'Mujahideen in Cyberspace' (Chapter 4), 'The "Inter-fada" and Global E-jihad' (Chapter 5) and 'Jihad for Peace' (Chapter 6). These chapters offer an opportunity to consider various Muslim statements and opinions emerging from 'western' and other contexts (from all 'sides') in terms of how they appeared online, especially those Muslim perspectives who were *opposed* to al-Qaeda, who sought to represent themselves on the Internet.

Chapter 7, 'Islamic Decision-Making and Advice Online', considers *fatwas* and other forms of decision-making and authority in Cyber Islamic Environments; in introducing the subsequent two chapters, it pays particular attention to databases and interactive fora disseminating notions of interpretation and understanding, drawn from diverse perspectives and 'schools' of thought, including new 'western' Muslim models.

Chapters 8 and 9, 'Sunni Religious Authority on the Internet I and II', discuss notions of online authority that have a connection with the numerically superior proportion of the Muslim world(s), which falls under the broad Sunni orthodox banner in majority (Chapter 8) and minority (Chapter 9) contexts. These sites have substantial content and facilities, necessitating within this section separate headings for designated online 'key players', who have been selected on criteria including site format, site content, projected influence and their affiliations.

Chapter 10, 'The Online Mujtahid: Islamic Diversity and Authority Online', offers a sketch of other online approaches to Islamic knowledge, especially Shi'a Islam and Sufism. Whilst these sectors of cyberspace are often not as extensive as their Sunni equivalent, they represent significant and individual understandings that are essential in formulating an effective and responsive overview of religious authority online.

Chapter 11, 'Islam and the Digital Age', concludes the volume by considering new Islamic interfaces and paradigms online. It draws together the essential points of the book, and seeks to chart a way forward for further detailed study of Islam, Muslims and the Internet.

The book contains Notes, a Bibliography (including URLs), a Glossary and an Index. Unless otherwise stated, all Internet references were correct and links functioned at the time of going to press.

To counter 'disappearing' websites or changing addresses, references to this book will be updated on the book's related website, as part of the online bibliography:

VIRTUALLY ISLAMIC

http://www.virtuallyislamic.com
The site will also contain related screen-shots of significant sites. Through this website, readers are welcome to contact the writer with observations, information and comments.

TRANSLITERATION

It was decided for this volume not to burden the reader with a complex system of transliteration of 'Islamic' and other terminology from Arabic and other languages into English. However, appropriate transliteration is provided in the Glossary. The general principles contained in the *Encyclopedia of Islam: New Edition* (Leiden: E.J. Brill, 1960) have been adhered to, with the popular model featured in Ian Richard Netton's *A Popular Dictionary of Islam* (London: Curzon Press, 1991) also applied. Quotations from Internet and textual sources retain their original transliterations; proper names maintain locally applied personal spellings and transliterations; Anglicised Islamic–Arabic terminology is applied where possible, i.e. 'mosque' for *masjid*. Where an Islamic term is contained in a quotation, the writer has given a general definition in parenthesis, i.e. *masjid* [mosque].

NOTES

1. See Edward W. Lane, *An Account of the Manners and Customs of the Modern Egyptians* (London, 1836).
2. Gary R. Bunt, *Virtually Islamic: Computer-mediated Communication and Cyber Islamic Environments* (Cardiff: University of Wales Press, 2000), pp. 66–103.
3. Ibid., p. 7.
4. David Gauntlett (ed.), *Web.Studies: Rewiring Media Studies for the Digital Age* (London: Arnold, 2000), p. 227.
5. *Al-Bawaba*, 'Algeria Hopes to Improve Telecommunications by 2010', 10 April, 2001; 'Egypt to Serve Less Privileged Areas with 100 Youth Centers Yearly', 27 July 2001, www.al-bawaba.com/news.
6. *UNESCO Webword News*, 'Only 4% of Internet Users in the Arab World are Women', 5 June 2000, www.unesco.org/webworld/news/000605_beijing.shtml.
7. Al-Huda, www.alhudapk.com.
8. Wissam El Solh, Netakeoff, Beirut, quoted in Steve Kettman, '1,001 Arabian Nights of Sex', *Wired*, 24 April, 2001, www.wired.com/news/print/0,1294,43243,00.html. Netakeoff is a Lebanon-based company developing and investing in Internet and technology firms. See www.netakeoff.com.
9. Such a figure is not necessarily indicative of trends throughout global Muslim contexts. See *al-Bawaba*, 'Expert: Rising Mideast PC Demand Bucks Global Trend', 15 August 2001, www.al-bawaba.com/ news.
10. United Nations Development Project, *Making New Technologies Work for Human Development* (United Nations Development Project, 2001).
11. Ibid., pp. 60–62, www.undp.org/hdr2001/. An early version of this element of the discussion in relation to Mediterranean contexts is contained in Gary Bunt, 'Islam Interactive: Mediterranean Islamic Expression on the World Wide Web', in *Islam and the Shaping of the Current Islamic Reformation*, Barbara Allen Roberson (ed.) (London: Frank Cass, 2003).
12. United Nations Development Project, *Making New Technologies Work for Human Development*, p. 40.

13. Peter Wolcott and Seymour Goodman, *The Internet in Turkey and Pakistan: A Comparative Analysis* (Stanford: Center for International Security and Co-operation, Stanford University, 2000), p. xii, http://mosaic. unomaha.edu/TurkPak_2000.pdf.
14. UNDP, *Making New Technologies Work for Human Development*, p. 41. The term 'digital divide' is explored by Pippa Norris, *Digital Divide: Civic Engagement, Information Poverty, and the Internet* (Cambridge: Cambridge University Press, 2001).
15. Mohamed A. El-Nawawy, 'Profiling Internet Users in Egypt: Understanding the Primary Deterrent against Their Growth in Number', Internet Society (2000), www.isoc.org/inet2000/cdproceedings/8d/s8.
16. Ibid.
17. The writer has raised this issue at conferences since the publication of *Virtually Islamic*, in particular at the Duke University Center for the Study of Muslim Networks 'Muslim Networks: Medium, Methodology & Metaphor' workshop, March 2001, 'Islamic Inter-connectivity in a Virtual World: e-jihad, e-ijtihad and online fatwas'.
18. For example, see Intifadat El-Aqsa, www.islamiccenterforstudies.org/ aqsa/drra.html [URL subsequently not functional]. Muhammad al-Durrah website, www.al-sham.net/al_quds.html.
19. Human Rights Watch, 'The Internet in the Mideast and North Africa', (Human Rights Watch, 1999), www.hrw.org/advocacy/Internet/mena/.
20. Human Rights Watch, 'Recommendations' (1999), www.hrw.org/ advocacy/Internet/mena/reco.htm.
21. Discussed in detail in *Virtually Islamic*, pp. 104–31.
22. See Jon W. Anderson, 'Technology, Media, and the Next Generation in the Middle East', *New Media and Information Technology Working Papers* (Georgetown: NMIT, 1999), http://nmit.georgetown.edu/papers/ jwanderson.htm; 'Arabizing the Internet', *The Emirates Occasional Papers*, No. 30 (1998); and Dale F. Eickelman (ed.), *New Media in the Muslim World: The Emerging Public Sphere* (Bloomington: Indiana University Press, 1999); 'New Media in the Muslim World: The Emerging Public Sphere', *ISIM Newsletter*, 5, www.isim.nl/newsletter/5/media/1.html.
23. Jon Anderson, 'Is the Internet Islam's "Third Wave" or the "End of Civilization"?', *Journal of Electronic Publishing* (1997), www.press.umich. edu/jep/archive/Anderson.html.
24. Dale F. Eickelman and James Piscatori, *Muslim Politics* (Princeton, NJ: Princeton University Press, 1996).
25. Arab Information Project, www.georgetown.edu/research/arabtech/. Similar class assignment work was being introduced in 2002 by George Mason University, in a course on 'Islam and the Internet', although it was too early at the time of writing to determine the validity of the findings.
26. Jon B. Alterman, 'New Media, New Politics? From Satellite Television to the Internet in the Arab World', summarised in *Policywatch*, 356, Washington Institute for Near East Policy, 11 December 1998, www. washingtoninstitute.org/watch/Policywatch/policywatch1998/356.htm.
27. Peter Mandaville, 'Reimagining the Ummah? Information Technology and the Changing Boundaries of Political Islam', in *Islam Encountering*

Globalisation, Ali Mohammadi (ed.), (London: RoutledgeCurzon, 2002), p. 88.

28. Ibid., p. 86.

29. For example, see Gary Bunt, 'Islam in Cyberspace: Islamic Studies Resources on the World Wide Web', *Muslim World Book Review*, Vol. 18, No. 1 (1997), pp. 3–13.

30. Wolcott and Goodman, *The Internet in Turkey and Pakistan*.

31. Yves Gonzalez-Quijano, 'Essai De Cartographie de l'Information sur Internet Au Liban', www.pisweb.net/mmm/3_quijano/3-quijano.html.

32. Rizwan Mawani, 'Community, Identity and the Internet: The Case of the Ismaili Muslims'. 'The Ismaili Community and the Internet: Exploring an Encounter', n.d., unpublished papers.

33. Lenie Brouwer, 'Muslimmail in the Netherlands', paper presented at the 'Writing Diasporas' conference, Virtual Diasporas strand, University of Wales, Swansea, 22 September 2000.

34. Debbie Wheeler, 'Islam, Community and the Internet: New Possibilities in the Digital Age', *Journal of Education, Community and Values*, No. 3 (2002), http://bcis.pacificu.edu/journal/2002/03/islam.php; 'New Media, Globalization and Kuwaiti National Identity', *The Middle East Journal*, Vol. 54, No. 3 (2000), 'Living At E.Speed: A Look at Egypt's E Readiness', in *Economic Challenges and Opportunities in the MENA Region* (Cairo: Economic Research Forum Publications, AUC Press, 2002).

35. Matthias Brückner, *Fatwas zum Alkohol unter dem Einfluss neuer Medien im 20. Jhdt* (Würzburg: Ergon-Verlag, 2000); 'Der Mufti im Netz', in Rüdiger Lohlker (ed.), *Islam im Internet, Neue Formen der Religion im Cyberspace* (Hamburg: Deutsches Orient-Institut, CD-Rom); 'IslamiCity – Creating an Islamic Cybersociety', *ISIM (International Institute for the Study of Islam in the Modern World) Newsletter*, No. 8 (2001) www.isim.nl/newsletter/8/bruckner.htm; Cyberfatwa: Index zu Fatwas und Muftis im Internet, www.cyberfatwa.de.

36. Rüdiger Lohlker, 'Der Koran im Internet', www.sub.uni-goettingen.de/ebene_1/orient/koran1.htm#Anmerkung_1a.

37. Henner Kirchner, 'Digital Jihad – Islam im Internet', *Quartalszeitschrift der Arbeitsgemeinschaft Kirchlicher Entwicklungsdienst*, No. 32 (1996) 4, 19–22, www.henner-kirchner.de/studies/cybermus.htm.

38. Jonah Blank, *Mullahs on the Mainframe: Islam and Modernity among the Daudi Bohras* (Chicago and London: The University of Chicago Press, 2001).

39. This was the Naqshabandi Sufi *tariqa* (order) led by Shaykh Nazim al-Qubrusi al-Haqqani, which has strong links with Lebanon. The Naqshabandis are also discussed in Bunt, *Virtually Islamic*, pp. 59–60. Sufism and the Internet are also considered in Gary R. Bunt, 'Surfing Islam: Ayatollahs, Shayks and Hajjis on the Superhighway', in Jeffrey K. Hadden and Douglas E. Cowan (eds.), *Religion on the Internet: Research Prospects and Promises* (New York: Elsevier Science, 2000), pp. 143–5. Results of the Transnational Sufism project had not been published at the time of writing. For a description of the project, see http://artsWeb.bham.ac.uk/mdraper/transnatsufi/projectdesc.htm.

40. Manuel Castells, *The Rise of the Network Society* (Oxford and Malden: Blackwell, 1996). Marshall McLuhan and Bruce R. Powers, *The Global Village: Transformations in World Life and Media in the 21st Century* (New York and Oxford: Oxford University Press, 1989); and Quentin Fiore, *The Medium is the Message: An Inventory of Effects* (London: Random House, 1967). Edward W. Said, *Orientalism* (London: Routledge & Kegan Paul, 1978); *Covering Islam: How the Media and the Experts Determine How We See the Rest of the World* (London: Vintage, revised edition, 1997).
41. See Kai Hafez (ed.), *Islam and the West in the Mass Media* (Cresskill, NJ: Hampton Press, 2000).
42. Whois. www.whois.org. Related services used in this research include: Sam Spade, www.samspade.org, Allwhois, www.allwhois.com, Betterwhois, www.betterwhois.com.
43. For a discussion on digital archiving, see Digital Preservation Coalition, www.dpconline.org, and Maggie Jones and Neil Beagrie, *Preservation Management of Digital Materials: A Handbook* (London: British Library, 2002).
44. Alexa Internet Archive Wayback Machine, http://web.archive.org.
45. Al-Neda, www.alneda.com. There were claims the new 'owner' of the domain was associated with the generation of pornographic websites. This confusing situation was not resolved by the time of publication. See discussion at http://cryptome.org/al-neda.htm and http://cryptome.org/alneda-wet.htm – suggesting the site was being monitored by US intelligence services in order to determine the origins of traffic to the site. Al-Neda content re-emerged in December 2002.
46. 'Al-Qaeda Hackers Hijack Sites', *The Age*, 27 October 2002, www.theage.com.au.
47. Alldas.de had been disrupted by a Denial of Service attack in September 2002, and had not resumed its service by November 2002. Attrition.org continued to function: www.attrition.org/mirror/attrition/.
48. *Moreover*, www.moreover.com, SANS Institute, www.sans.org, *Wired*, www.wired.com, *al-Jazeera*, www.aljazeera.com, *al-Bawaba*, www.albabawa.com, *The Register*, www.theregister.co.uk, mi2g, www.mi2g.com, *News Now*, www.newsnow.co.uk See the writer's news feeds at Virtually Islamic News and Islamic Studies Pathways, both linked at www.virtuallyislamic.com.
49. International Policy Institute for Counter-Terrorism, www.ict.org.il, Middle East Media Research Institute (MEMRI), www.memri.org, Anti-Defamation League, 'Jihad Online: Islamic Terrorists and the Internet', www.adl.org/internet/jihad.asp, 2002, Jewish Internet Association www.jewishinternetassociation.org, Simoky Fed, www.simokyfed.com (in late 2002, these pages became part of Internet Haganah, http://haganah.org.il).

2 'The Digital Sword'? Defining 'E-Jihad'

And fight in God's cause against those who wage war against you, but do not commit aggression – for, verily, God does not love aggressors.[1]

The thesis that the hyperlinks between one site and another are indicative of specific allegiances of an individual or an organisation is a problematic one. Such links *can* suggest networking and affiliations that transcend some forms of mainstream or conventional knowledge about Islam in the contemporary world. Many sites, including those discussed below, issue disclaimers as to the content of external sites. Some issue disclaimers regarding the content of their own sites too! The extent to which these disclaimers should be observed is open to question and probably dependent on the type of site visited. There can be substantial crossovers and linkages between Cyber Islamic Environments, in terms of content, ideology, religious affiliation, symbolism and hyperlinks. It is not feasible to quantify these links. It will be seen that Islamic sites that were vocal in their support for al-Qaeda may share some elements of design and content with those sites that vehemently criticise the actions of 11 September 2001. Neither is necessarily less 'Islamic' than the other, and it is certainly not the purpose of this book to suggest this. Rather, it is to evaluate the ways in which pan-Islamic concepts are used and applied in a variety of contexts online. Connections of place and time are not always easy to determine online, given the ways in which information can be cloaked, and also because websites can be global in nature. A sense of geographical place *can* be useful to 'locate' a group or individual – politically, religiously, socially and culturally – within a Muslim framework. Consequently, universal web-based location tools are applied within the book to present material in this discussion such as a site owner's locations, where that information is not always obvious.

THE SYMBOLISM OF JIHAD

There has been a massive increase in online activities, particularly in relation to the conflict in Palestine and Israel (and more recently, associated with 9-11), which has been labelled 'e-jihad' (or alternatively described as an 'inter-fada') by many groups (on all 'sides').[2] The application of the term jihad is itself interesting, given that it has also entered English in relation to other forms of activism.[3] In the context of cyberspace, the traditional concept of jihad as an inner Muslim spiritual striving has frequently been negated in favour of a digital sword striking in a number of different ways at a broad selection of targets.

The phenomenon of online activism in the name of Islam in relation to Cyber Islamic Environments was introduced in *Virtually Islamic* as an area in which tensions might escalate as Internet technology becomes more widely available and accessible. Various 'Islamic' groups, especially in relation to conflicts in Chechnya, Palestine, Kashmir and Afghanistan, have proved this in online campaigns seeking to promote their cause, and at times disrupt the online activities of their ideological and military opponents. The term e-jihad perhaps has some flexibility within our discussion. It could be associated with hacking, cracking and disruptive technological application; more widely, it could also be applied as a form of propaganda (or e-*da'wa*?) in order to present specific worldviews – perhaps to a selective and sympathetic audience, but also to a wider global audience (Muslim and other). E-jihad could be extended to discussions on how information technology was applied by groups such as al-Qaeda in order to organise logistics for their campaigns, through the application of e-mail and encrypted files, as well as a means for developing their own strategic intelligence. The notion of jihad in classical Islamic contexts is much broader than the violent associations it has acquired. The term accommodates peaceful spiritual 'striving' and effort in the name of Islam, as well as militaristic activities: just as it could be said that not all battles are conducted by military campaigning, so the battles of the individual Muslim (for example, against the pressures and temptations of the mundane world) can be described as jihad. So whilst e-jihad is a convenient label, technically it could seen as a misnomer, and many of the expressions of Islam contained on the web might represent this so-called sixth 'pillar' of Islam.

In order to determine whether the term 'e-jihad' itself is appropriate, it is intended here to explore some of the traditional aspects and applications of jihad. It is impossible to place a quantifiable value on jihad's role in Islam, and it cannot be suggested that one component of Islam has a greater or lesser role than any other. Without any 'component', Islam would be incomplete: to ignore one portion of God's Word would be – for a Muslim – to deny the immutability and rigidity of the entire Qur'an; to place a quantifiable value on jihad would be to suggest inner personal knowledge of Allah, (often) denied to the greatest Muslim saints, imams and scholars.

However, a relative indication of jihad's importance might be ascertained by analysis of the social, economic, historical, political and theological 'Islam' contexts jihad has been placed into – particularly relevant when discussing its online manifestations. This is a complex process, to which allusion can only be made here. To commence such an analytical process, a definition of jihad must be acquired, and indeed an understanding of what is meant by 'Islam', whether on an individual, community or universal level.

A single, arbitrary and concise definition of 'Islam' can be difficult to provide. Essential core beliefs can be similar, but there can be significant differences in understanding within and between various Islamic frameworks as to what 'Islam' really means. The Internet itself illustrates the nuances of definition associated with 'Islam'. To pursue the question of jihad's role in 'Islam', these factors, and the problems of separating ideals and realities, are kept firmly in mind. The word 'jihad' is the abstract noun of the verb *jahada* (exerted), and suggests exertion 'of one's power in Allah's path'.[4] Whilst jihad is commonly translated, especially in 'the West', as 'holy war', military action sanctioned (purportedly or otherwise) in the name of God is the lesser jihad. The greater jihad could be explained as a spiritual and religious striving on a path towards – and/or in the name of – God. Understandings of jihad can have both exoteric and esoteric emphasis, and can be examined on its external aspects alone and on its deeper, exegetical meanings.

The greater jihad, a personal striving of *ma'ruf* (good) over *munkar* (evil), should be a continual process for individual Muslims. The Qur'an addressed Muhammad's Companions on their role, and by analogy this statement could now apply to the greater community, or *ummah*:

You are indeed the best community that has ever been brought forth for [the good of] mankind: you enjoin the doing of what is right and forbid the doing of what is wrong, and you believe in God.[5]

Observation of the basic precepts of Islam contributes to jihad, and vice versa.[6] The greater jihad, when seen as a striving of an inner perfection, is an 'essential' component of Islam, and it could be argued that Muhammad – the 'Last Prophet' – was so successful on his jihad(s) that he initiated what some commentators describe as a 'Golden Age of Islam'. This would be dependent, perhaps, on whether attribution for good and noble deeds rests solely in the hands of Divine Providence, or on individual human effort:

And [thus, O Prophet,] We have sent thee as [an evidence of Our] grace towards all worlds.[7]

Did Muhammad receive Revelation because of his 'purity', as part of a *jihad fi-Allah* – 'Quest for Allah' – initiated when he was on a 'retreat' prior to receiving his first Revelation? Or was this the role of earlier prophets? Whatever the answer, it indicates a crucial role for jihad in Islam, one that is frequently expressed online.

Definitions of greater jihad in Islam may suggest the power of an individual to have an overall effect on the whole society. Humanity is the *khalifah*, or vice-regent of God. The moral and spiritual quest is guided and dominated by the Qur'an, which suggests both a love of God and a fear of God (and Divine Judgement). Although the greater jihad may impose what seem like impositions and hardships, these bonds and fetters are, in the words of the Egyptian Islamist writer Sayyid Qutb (1906–66), 'in reality ... aspects of movement, liberation, and vitality'.[8] If a Muslim does 'lose', the loss is imposed by God to prevent a greater loss. God cannot be questioned or doubted within the ideal universal Islamic state.

Some Muslim 'theologians' and scholars suggest the greater jihad does not impose unnecessary hardships, but rather attempts to strike a balance. The Pakistani Islamist Sayyid Abul A'la Mawdudi's (1903–79) perspective was that an ascetic life of deprivation – such as that practised by some Sufis – would not assist in the (non-mystical) jihad, rather:

To seek spiritual elevation, moral purity, nearness to God, and salvation in the life to come, it is not necessary to abandon this world. Instead, the trial of man [*sic*] lies in this world, and he should remain in its midst and follow the way of Allah here in it. The road to success lies in following the Divine law in the midst of life's complexities, and not outside it.[9]

Humanity's ultimate 'role model' in such exemplary conduct must be the Prophet Muhammad:

> Verily, in the Apostle of God you have a good example for everyone who looks forward [with hope and awe] to God and the Last Day, and remembers God unceasingly.[10]

The actions and conduct of the Prophet offer a source by which the importance of greater jihad in Islam can be ascertained.

From a contemporary 'western' historical and social perspective, it is the lesser jihad that has made the greatest impact and received the most attention – academically, politically and socially. This is particularly true when ascertaining its online manifestations, and the pronouncements of prominent activists, ideologues and organisations. The concept of jihad, erroneously or not, is significant in the 'western' perception of Islam – as a term synonymous with ultra-violent terrorism, 'anti-western' political movements seeing a return to 'Islamic roots', and/or as a convenient 'orientalist' reductive label often applied by secular/non-Muslim/Muslim societies to explain movements that may or may not have 'mysterious' 'Islamic' religious motivations behind them.

The first military jihads took place in the lifetime of the Prophet: whilst the concept of 'holy war' pre-dates Muhammad, the origins of 'lesser jihad' could be demonstrated when applying the Qur'an, hadith and sunna as primary documentary texts. Military victories – and defeats – during Muhammad's lifetime are referred to in the Qur'an, hadith and sunna, and are exemplified in biographical sources and histories associated with the life of Muhammad. However, militaristic activity is but one part of the lesser jihad, which can incorporate religious missions and persuasion, and the application of religious jurisprudence falling under the broad spectrum of the 'shari'ah'. The militaristic stereotype of jihad has been applied as a tool *against* Islam, especially in statements suggesting that conversion 'by the sword' was the principal way in which Islam spread. It is not the purpose to debate that paradigm here, simply to state that whether by the sword or the Qur'an, the lesser jihad has played an important role in the propagation of Islam. The emphasis within the Qur'an between violent and persuasive jihad varies, according to the period of the Revelation. The Qur'an itself states that 'There shall be no coercion in matters of faith'.[11]

In the face of adversity, Muslims must be prepared to make the ultimate sacrifice and defend Islam to the death, as stated in *Surah al-Anfal*:

> And fight against them until there is no more oppression and all worship is devoted to God alone.[12]

Surah Baqarah, (especially verses 190–4) emphasises the physical 'external' jihad, which has been synonymous with the term in the 'western' perspective of Islam:

> Your enemies will not cease fighting with you until they turn you, back from your religion, if they can.[13]

The 'correct application' of the 'jihad' concept continues to be a discussion point within Muslim communities, as it has been since the lifetime of Muhammad. The Iranian 'reformer' Ali Shariati explored this in his writings, when discussing 'intra-Muslim' conflict:

> Swords engraved with the Quranic verses on holy war were pointed towards us. His representatives stepped into our houses and took our youth as slaves for the chieftains of their tribes, sold our mothers in the distant markets, killed our men in the name of struggle in the way of God, and looted our belongings in the name of charity.[14]

Some commentators attribute the rapid spread of Islam to the strength of jihad as a military force alone, relegating socio-political, economic and legalistic factors, and disregarding any purely theological arguments of sincerity and belief altogether. However, military jihad has frequently acquired a dominant role in the modern, 'western', conception of Islam of people who are not Muslims, fuelled by activities that many Muslims (not actively involved in the particular political-social-economic struggles arbitrarily referred to as jihad) might deem 'un-Islamic'. Whether such jihads are un-Islamic or not should not be determined here.

There are many approaches that can assist in determining the importance of the lesser jihad as a component of Islam: historically (i.e. success as a means of spreading Islam, and uniting diverse ethnic-cultural groups); socially (i.e. as a means of motivating socio-political change); legalistically (i.e. provision of divorce and property laws for women, implementation of 'Islamic law'); and economically (i.e. in attempts to prevent usury). Assessing the relevance of jihad might require contextually analysing the people it was applied against, either theoretically or in practice, and those who instigated it, and the form of authority that was applied in order to justify the term's application. The role of jihad now has an electronic dimension in its articulation in cyberspace, and in some cases a digital sword has been applied to strike in jihad's name.

The term itself can be interpreted in many different ways, and in this overview can only be determined with generalisations here. Historically, in Shi'ism, an imam's sanction was required to justify a jihad, the imam being a descendant of the *ahl al-bayt* (literally, people of the Prophet's house, essentially his family). A Shi'i might require allegiance to an imam when undertaking a jihad – an allegiance known as *walaya*. In Sunni Islam (where there can be a different concept of religious leadership), the question arises of who has the capacity to judge instigation (or not) of lesser jihad. Whether this lies in the hands of a *caliph*, an '*alim* (religious scholar) or some other form of ideologue is an open question. Elements of historical revisionism *can* interpret military campaigns as being under the banner of jihad, where the protagonists might not have applied that term. Similarly, the symbol of jihad has been applied in recent conflicts – occasionally on both sides – in order to justify military campaigning.[15]

Different types of jihad have different names: *al-Muharibun* (against secession), *al-Ridda* (against apostasy), *al-Baghi* (against dissention). These terms were influential during the development of Islam, especially during the expansion of Muslim influence after the death of Muhammad in 632 CE. If there were to be a consensus about lesser jihad amongst various factions of Islam, it would be that *ribat*, or defence (i.e. on the frontiers), of Islam is imperative, with a hadith stating the importance of *ribat*:

It is related from Sahl ibn Sa'd as-Sa'idi that the Messenger of Allah, may Allah bless him and grant him peace, said, '*Ribat* for one day in the way of Allah is better than this world and what it contains. The place of the whip of one of you in the Garden is better than this world and what it contains. A morning or an evening spent in the way of Allah is better than this world and everything it contains.[16]

Perception of the importance of both greater and lesser jihad, therefore, is dependent on the sources used, i.e. from 'orthodox' Conservative Islam through to non-conformist Islam; from Sunni to Shi'a to Druze to ...; 'establishment' to 'social' Islam; whether jihad is perceived through a single representative example or a collective whole, and whether it is from within or outside the Islamic community.

In the final analysis, there is no general consensus, except perhaps in the use of the Qur'an as a source of inspiration: essentially, within the main ideals and traditions of Islam, the central tenets of jihad remain the same. One hadith suggests:

> Some one who does jihad in the way of Allah is like someone who fasts and prays constantly and who does not slacken from his prayer and fasting until he returns.[17]

In hindsight, it could be said that Muhammad fought a personal inner jihad and an external jihad of conquest and propagating Islam.[18] Jihad could be seen as having been the essential requirement that prevented Muhammad's Revelation being consigned to historical and theological footnotes: Qutb (and others) described jihad as the 'miracle' of Islam, in that it was responsible for such a rapid transformation of a tribal society in such a small period of time. However valid the Revelation is, without jihad it could not have survived, at least in its present form.

Jihad was the determining factor in the development of Islam: its role today – whether lesser or greater jihad – ensures the spread and/or survival of Islam on many levels. An inner inspiration and an outer tool; a means of finding God within and of spreading God to others; a source of scepticism, salvation and suffering. If not a 'Sixth Pillar', although 'unquantifiable' in many ways and 'misused' in many others, jihad is and always has been a 'fundamental' component within the many forms and categories of Islamic expression.

Substantial divergence can appear between different Muslim perspectives on jihad, not just *between* Sunni and Shi'a, but within Sunni and Shi'a factions.[19] The term 'jihadist' has also emerged to promote the militaristic definition of jihad, and has to an extent become interchangeable (for some commentators) with that of 'Islamist'. Khalid Duran controversially noted that:

The primacy of Jihad as a violent means of establishing a theocracy is an essential ingredient of the modern political ideology of Islamism. For this reason the terms 'Islamist' and 'Jihadist' are basically interchangeable. The minor difference between the two is that the Jihadists are less diplomatic, they blur out publicly what other Islamists say in private.[20]

Duran has been heavily criticised by Muslim organisations, including the Council on American-Islamic Relations, for his comments about 'Islam' and 'Muslims'.[21] However, this point about what is said in public and private about jihad is still an interesting one, especially when considering the expression of Islam on the Internet. The extent to which jihad appears on websites and in chat rooms (or not) will be seen in the discussion below. Clearly, many organisations and individuals are happy to express their views on jihad in public. These have been criticised by other activists, who themselves might be described (or describe themselves) as jihadi in orientation.[22]

The question as to whether the 9-11 attacks were legitimate expressions of jihad became a dominant question. It was associated with the question of whether suicide bombing was 'legitimate' or 'prohibited' in Islam. Sheikh Abdulaziz al-Sheik, Grand Mufti of Saudi Arabia, said it was 'strictly forbidden in Islam'. Abdul-Moti Bayoumi of al-Azhar agreed. However, Yusuf al-Qaradawi, an influential 'modernising' scholar (discussed below), indicated that 'rulings against suicide bombings were issued by "people who are alien to Sharia (Islamic laws) and religion"'.[23] These discussions relating to the legitimacy of jihad were also played out in cyberspace, as will be seen below.

THE GREATER AND LESSER E-JIHAD

Many of these diverse factors are represented in the online manifestations of jihad, especially on the World Wide Web. As such these may reflect the political dimensions of contemporary Islam, although the nature of the articulation may be more pronounced by some groups, platforms and individuals in comparison to others. These can be because of specific beliefs relating to jihad, although issues of potential censorship and 'freedom of expression', together with levels of access to the Internet, will also influence this articulation of jihad.

'E-jihad' can take many forms, particularly in its more militaristic capacity, and does not require publication on a website to be effective.

The term 'e-jihad' has even been applied to describe hacking, cracking and other online activities by people who are *not* Muslims, and this perhaps can be associated with what some critics might describe as a romanticisation of language. Arquilla and Ronfeldt, who accept that certain types of networks and organisations are more likely to be involved in such activities than others, have applied the terms 'net-war' and 'cyber-war' since 1993:

> Through netwar, numerous dispersed small groups using the latest communications technologies could act conjointly across great distances.[24]

These terms could be seen as equivalent to e-jihad, although in the context of this discussion the term is applied to forms of Muslim online activities related to electronic 'jihad' (in its various definitions and guises). More specifically, it is utilised when protagonists themselves see their activities as jihad-like.

The term was highlighted in a 'virtual conflict' in cyberspace between pro-Palestinian and pro-Israeli interests.[25] Digital activism in the name of religion is not a new phenomenon, although its association with religion has now become more pronounced, and religion forms one theme of this current conflict. Certainly, questions may emerge as to whether cracking and/or hacking can be justifiably interpreted as Islamic activities. It may be that dialogues are similar to those attempting to determine the forms of jihad and whether they are appropriate, perhaps illustrating the dichotomy of lexical and conceptual differences associated with jihad. Many kinds of issues emerge with this kind of campaigning, and questions appear as to whether they are truly significant and influential on Muslim worldviews and opinion. If the 'spiritual striving' aspects of jihad can be located within online *fatwas*, then the more militaristic or combative aspects as expressed online can be located in what can be labelled 'e-jihad' and hacking/cracking. This jihad could be in the form of campaigning individuals, groups or platforms (it can be difficult to distinguish between the output of an individual author and a 'collective' site). Many such expressions can be found associated with political and military conflicts, and related activism.

NOTES

1. The Qur'an, *Surah al-Baqarah* (The Cow), 2:190. Note: all extracts from the Qur'an follow the Asad translation, unless part of quotations from

other sources or otherwise stated, and are referenced as 'The Qur'an'. The notation is as follows: *Arabic title* (English translated title), *surah* (chapter) number: *aya* (verse) number. *The Message of the Qur'an, translated and explained by Muhammad Asad* (Gibraltar: Dar al-Andalus, 1980, 1984, 1993).

2. The 'e-' stands for 'electronic', and is also used in this book in relation to *ijtihad*.

3. One example is Queer *Jihad* (writer's emphasis), initially a response by British gay activists responding to al-Muhajiroun, the UK 'back to the caliphate' group who frequently articulate a more militaristic and aggressive approach to the term, especially when pronouncing on 'appropriate' treatment for homosexuals. A separate 'Muslim' gay and lesbian group online later adopted the term. See Gary Bunt, *Virtually Islamic: Computer-mediated Communication and Cyber Islamic Environments* (Cardiff: University of Wales Press, 2000), p. 118.

4. Majid Khadduri, *War and Peace in the Law of Islam* (Baltimore: Johns Hopkins University Press, 1955, 1962), p. 55.

5. The Qur'an, *Surah al 'Imran* (The House of Imran), 3:110.

6. These precepts are often described as the Five Pillars of Islam: The Declaration of Faith (*shahadah*), Prayer (*salah*), Alms (*zakah*), Fasting during Ramadan (*sawm*) and the Major Pilgrimage to Mecca (*hajj*).

7. The Qur'an, *Surah al-Anbiya* (The Prophets), 21:107, Asad, p. 502.

8. Sayyid Qutb, *This Religion of Islam (hadha 'd-din)* (Damascus: IIFSO, 1977), p. 30.

9. Sayyid Abul A'la Mawdudi, *Towards Understanding Islam* (Safat, Kuwait: Sahaba Islamic Press), p. 160.

10. The Qur'an, *Surah al-Ahzab* (The Confederates), 33:21, Asad, p. 642.

11. The Qur'an, *Surah al-Baqarah* (The Cow), 2:256, Asad, p. 57.

12. The Qur'an, *Surah al-Anfal* (Spoils of War), 8:39, Asad, p. 244.

13. The Qur'an, *Surah al-Baqarah* (The Cow), 2:217, Asad, p. 47.

14. Ali Shariati, *Reflections of Humanity – Two Views of Civilization and the Plight of Man* (Houston: Free Islamic Literatures, 1984), p. 7.

15. For example, during the Iran–Iraq war (1980–88), and during the Gulf War (1990–91), the term jihad was applied on all sides. One discussion on the legitimacy of 'martyrdom operations' within the context of jihad can be found in Abu Ruqaiyah, trans. Hussein El-Chamy, 'The Islamic Legitimacy of The "Martyrdom Operations"', *Nida'ul Islam magazine*, 16, 1996, www.islam.org.au/articles/16/martyrdom.htm.

16. Aisha Bewley (trans.), *The Sahih Collection of al-Bukhari* (Muhammad ibn Ismail Bukhari), Chapter 61, Book of Jihad and Military Expeditions. LXXII: The Excellence of *ribat* in the way of Allah, 2735, http://bewley.virtualave.net/bukhari23.html#jihad. Note: it is not intended here to determine the validity of specific hadith sources, nor their chains of transmission. See Bunt, *Virtually Islamic*, pp. 33–4.

17. 'Book of Jihad', 21.1, *Al-Muwatta, Imam Malik* (Malik ibn Anas), trans. 'A'isha 'Abdarahman at-Tarjumana and Ya'qub Johnson, (Norwich: Diwan Press, 1982), p. 197.

18. To explore the role of jihad in the early development of Islam from a perspective featuring hadith sources, see Muslim b. al-Hajjaj al-Qushayri, *Sahih*, trans. Abdul Hamid Siddiqui, Book 19, *Kitab al-Jihad wa'l-Siyar*

(*The Book of Jihad and Expedition*), International Islamic University, Malaysia, www.iiu.edu.my/deed/hadith/muslim/019_smt.html. This is based on the printed translated version: *Sahih Muslim* (Lahore: Sh. Muhammad Ashraf, 1971–75). Also see Martin Lings, *Muhammad: His Life Based on the Earliest Sources* (London: George Allen and Unwin, 1983), F.E. Peters, *A Reader on Classical Islam* (Princeton, NJ: Princeton University Press, 1994), pp. 154–65. An overview of Islam's historical development and spread is contained in Neal Robinson, *Islam: A Concise Introduction* (London: Curzon Press, 1999), pp. 17–39. A detailed interpretation of jihad is contained in *The Encyclopedia of Islam: New Edition*, II, C-E, eds. H. A. R. Gibb, et al. (Leiden: E.J. Brill, 1965), E. Tyan, '*Djihad*', p. 539.

19. Bruce Lawrence, who gives examples of intra-Shi'a differences regarding jihad, discusses this issue in detail. See Bruce Lawrence, *Shattering the Myth: Islam beyond Violence* (Princeton, NJ: Princeton University Press, 1998), pp. 172–83. Also see Amal Saad-Ghorayeb, *Hizbu'llah: Politics and Religion* (London and Sterling: Pluto Press, 2002), pp. 121–8.

20. Khalid Duran, 'Jihadism in Europe', *The Journal of Counterterrorism & Security International*, Vol. 7, No. 1, 2000, pp. 12–15.

21. Council on American-Islamic Relations, 'Muslims question choice of author for book on Islam', www.cair-net.org/asp/article.asp?articleid=347&articletype=3, 4 April 2001.

22. For an attack on Osama bin Laden, the Taliban, the United States and a number of 'Muslim' states and organisations, see Abdalqadir as-Sufi al-Murabit, 'The Kuffar Move to the Endgame', Murabitun of the Americas, www.geocities.com/Athens/Delphi/6588/endgame.html, accessed April 2002. The Murabitun also promote a form of 'Islamic finance', based in part on an electronic e-dinar. There were accusations that al-Qaeda might have utilised this system to transfer funds, although the Murabitun publicly expressed their distaste for bin Laden and his ideology. See Julian Dibbell, 'In Gold We Trust', *Wired*, 10.01, January 2002, www.wired.com/wired/archive/10.01/egold.html.

23. *The Star* (Malaysia)/*Associated Press*, 'Muslim Scholars Debate Legitimacy of Suicide Bombings', 17 September 2001, http://thestar.com.my.

24. John Arquilla and David Ronfeldt (eds.), *Networks and Netwars: The Future of Terror, Crime and Militancy* (California: RAND, 2001), p. 2. They note that they first applied this term in 1993. See John Arquilla and David Ronfeldt, 'Cyberwar is Coming!', *Comparative Strategy*, Vol. 12, No. 2, Spring 1993, pp. 141–65.

25. An introductory discussion on e-jihad, written prior to 9-11, appears in Gary R. Bunt, 'Islamic Inter-connectivity in a Virtual World: e-jihad, e-ijtihad and online fatwas', in miriam cooke and Bruce Lawrence (eds.), *Muslim Networks Across Time* (Chapel Hill: University of North Carolina Press, forthcoming).

3 Hacktivism, Hacking and Cracking in the Name of Islam

The term 'hacktivism' has been applied to describe 'the convergence of hacking with activism ... Hacktivism includes electronic civil disobedience, which brings methods of civil disobedience to cyberspace.'[1] 'Hacking' can 'refer to operations that exploit computers in ways that are unusual and often illegal, typically with the help of special software ("hacking tools")'.[2] The term 'cracking' is also used to describe 'the art of breaking the registration ... time limits and various other aspects of a piece of software'.[3]

Questions emerge as to whether the disruption of websites through hacking and cracking really represents a form of e-jihad, or (in this context) simply an imaginative application of electronic technologies as a means of disseminating a (religiously-oriented) message. The effectiveness and importance of such activities also needs to be challenged. The romantic notion of the online celebrity hacker-activist (or 'hacktivist') has been questioned in some quarters, although in the context of some pronouncements relating to Islam, the hacks go beyond the activities of so-called 'script-kiddies' (undertaking a hack in part for self-fulfilment purposes) into the realms of serious politics and effective service disruption. The message of the hackers also reaches a wider public, as online activism associated with Islam has received substantial press coverage.

Perhaps this is because the juxtaposition between Islam and information technology is seen by some as unusual, but this perhaps reflects erroneous 'western' perceptions of Muslims and Islam as 'technologically backward'. This patronising assumption has at times worked in the hackers' favour, given the levels of publicity achieved, and it could be one indicator why some of the 'victims' of e-jihad – including major corporations and organisations that may have sensibly calculated that they *would* become targets – did not provide adequate defence mechanisms for their databases and servers.

Like hacking in other contexts, many hacks in the name of Islam may lack a relative technical sophistication, but are no less effective. It is quite straightforward to visit a hacking resource website and through generic tools launch some form of disruptive activity, although the success rate is dependent on the target, its defences and the originality of the attempted attack. A level of dedication and study to the task will reap a greater reward. There are a number of resources that are interested in programming and networking issues, which conceivably could be applied by those interested in 'hacking' activities, although that is not the stated intention of the resources' authors. There is a vast range of material available, both online and in printed form:[4]

> Richard Hollis, a computer security consultant, said there were now more than 400,000 web pages offering would-be hackers tools for downloading.[5]

One example of such a resource is Hackerthreads.com, which provides an authoritative guide to hacking-related issues and links to associated sites, whilst stating:

> We are not interested in teaching people how to apply a crack or where to get a serial.[6]

Computer technicians are one group who would be interested in such a resource in order to develop defence mechanisms against so-called 'hackers'. The term itself is contentious, and some are scathing of the so-called 'script kiddies' who are able to launch relatively straightforward Denial of Service attacks on networks. It may be that the term 'hacker' is a misnomer in many of the contexts in which it has been applied, particularly when utilised in an Islamic framework.[7] For the purposes of this discussion the term will be used (albeit with caution) as the technical considerations are secondary to the description of the so-called Muslim hacking activities.

HACKING FOR ISLAM

A number of Muslim electronic 'activists' apply the term 'hacker', but determining who is a 'Muslim' hacker is an interesting issue. In the Philippines, for example, a hacker (or group) were using the name Abu Sayyaf Boys. This name reflects an Islamist group alleged to have connections to al-Qaeda. However, the hacks are not distinctly 'Islamic' in nature, with their local references and demands to 'stop kitty porn'.[8] Similarly, a number of hackers may proclaim regional alliance to a predominantly 'Muslim' country, but their content may not necessarily reflect Islam, Muslims or 'Islamic' issues.

This factor can even apply when a group has the descriptive 'Muslim' in their title, such as the Muslim Hackers Club (MHC), who presented themselves online as an 'educational' resource. At the time of writing, the contents of their site had not been updated since 1999.[9] However, there were functioning links to a variety of resources, including encrypted e-mail services. MHC and their members seem to have been involved in the pro-Palestinian activities of 'cyber-war', and had (non-functioning) links to the Pakistani Hackerz and Doctor Nuker (discussed below).

Through a 'Virus Tutorial', the MHC site provided hyperlinks to a number of resources which could be applied by individuals pursuing hacking agendas. Such 'beginners' tools are straightforward to use, being drawn primarily from generic hacking websites. They are only presented in a Cyber Islamic Environment. The pages of the site apply some Islamic calligraphy and terminology (*Nabi* or Prophet, *insha-Allah* or 'God Willing' and *ummah* or community being three examples). MHC seek the reader's identity on entry to their pages, although it is not necessary to enter this information to fully access the site. Some of the 'identity' issues associated with being Muslim *and* a hacker are explored on the site:

Why Muslim? Muslim because we are proud to be Muslims and to belong to the *Ummah* of our Nabi Muhammad (saaw); Club because you do not need to be a 'hacker' to be a member, or supporter. You don't need to be a cricket player to belong to a Cricket Club, or to support it.

We believe that there is nothing wrong in associating the word 'Muslim' to the word 'hackers'.

The very first known virus the Pakistani 'Brain' was developed by two brothers from Lahore. We hear constantly of hacking and many other fringe computer related matters that seem to be so complicated. So why not a platform for the Muslims to discuss hacking, virus making etc.? We hope we can somehow help each other by freely debating and learning – insha-Allah!

There are many who believe that hackers, crackers, phreakers and pirates (warez traders) are one and the same thing! This isn't all true! There's a lot of difference as a hacker is a person who loves IT and likes to explore to utmost the capabilities of computers, networks and learn all about them. A hacker does not exchange or sell illegal software (anyone who does that is a pirate or warez trader). A hacker does not destroy a system that he/she has hacked (anyone who does that is a cracker). A hacker's aim is just to seek knowledge.

Seeking knowledge may not be destructive. We don't advocate anyone's going out and infiltrating or infecting an innocent party's computer systems with a malicious intent designed to destroy valuable data or bring their system to a halt. Don't ever do that as you may end up in jail or find yourself in lots of trouble. Be responsible and use the knowledge you may obtain here for your own education. *The programs and information provided on this site can be dangerous if you do not use them properly. They can be a lethal weapon.*[10]

MHC refer here to the Brain Virus: ironically, perhaps, Brain's developers in the 1980s, Basit and Amjad Alvi, subsequently went on to run Brain.net.pk, Pakistan's largest Internet Service Provider. As an ISP company, 'insider' knowledge of potential intrusion techniques is invaluable. Coincidentally, the Taliban used it as the ISP for their website.[11]

The MHC's intention to 'seek knowledge' is *perhaps* a reflection of a hadith (saying) of Muhammad, to 'Seek knowledge, even if you have to go to China'. Certainly, the 'Hacking Tutorial' contained on the site represents a substantial and eclectic archive of reproduced files and links relating to hacking, including beginner's guides, various encyclopedias, the Anarchist Cookbook, and basic introductions to specific scripting and hacking procedures. Much of this has been cut and pasted from other sources onto MHC pages, and a considerable percentage dates back several years – it is not new material. There has been limited editing for the 'Muslim' readership: some of the files have profane language on them (for example, 'Hacking FTP').

During the period (19 November 2001–26 December 2001) Alldas.org logged 28 hacking attacks linked to MHC. The majority of these were '.com' domains with affiliations to India. One defacement, of a Jaipur Hotel site, gives 'gr33ts' to 'PHC – GForce – AIC – SILVERLORDS – WFD – War4 – MHC – xst – Pakistan Cyber Warriors [PCW] – All Muslim Hackers'. Many of these were active hackers, such as PHC (Pakistan Hackers Club), Silverlords and GForce (discussed below). The page also includes the statements 'FREE KASHMIR, FREE PALESTINE … We are her3 to Fuck Up INDIANZ …

The *WAR* Has Just Begun'.[12] Similar pages appear elsewhere credited to MHC, including one describing MHC as the Matrix Hacking Club – but giving the same list of 'gr33ts' as the example above.[13] Another has a photo gif of two women using a laptop and a cartoon from the cult 'Joy of Tech' series – hardly examples of 'Muslim' symbolism.[14] Different members, who seem to leave their own trademarks on 'defacements', undertake MHC hacks.

Silverlords, cited by MHC, are logged by Alldas.org as having undertaken 1,436 defacements between 20 November 2000 and 14 April 2002. However, these figures are deceptive and represent rivalry for the Silver Lords moniker between Brazilian and Pakistani hackers. These can be seen through examination of the archive: some of the earlier (Brazilian) hacks are simply 'shouts' to other hackers or replace index pages with other images (such as Pokemon characters); some of the information was in Spanish. However, the December 2001 'Silver Lords' hack of paintcompany.com presented a pro-Kashmiri page, with graphic photographs of human rights violations. One example had the statement (in capital letters):

> STOP THE INDIAN GENOCIDE AGAINST THE PEOPLE OF KASHMIR. FREE KASHMIR, PALESTINE, CHECHNYA, KOSOVA, AND BOSNIA. END THE INJUST U.N. SANCTIONS ON IRAQ.

The site provided a history of Kashmir in the period of Partition, highlighting the role of India:

> Kashmir was a majority Muslim state, and since Pakistan was to become a Muslim nation, it made sense. Not to India however. India immediately dispatched troops all over Kashmir to suppress the will and voice of the Kashmiri people.[15]

Amongst the shouts was (ironic?) acknowledgement of various Brazilian sites and individuals. At the time of writing, there appeared to be continuing and intense rivalry between the pro-Kashmiri and Brazilian users of the name Silver Lords, with the parties using hacks to abuse one another.[16] It indicates one problem when trying to define 'Muslim' hacktivists.

Perhaps slightly clearer are the activities of the World's Fantabulous Defacers (WFD). WFD include mOrOn and Nightman, who have also worked separately, and are responsible for 63 archived defacements between 23 September and 18 December 2000, primarily against Israeli targets, with some Indian, .tw, .com and Yugoslavian sites also attacked.[17] These hacks were more 'basic' in terms of on-page content than the WFD hacks, and several were focused on non-political interests, such as an attack on an online bank in Karachi.[18] Several other names contribute to various WFD hacks.

The WFD Alldas.org archive includes 334 defacements between 20 November 2001 and 21 March 2002. However, as with any archival statistic relating to hacking, this figure must be treated with caution, as other groups not associated with Islamic issues also use the name. Taking this consideration in mind, the pro-Palestinian WFD have undertaken a number of high-profile hacks, with 79 archived attacks on .il domains. A spectacular post-9-11 example came on an Israeli site, featuring a Flash movie on the intifada, backed by a music soundtrack. It also featured commentary on 9-11:

> If you are still shaken by the horrifying scenes of September 11, please observe a moment of silence for the 5,000 civilian lives lost in the New York, Washington, DC and Pennsylvania attacks.
>
> While we're at it, let's have 13 minutes of silence for the 130,000 Iraqi civilians killed in 1991 by order of President Bush Sr. Take another moment to remember how Americans celebrated and cheered in the streets.[19]

The page continues (proportionally) seeking minutes of silence for other victims of ('American-related'?) conflicts. They include a link to the Alldas.org archive to highlight their work, and include a typical hacker 'shout' at the end of the page:

> We will deface sites from time to time, spreading our message, though we've not been involved in too many defacements lately but we were & are the most powerful hacktivist group in the world, there is no denying to this fact & the reason is our sheer determination & our will not to leave the hands of truth no matter what, the cyber resistance will go on...[20]

The impact of such an activity may be limited, given that the hacked site was simply an exhibition and trade show company. There is no doubt that such hacks will generate interest amongst the hacking community and amongst others who wish to inspect their handiwork.

Of great impact was the WFD hack of Ariel Sharon's Election Campaign 2001 website. This applied a degree of satire in reproducing the original format, but replacing the text and images. Sharon is described as a 'war criminal'; the photos are extremely graphic, including one of a badly scarred child whose horrific injuries were the result of his house being 'burned down by illegal Jewish settlers in the West Bank'. The page includes the statement: 'Long live Hizballah! Long live Palestine! Long live Chechnya, Kashmir, Kosovo and Bosnia!' There is also a note on the role of a hacker, which perhaps puts such activities in proportion:

> We are not heroes ... But merely hackers ... While we understand that it is not feasible for us to successfully make a legitimate difference in oppressed and tortured lives in Palestine and other places in the world, we will continue to deface, not destroy, for the cause ... until there is reform ... until there is change ... until when Palestinian, Chechen, Kashmiri, Iraqi, Albanian, African, Irish, and all suffering children in the world can wake up to a world of peace, not a world of death, destruction, and chaos, a world devoid of war.[21]

Such a high-profile hack is significant, however, especially in that it generates media interest on a notable target. The fact that the page continues to exist on the Alldas archive is also important for the hackers. Other WFD hacks include commentary on contemporary events and links to news resources. A hack on Ramat Gan's local government site (in Israel) included links to Intifada Online, the Palestine Information Centre and the Islamic Association for Palestine.[22] The extent to which these might be read by the 'usual' readers of the site is open to question. Their 'shouts' indicate some awareness of other 'Muslim' hackers, for example in giving the names of the GFORCE members, and acknowledging Bosnian hackers:

> GForce Pakistan (Sniper, heataz, Rsnake, instinct, miller, rave- and amnesiac) Salute! For hacking against India and showing THE WORLD HOW CORRUPT, UNSCRUPULOUS, PERVERT [sic] AND UNETHICAL INDIAN POLITICIANS AND INDIAN MEDIA (ZEE NEWS) ARE![23]

The same page contains lengthy statements relating to Palestine, a Flash movie of the shooting of Muhammad al-Durra by Israeli

Defence Forces and a list of the WFD hacks on 40 Israeli technolog-ical companies. Several of the WFD hacks offer e-mail addresses as points of contact, although these change rapidly; the service provider suspended the use by WFD of the anonymising HushMail e-mail.[24]

Hacking can also form part of the contents of websites with Islamic interests. One example is the Sweden-based Alforatein site, which incorporates a hacking section amongst pages on Iraq (its central interest), poetry and anti-dictators sections. 'Humam', a student in the Royal Institute of Technology in Sweden, created the site.[25] The index page suggests a Shi'a linkage, with its picture of Karbala in Iraq. A substantial proportion of the materials are in Arabic, including 'Window's Secrets', 'How to delete a trojan' and 'Spying programmes'. The spying tools and programs section provides information in Arabic about the use of a variety of tools (all from external sources, some written in the Arabic language), together with substantial warnings about the implications for their use. There is also a listing of viruses, including Melissa, which whilst they would not necessarily be effective against an 'inoculated' system (i.e. one with an up-to-date virus checker), could be effective if adjusted or re-coded. Some of the programs log themselves on to individual PCs and are difficult to remove.[26] Generic information is also available. The facilities on offer are more sophisticated than those on the MHC site, including various key-logger programs (which record computer keyboard outputs and e-mail them to a specific address) and preventative measures to protect against unwanted intrusions. It contains a long list of pages associated with Arabic hackers, such as Mr Linux Lover, whose attacks on a number of Israel-based sites are listed (together with links to their Attrition.org 'mirror' copies).[27] There is also a listing of Swedish and English hacking-related sites, unconnected with Islam, which offer further resources and guides.

Whilst several of the other sites on the list had non-functioning links, there was a link to the regularly updated Gebal ('Mountains') site, which contains substantial Arabic information and discussions on a broad range of computer-related issues.[28] Although there is a lot of general information on the site, there is a section containing discussions relating to hacking activities, including advice on entering specific sites, virus information and warnings, and coding issues. The extent to which this represents a process of 'Islamic' hacking is perhaps open to question. Whilst the discussions include individuals living in Saudi Arabia, and some of the language naturally contains 'Arabic Islamic' protocols ('peace be upon you', 'God willing', etc.), the site does not itself indicate a direct Islamic ethos – although the resources themselves conceivably might be useful to 'Muslim hackers' (and other Arabic speakers). There is, of course, no need for a Muslim hacker to go to a specific 'Islamic' site or a site produced in a specific language. Many resources are generic, and the 'Islamic' hacking sites themselves are often mirrors or adaptations of other resources. In themselves, these sites cannot be conceived as a major 'threat' or source of knowledge for potential or existing hacking activity. Those most likely to conduct any 'serious' form of e-jihad relating to service disruption, hacking or cracking are more than likely to already be proficient at the basic coding on offer.

Can hacking or e-jihad really be deemed an Islamic activity, and is this blowing the issue out of proportion? There was a brief discussion of this in the Madinat al-Muslimeen chat room, which contained concerns of the illegality of the activity and its incompatibility with Islam. The stream of discussion was started by one reader, 'Al-Basha', who was asking about the ethics of hacking, whether it equated with jihad and whether it was completely *haram* (forbidden). A response came from SuperHiMY:

'What would the Prophet do with the Internet?'
'I can't answer that for you.'
'Use your gifts to create something.'
'Something good.'
'Not something, that IF you bragged about it, would get you a one way ticket to Club Fed ...'
'At some point the mental gymnastics one allows Shaytaan to suggest in your mind will break down and the incompatibility of being a Muslim and ripping off someone either through Cracking Warez, etc. will confuse you. Be a MUSLIM Boy. Don't be a Mafia Boy.'[29]

'Club Fed' are the federal authorities, and Mafia Boy is a reference to a hacker who had boasted of his activities through chat rooms, and was finally caught. The channel's administrator, Jannah, noted:

I think in many people's minds hacking is a form of jihad or 'pride' but it is illegal and more trouble than it is worth so you have to weigh the pros and cons carefully. A pro is definitely the psychological impact, for too long muslim youth have felt like they were backwards and inferior to the West and can't affect anything in the world.[30]

Elsewhere, Islam Online produced an online *fatwa* on this subject, in a live *fatwa* session with Sheikh Faisal Mawlawy, vice president of the Islamic European Fatwa Council.

Launching any attacks on anti-Islamic and Zionist Websites is strongly prohibited, unless they start attacking Islamic ones ... When asked about Zionist sites that libel Islam and slander Islamic symbols, Mawlawy said that Muslims could answer back only if attacks on Islamic sites had been offensive and had disrupted the site's online status. When asked about Christian and secular sites which 'spread corrupted beliefs and wicked ideas,' Mawlawy said that Muslims had a mission to make things clear peacefully.[31]

Mawlawy did state that Israeli banks in the occupied territories were legitimate targets. He also proclaimed that visiting secular, and 'Zionist', websites was permissible for Muslim surfers as information-gathering exercises. The role and actual authority of Mawlawy and his European Fatwa Council is itself an important question.[32]

In this context, the term e-jihad is descriptive, and applied by both (cr/h)activists and commentators. It particularly applies to the hacking of Israeli sites, although it should be stressed that hackers do not always have an overtly Muslim identity and are not always Palestinian. There are Christian Palestinian hackers in cyberspace. The application of religious language and justification for the activities of hackers is mixed. In some cases, the conflict might be described as 'Zionist'-Palestinian not Jewish-Christian/Muslim. E-jihad may be a useful description, rather than an accurate definition of activities in this regard.

The 'Palestinian–Israeli Cyberwar' brought the term 'e-jihad' to prominence during a prolonged exchange of attacks between various groups and individuals, which accelerated after the outbreak of the so-called Al Aqsa Intifada on 28 September 2000. 'Pro-Palestinian' hackers targeted sites associated with Israel, whilst US sites were also considered appropriate targets. Notable victims of hackers and crackers included Israeli Defence Forces, the Israeli government, the *Jerusalem Post*, technology companies and academic institutions.[33] Israeli ISPs were also hit: these included Israel's biggest ISP, NetVision, which at that time also hosted the Palestinian National Authority's website.[34] Attacks on ISPs were particularly disruptive to the Israeli public, given their relatively high level of Internet access in relation to their regional neighbours.[35]

The results of such hacking (on both sides) included e-mail overload, system failure, the defacement of web content, database acquisition and dysfunctional and crashed sites. E-mail servers were attacked by tools such as EvilPing and QuickFire, which crashed systems by sending multiple messages to the same e-mail address:

> The most common weapons used were variations on denial-of-service and 'ping-flood' type tools with nefarious names like 'EvilPing,' 'Winsmurf,' and 'QuickFire.' EvilPing – a variation of a tool known as the 'Ping of Death' – sends a single 64K packet that can completely crash most machines ...
>
> Once one side distributes an attack tool, that same tool is then reconfigured and used against the attacker's Web sites.[36]

This form of hacking required only basic hardware, including a 56k modem, although the results are enhanced with the use of an Asynchronous Digital Subscriber Line (ADSL). Similar hacking resources are available on 'pro-Israeli' and 'pro-Palestinian' sites, as well as generic, 'neutral' sites. Hacking technology 'improved' during the conflict, as special tools were created and refined on both sides as weapons. It is interesting to note that this conflict involved not only pro-Palestinian Muslim participants from outside the region (including Iran and Pakistan) and pro-Israeli support from outside the region, but also Brazilian hackers who chose to hit both sides (sometimes simultaneously).

One example of this phenomenon came from the UNITY group, whose website was part of the UK registered ummah.net domain (see above). The founder of the UNITY website noted the importance of so-called 'cyber-war':

> 'As information technology comes to rule every part of our life, it is no longer necessary to have rockets to destroy an electrical facility,' explained Faris Muhammad Al-Masri, founder of UNITY (www.ummah.net/unity), a website with an Islamic ideology. 'Instead, penetrating the enemy's networks and planting your code will get a better result.'[37]

The UNITY website contained campaigning materials in several European languages, focusing on Palestinian-Islamic issues. There was also UNITY hacking, under the 'Iron Guards' banner. They were allegedly involved in attacking Israeli ISPs, as part of a cohesive strategy:

'Phase one of our objective consists of disabling official Israeli government sites,' explained Al-Masri, in an e-mail interview.
'Phase two focuses on crashing financial sites such as those belonging to Israel's Stock Exchange and central bank; phase three involves knocking out the main Israeli ISP servers; and phase four consists of blitzing major Israeli e-commerce sites to cause the loss of hundreds of online transactions.' [38]

Israeli infrastructures were affected by hacking activities. This type of disruption went beyond site defacement to attack complete networks and facilities. It can be difficult to determine the level of 'success' groups such as the Iron Guards have, but they represent one manifestation of the hacking ethic in relation to Islam. Whilst this may be seen as a 'macro'-hacking activity, defacements in the name of the 'Iron Guards' have also included attacks on mundane personal home pages seemingly unconnected with Israel or Judaism. One example on a personal home page included photos of victims in Palestine, graphics of 'Muslim' flags facing a burning American flag and links to Hizbullah and Unity websites. The line 'Jihdad till Victory' was an unusual typographical mistake on this defacement, which would have had a very limited readership.[39]

The role of language in these hacks is perhaps a separate issue, but certainly some of the pro-Palestinian hacks have used 'profane' language, whilst identifying themselves as 'Islamic' in orientation. A hack of an Israeli astronomy site by 'Root-X' in April 2002, for example, stated:

Fuck Israel.
Free the World This Goes Out To All The Bro's , Sis's In Palestine.[40]

The defacement page contained 'Greetz' to several individuals whose names indicated that they were Muslims.

In October 2000, two Hizbullah websites were victims of pro-Israeli hacking, but they continued to operate several 'back-up' sites. The attacks were in the form of 'e-mail bombing' or through 'virtual overwhelming traffic'. Ali Ayoub, the Hizbullah web master (previously interviewed for *Virtually Islamic*) noted that:

> the Lebanese group [Hizbullah] considers the Internet 'a public domain and a means of expression for everyone'. 'We also considered that our presence on the Internet was the most important thing for us, our sole objective is to remain up and running ...
>
> 'There is a power balance in this field. All it takes is a computer and brains. Like the Israelis, we proved to everyone that we have the technology and the brains to do it and win this war,' he said.[41]

In 2002, Hizbullah became less dependent on external resources, when it organised its own private server. Plans were underway to establish a Hebrew language channel as part of a major upgrade of party sites.

The pro-Israeli group 'mOsad' claimed responsibility for attacking the Hizbullah sites' Internet Service Provider ITX in January 2001, part of a phase of activity by mOsad which commenced in November 2000, and including attacks on commercial Arabic sites, Qatar's Ministry of Awqaf and Islamic Affairs, Mohammed Khatami's official site and various other sites in Pakistan, Saudi Arabia and Qatar.[42]

During this phase of the 'cyber-war', other notable hits for 'pro-Israeli' hackers were the linking of Hamas and Hizbullah websites to hard-core pornography. Shortly after a bombing attack in Netanya on 5 March 2001, visitors to the Hamas site were diverted to a pornographic site (entitled Hot Motel Horny Sex Sluts). The leader of Hamas, Sheikh Ahmad Yassin, determined this hack as an attack on Islam and responded angrily:

> I'm telling them to die of their own fury ... They are trying to disfigure the image of Islam and Muslims. These are the people who are shedding our blood and massacring our people every day, so it is not difficult for them to do something like this. As much as their anger and fire rises, they will try all and crazy ways to extinguish it.[43]

However, Yassin was also quoted as saying in 2000 that 'We will use whatever tools we can – e-mail, the Internet – to facilitate jihad.'[44] Other pro-Palestinians have interpreted such attacks as being anti-Arab, rather than anti-Islamic.

Hackers on all 'sides' applied ingenuity to create, develop and distribute attack strategies. A prime example was Doctor Nuker, founder of the Pakistan Hackerz Club (PHC). Nuker had previously hacked into Indian sites associated with Kashmir, together with other members of the Pakistani Hackerz Club:

> 'Our goal is to bring attention to violence in Kashmir, but that's just not going to be our only goal. PHC will hack for all the injustice going in this world, especially the killings and injustice with Muslims. [The] United Nations and [the] United States never forget to act urgent on other small issues but they never give a damn about the Kashmir issue. We not only say, but we really care for Kashmiris and take them as our brothers and sisters', Doctor Nuker said.[45]

PHC and Nuker became interested in the Palestinian conflict because 'we share the religion and we think alike'.[46] Nuker compromised the American Israel Public Affairs Committee (AIPAC) website, and obtained its e-mailing list of 3,500 names, together with another list containing about 700 credit card account details of AIPAC donors, which were published online.[47] The hack replaced the AIPAC site with hyperlinks to photos of the victims of conflict, together with other information and a summary of some of the database content. AIPAC were eventually able to take their site offline, leaving an Error 404 message in place of conventional content, but the content of Nuker's hack was already circulating in cyberspace by this time, including on several Muslim e-mailing lists.

Nuker obtained substantial publicity from the technology and mainstream press (on- and off-line), primarily because of the security issues that were raised by obtaining and publishing the credit card database. The AIPAC press spokesman noted that, despite the intrusion, there were only three incidents of fraud associated with information obtained from the database.[48] Whilst it is not intended to construct a psychological model of such 'hacktivist' agendas, it could be noted that one motivation of such hacking is the opportunity to demonstrate technological skill.[49] Nuker made a particular effort to give 'shouts' to hacking friends and colleagues, boasting of the achievement. However, Nuker also provided links to sites relating to what were perceived as human rights atrocities committed against the Palestinians. It was, perhaps, one example of a 'successful' hacking activity, going beyond simple disruption and displays of technological plumage. Whether it can be described as an 'Islamic' hack is open to discussion. There is a political dimension, with a religious undercurrent and focus (in terms of the target). The application of Islamic terminology is restricted, and indeed the exercise of 'profane' vocabulary was a prominent feature of the hack.

On 21 September 2001, 'Nuker' hacked the commercial Worldtradeservices.com site, condemning bin Laden's attacks, whilst attacking the United States' activities in the Middle East and Kashmir:

> Part of the defacement said the CIA had the most to gain by last week's attacks on the World Trade Center in New York, as they legitimise long-standing US efforts to hunt down Osama Bin Laden, the prime suspect for the terrorist attacks ...
>
> 'The attack is nothing to with muslims [*sic*] or Osama-bin-Laden. If you want to compare what Israel has done against the Palestinians, it is 10 times worse than what they Muslim terrorists, only if they are behind it, have done to the US now.'[50]

The Alldas.org archive lists 47 defacements attributed to Pakistan Hackerz Club (PHC) between 12 July 1999 and 24 October 2001. These PHC hacks cite Doctor Nuker as founder of the club. Typically, they contain his logo, a reference to Kashmir and 'greets' to other individuals and organisations. The June 2000 hack of Silicon India, for example, mentions 50 other names, together with an extract of a CNN interview with Pakistan's President Musharraf stating that the Kashmir issue was central to future peace in South Asia. It also sends a message to the server's administrator, noting the inadequacy of the firewall, and that PHC had obtained credit card details through the hack.[51] Other hacks feature information about Kashmir and comments on political issues in the region.[52]

In October 2001, the FBI identified 'Doctor Nuker' as being a Karachi resident, Misbah Khan, who was indicted (although he had not been located) by the US authorities.[53] Despite his 'shouts' of technical wizardry, it seemed that these were not sufficient to mask his identity:

> The four-count indictment charged Khan with knowingly causing the transmission of a computer command which intentionally caused damage to AIPAC's computers; intentionally accessing AIPAC's computer without authorization and obtaining information from that computer; knowingly and with intent to

defraud possessing fifteen or more unauthorized 'access devices' (credit card account numbers); and causing the use of unauthorized access devices to obtain things of value of more than $1,000. The two computer offenses are punishable by up to five years in jail; the credit card offenses are punishable by up to ten years in jail; all four offenses carry fines of up to $250,000 and terms of supervised release of up to three years.

FBI Special Agent-in-Charge Lynne Hunt said that 'doctornuker' was recently identified as Misbah Khan by the FBI computer crime squad with the assistance of the FBI legal office or 'legat' at the U.S. Embassy in Islamabad, Pakistan. SAC Hunt said that the investigation demonstrates that 'computer hackers often leave behind a more elaborate trail of evidence than they realize, and we will follow that trail no matter where in the world it leads.' United States Attorney Thomas DiBiagio commended the FBI's investigation and noted that the U.S. Attorney's Office has prosecuted a number of computer intrusion and intellectual property crimes during the past year.[54]

This led to some confusion, as another individual claiming to be the 'real' Doctor Nuker emerged, together with the allegation that several individuals were using the same name.[55] At the time of writing, the 'real' Doctor Nuker seemingly had not been found.[56]

Nuker was one of several Pakistan hackers operating on the Internet singly (or potentially as a group under the single moniker). GFORCE was another which achieved notoriety, for example through hacking the US Defense Test & Evaluation Processional Institute (DTEPI) in September 2000. The original defacement had contained strong language and profanity:

The US has always seen itself as the moderating power of the world but it has supported Israel in its cause and has remained silent on the Kashmir Issue for Too [sic] long. A Must we remind everyone that almost all the people in the world is owned by the Muslims? Is that why the US kisses Saudia Arabia's ass while committing such injustices deep inside? And they call Pakistan a corrupt country? Just how fucking corrupt can you get when the President of the most powerful nation in the world gets a blowjob from an intern working in his office??? We have suffered throughout the ages and will suffer no more. This is the era of cyberwarfare, where once again the Muslims have prevailed. We will not rest till every node, every line, every bit of information contained in our suppressors has not been wiped out, returning them to the dark ages. Well will not tolerate anymore, and we will not fail. As I type this from the confront of my home ... far away in a valley the blood of innocents paints the mountains red...[57]

GFORCE also succeeded in hacking US government agencies, military and other targets via Taiwan-based platforms.[58] GFORCE has been seen as one of the most prominent (group of) hackers to emerge from Pakistan, along with Doctor Nuker and associates in the Pakistani Hackerz Club. GFORCE applied specific compromise techniques in order to exploit Internet vulnerabilities, and download their own data onto a system.[59]

In October 2001, there were unsubstantiated rumours of an 'al-Qaeda Alliance Online':

> Referring to recent attacks by the pro-Pakistani hacker group G-Force Pakistan against U.S. government and military websites, the Indian publication 'The Statesman' claims that an 'Al-Qaida Alliance Online' has been formed to wage 'full-fledged cyber-terrorism' against the U.S., the UK and India. There has been no official confirmation to support the creation of such an alliance, which is said to include G-Force Pakistan, the Pakistan Hackers Club, Dodi and WFD.[60]

A later report suggested there were 25 hackers in the group, from Australia, Afghanistan, Pakistan and Kashmir.[61] However, to date, very little activity has registered in the 'al-Qaida Alliance Online' name.

Reuters separately reported a 'Bin Laden Worm', which came in the form of 'an e-mail file attachment with the name binladen_brasil.exe'.[62] The 'brasil.exe' suffix suggests its regional origins, whilst associated statements (for example, the e-mail subject headers including 'Bin Laden toillete paper' and 'Sadam hussein & BinLaden IN LOVE') indicated that it was not a product of pro-al-Qaeda hackers.

Various Muslim hackers started action in the name of bin Laden or the Taliban, including Pakistan GFORCE (attacking US government sites) as part of a 'cyber jihad' campaign. For example:

> A crew known as GForce Pakistan replaced the home page of the Defense Test & Evaluation Processional Institute (DTEPI) site with

a text message about terrorism and Islam. The defaced page also included several photographs described by the attackers as depicting Muslim children killed by Israeli soldiers.[63]

This was their second attack on the site, an earlier defacement taking place in September 2000 (see above). The 2001 defacement was quickly taken off-line, and the archive unavailable at the time of writing. Although GFORCE's main player was arrested in November 2001, the group continued to be active,[64] allegedly placing trojan sniffers onto US sites via Taiwanese platforms, in order to obtain secret data, which they threatened to pass onto bin Laden.[65]

During the escalation of violence in Israel and Palestine in 2002, there was also an attendant increase in hacking activities against Israeli targets. Writing on 15 April 2002, the mi2g company noted that:

> The Israeli domain '.il' has been the biggest victim of web defacements (548) in the Middle East (1,295) by a wide margin over the period July 1999 to mid-April 2002 inclusive. This includes the start of the second Intifada, the Palestinian uprising, in September 2000.
>
> Israel has suffered 42% (548/1295) of the Middle East overt hack attacks, while Turkey (13%), Morocco (12%) and Egypt (12%) were also targeted. Israel's digital risk is greater because it has the most Internet connections (1.1 million) in the Middle East (more than all 22 Arab countries combined).
>
> During the past 14 days, Israel was the victim of 67% (10/15) of significant web defacements in the Middle East according to the mi2g Intelligence Unit.[66]

The same report noted that other Middle Eastern countries were also victims of such activities.

By September 2002, 'pro-Islamic' hacking had increased substantially, with various groups under the Unix Security Guards banner making 355 attacks between May and September 2002, including denial of service attacks and 'protective hacking', highlighting security loopholes in Islamic sites and advising site administrators of these deficiencies.[67] By October 2002, they were claiming that they had made 1,511 attacks in one single month. Related disruptive activities also substantially increased, with the pro-Islamic FBH (Federal Bureau of Hackers) and TheBuGz also substantially increasing their hacking activities.[68]

The motivation for such activity is a key issue, whether it is 'for fun' or for more 'serious' reasons. In an article on hacking in Pakistan, which contained interviews with several Karachi-based hackers, Khalid Hussain noted a variety of reasons for hacking:

> It's the urge for global recognition. The desire to get media attention, as one local IT expert believes. 'Defacing a major Indian website and putting some pro-Kashmir literature or posters on it will attract instant attention from the world media,' the IT expert, who requested anonymity points out. 'Your work will be flashed and discussed in some of the biggest TV channels like the CNN and leading newspapers like the New York Times. An average hacker, who is I believe a person with a bigger than normal ego, will get a lot of satisfaction and pride from such a thing.'...
>
> 'I don't think these guys are actually interested in any cause,' says Junaid. 'They are very serious when it comes to hacking, but otherwise most of the ones I know don't really care about what's happening in the world. I believe they mostly do it for fun and maybe publicity.'[69]

Perhaps the significance of such hacking activities should not be blown out of proportion within academic contexts, although the phenomenon can be representative of a minority of 'Islamic' activities online. Despite warnings from Internet watchdogs,[70] and fears of 'cyber-attacks' 'as retribution for the US campaign in Afghanistan',[71] there was no evidence of an increase in general hacking activity post-9-11, according to the US Federal Computer Incident Response Center (FedCIRC).[72] It is possible that there was an increase in relation to Islam and 'Muslim issues' (for and against). This is an area of interest to legislators, notably in the drafting of various surveillance and anti-terrorism legislation, and following 9-11 greater attention was being paid to hacking related computer crime.[73] 9-11 stimulated the development of specific governmental and international computer monitoring units, such as the pan-European Europol:

> The unit will use databases to keep track of the nicknames and e-mail addresses of suspected criminals. Analysts will be able to draw on software to look for linguistic similarities in communications or to monitor changes made to Web sites.[74]

High-tech crime may have a broad definition, but the technology used to track it may be similar, whether the criminals are involved in financial fraud, hacking or 'terrorism'. It will be interesting to observe the extent to which issues of cyber-law will enter into the fields of 'Islamic legal scholarship', particularly as these issues are certainly relevant within various Muslim majority governmental contexts.

THE NEW EXEGESIS: ENCRYPTION AND THE USE OF E-MAIL

The use of encryption by al-Qaeda led Allied forces to seek possession of al-Qaeda and Taliban computers during their operations in order to obtain encryption keys. Barak Jolish, in a 2002 article for Salon.com, suggested that al-Qaeda had been 'an avid consumer of computers over the last seven years, and is especially fond of laptops'.[75] For example, Jolish notes the use of laptops by an alleged member of the 9-11 hijackers, Zacarias Moussaoui (who was arrested prior to 9-11 and subsequently indicted), and also their use by the 1993 World Trade Center bomber Ramzi Yousef.[76] As Jolish states:

> Ironically, though, winning possession of this equipment on the battlefield may be the easy part; terrorists today have the capacity to protect data with encryption schemes that not even America's high-tech big guns can crack. The number of possible keys in the new 256-bit Advanced Encryption Standard (AES), for example, is 1 followed by 77 zeros – a figure comparable to the total number of atoms in the universe.[77]

Without keys or clues to passwords, attempts to control the export of, or access to, encryption technology have been largely unsuccessful. One of the most successful producers and exporters of encryption products has been Israel, which deemed it impossible to prevent the use of such software, even by the 'enemy':

> Both the Israeli army and the FBI have confirmed that Hamas and other Islamic militants regularly use the Internet to transmit encrypted instructions for terrorist attacks – including maps, photographs, directions, codes and technical details about how to use bombs. On the other hand, Israel's economy is among the most reliant in the world on high technology exports.[78]

Encryption technology is available 'off-the-shelf' from any software store. It is also easy to purchase through the Internet, as well as being built into e-mail packages such as Microsoft Outlook Express. Anonymiser e-mail, such as HushMail, can also be used to send material in 'secret'.

To demonstrate the ease in which encryption software might be obtained, the writer selected, at random from the net, a German company offering Shyfile online, advertising it as 'a 6144bit Email Encryption Software product' with 'Military strength encryption for 1on1 mail'.[79]

> ShyFile will also encode all kinds of binary files [e.g. those having a -jpg, -gif, -bmp, -doc, -xls, -cls, -mp3 or even an -exe extension]. It has never been easier to encrypt, e.g. your MS Word-document in a way no Secret Service on this planet could snoop into. But those files containing encoded binary information cannot be opened using an Internet browser alone, i.e. they require the actual ShyFile software to decode. Any ShyFile installation can be used to decode, regardless whether it's the full version or even an expired evaluation copy ...
>
> According to German Law we do not have to leave a backdoor open for any public agencies, so we didn't.[80]

It was straightforward to download the free evaluation version or purchase and download the full version, and the package also provides a File Shredder to destroy any files. This software is similar to several other products the writer has viewed and used.

Faced with such technology, intelligence sources have been limited in the effectiveness of using software such as 'Magic Lantern', designed to obtain encryption keys through placing a virus (via e-mail) on a specific computer. Other invasive information-seeking software, such as DCS1000 (previously known as the Carnivore Internet surveillance system), is apparently ineffective against encrypted data.[81] The application of such software had been questioned by civil rights organisations, although their demands may have been tempered following 9-11.

There were indications that Osama bin Laden and supporters of al-Qaeda were applying the net to disseminate strategic documents and messages, utilising encryption software, and coding messages in other digital packets and posting them on the web. The favoured packet, according to some 'cyber experts', was the undraped female form.

These pornography sites could be accessed with the correct digital keys in order to decode the hidden messages.[82] In December 2001, this writer contacted Internet security experts (who wish to remain anonymous), who expressed scepticism at the use by al-Qaeda of such means of communication. The FBI had also suggested that clear text messages (via Hotmail and Yahoo) were the traditional means of communication.

On 31 December 2001, however, two journalists from the *Wall Street Journal* published a story in which they described how they had obtained, from a Kabul market, two computers which they later claimed had been used by al-Qaeda.[83] These contained encrypted information, which was decipherable. There was substantial logistical information, details on strategies and operatives, and a 'primer on coding and encryption of documents. Other files outline procedures for transmitting messages via Pakistan.'[84] Given the limited access to e-mail and the Internet in Afghanistan, it can be assumed that any messages might be copied onto disk and then e-mailed from Pakistan.

The same *Wall Street Journal* story details the similarities between the itinerary of one 'Abdul Ra'uff' and Richard Reid, who was convicted in 2003 of trying to detonate explosives contained in his footwear, whilst flying between France and the United States on 22 December 2001. Authorities subsequently attempted to track down the routes of the e-mails Reid was alleged to have sent via an e-mail café in Paris:

> Investigators have determined Reid was constantly using e-mails for communications, not only from Paris, but elsewhere in France and in Belgium. They said that Reid was in touch with at least 10 people.
>
> In another e-mail that he thought would be received after his death, Reid wrote his mother in Britain, explaining his reasons for targeting the jet and urging her to convert to Islam. The French police sources said that Reid appeared to be saying good-bye to his mother.[85]

When Reid was unable to board an earlier flight, he was alleged to have e-mailed an address in Pakistan for instructions and was told to board a later flight. It was suggested he used Hotmail and Yahoo web e-mail services:

> NBC's Robert Windrem, citing U.S. officials who spoke on condition of anonymity, said intelligence services have long

identified Yahoo and Hotmail as the al-Qaida terrorist network's preferred means to send e-mail.

The benefits to al-Qaida are that such services can be accessed from any computer in the world with an Internet connection, can be encrypted if necessary, and accounts can be opened and closed quickly. Moreover, the services do not retain records of emails for a long period of time.[86]

A later despatch by Windrem discusses how al-Qaeda couriers might transport data (for example, through the use of floppy disks and Zip disks – although rewritable CDs would also be viable) containing 'encrypted data to a third party who in turn takes it to the cell planning an attack'.[87] This could be interpreted as a 'low-tech' solution to communication, in conjunction with the application of web-based e-mail (discussed above). Windrem suggests that al-Qaeda have also used instant messaging and chat rooms to convey information, perhaps through the use of coded messages. The application of steganography to transmit information in encoded form was also raised, although no further details are provided. One of the significant issues associated with research and journalism on this application of technology is that a certain proportion of data is not available in the public domain. Perhaps in the future, a more detailed picture of the application of this technology will emerge.

Coincidentally, John Walker Lindh, an American accused of membership of the Taliban and al-Qaeda who was captured by Allied forces in Afghanistan, was said to have used e-mail to correspond with his family. There was no suggestion that he was using the medium in an encrypted format for other purposes.[88]

In January 2002, the kidnappers of Daniel Pearl, a *Wall Street Journal* bureau chief, used e-mail (including Hotmail) to deliver photos of their captive together with ransom demands. Pearl had previously been in e-mail contact with alleged leaders of Islamist groups in order to arrange the assignation in Karachi that resulted in his kidnap (and eventual murder). Police in Pakistan were able to track down three suspects, although at the time of writing it was unclear whether this was through e-mail surveillance technology. Ian Brown, of the computer science department at University College, London, noted that it would have been straightforward for the kidnappers to set up an anonymous e-mail account:

'You could set up an anonymous Hotmail account in a cyber-cafe but you would only ever be able to send one message via that account. The more information you send, the easier it is to trace you ...

'For a computer enthusiast with some knowledge of how email works, it is possible to send fairly disguised messages.'[89]

Keeping e-mail activity and web access anonymous is uncomplicated (at a basic level), and there are a number of online explanations available which explore the ways in which anonymity can be configured through the use of proxies and downloadable software applications.[90]

In December 2001, the Canadian Office of Critical Infrastructure Protection and Emergency Services published a report, which emphasised the potential for future online attacks by supporters of al-Qaeda. It acknowledged the lack of IT infrastructure in Afghanistan meant that any attacks would be organised outside the country. It referred to the 'Iron Guard' (discussed above), and the potential of Osama bin Laden's utilising his wealth to invest in technologies for such cyber-attacks. It also noted the activities of a pro-United States group, who were indiscriminately attacking 'Islam', the 'Middle East' and related websites:

On 14 September, a group calling itself the 'Dispatchers' posted a statement on the Web saying it has already disabled Internet Service Providers (ISPs) in the Middle East and has been targeting ISPs in Afghanistan with the explicit goal of destroying them. The Dispatchers, claiming to be approximately 300 strong, said it would target Pakistan, Iraq and several other Middle Eastern countries. The hacker group said it is planning a coordinated attack against Internet infrastructure in targeted countries and other critical information systems. The US National Infrastructure Protection Center has issued an alert suggesting that the Dispatchers may inadvertently cause collateral damage to American computer systems during attempts to damage Arab/Muslim foreign computer systems via distributed denial of service attacks.[91]

The Dispatchers were criticised by other hacking groups (such as Chaos Computer Club) as well as the FBI for their disruptive activities and inappropriate targeting of 'innocent' sites.[92]

A number of groups affiliated to or supportive of bin Laden remained on the web after 9-11, and several made statements in support of bin Laden and/or the Taliban (if not of the bombing). In the weeks following 9-11, a number of Islamic sites fell victim to hacking, such as the Taliban site and Hamas. InfoCom, a host company for Arab websites based in Dallas, Texas, was shut down on orders of the Federal authorities.[93] An Islamist mailing list was cracked on the qoqaz.de website, and details about its e-mail subscribers were published on the web.[94] An Islamic Usenet discussion group (soc.culture.islam) was flooded by e-mails, causing catastrophic disruption.[95] Several hacking groups initiated anti-Islam campaigns and there was an ensuing dialogue (on all sides) relating to the 'ethics' of hacking.

NOTES

1. Dorothy E. Denning, 'Activism, Hacktivism and Cyberterrorism', in John Arquilla and David Ronfeldt (eds.) *Networks and Netwars: The Future of Terror Crime and Militancy* (California: RAND, 2001), p. 263.
2. Ibid.
3. DMOZ Open Directory Project, http://dmoz.org/Computers/Hacking/desc.html.
4. For examples of popular books about cyber-security issues and hacking, see Joel Scambray, Stuart McClure and George Kurtz, *Hacking Exposed* (Berkeley and London: McGraw-Hill Professional, 2nd edn, 2000); Ankit Fadia, *Unofficial Guide to Ethical Hacking* (New York: Macmillan, 2001).
5. David Leppard, 'Cyber Criminals Cost Companies £10 billion a year', *The Sunday Times*, 14 April 2002.
6. Hackerthreads, www.hackerthreads.org.
7. David Condrey, *Black and White*, Hackerthreads, www.hackerthreads.org/downloads/black_white.pdf25 (Adobe Acrobat file).
8. Alldas.org archive of defacement of a Philippines government site, 12 February 2001, http://pasay.gov.ph, http://defaced.alldas.org/mirror/2001/02/12/www.pasay.gov.ph.
9. Muslim Hackers Club (MHC), message online posted on BIC (Belfast Mosque and BIC News, 15 July 1998. www.ummah.net/bicnews (message now deleted). Muslim Hackers Club, www.ummah.net/mhc.
10. Muslim Hackers Club, www.ummah.net/mhc.
11. Patrick di Justo, 'Does Official Taliban Site Exist?', *Wired*, 30 October 2001, www.wired.com/news/0,1294,47956,00.html.
12. Alldas.org archive of defacement of Hotels in Jaipur, www.teenkadabba.com, 26 December 2001, http://defaced.alldas.org/mirror/2001/12/26/www.teenkadabba.com.
13. Alldas.org archive of defacement of Real Estate Bazar, www.realestatebazar.com, 21 November 2001, http://defaced.alldas.org/mirror/2001/11/21/www.realestatebazar.com/.

14. Alldas.org archive of defacement of Viveka Foundation, www.viveka foundation.com/, 21 November 2001, http://defaced.alldas.org/ mirror/ 2001/12/18/www.vivekafoundation.com/.
15. Alldas.org archive of defacement of www.paintcompany.com, 15 December 2001, http://defaced.alldas.org/mirror/2001/12/15/ www.paintcompany.com.
16. For example, see Alldas.org archive of defacement of www.dit24.com.pk, 25 March 2002, http://defaced.alldas.org/mirror/2002/03/25/www.dit24. com.pk/.
17. Alldas.org, http://defaced.alldas.org/?attacker=m0r0n+and+nightman, 18 April 2002.
18. Alldas.org archive of defacement of www.bankalfalah.com, 7 December 2000, http://defaced.alldas.org/mirror/2000/12/07/www.bankalfalah. com/.
19. Alldas.org archive of defacement of www.zaurus.co.il, 21 May 2001, http://defaced.alldas.org/mirror/2001/12/05/www.zaurus.co.il/.
20. Ibid.
21. Alldas.org archive of defacement of www.sharon.org.il, 30 January 2001, http://defaced.alldas.org/mirror/2001/01/30/www.sharon.org.il/.
22. Alldas.org archive of defacement of www.ramat-gan.gov.il, 1 March 2001, http://defaced.alldas.org/mirror/2001/03/01/www.ramat-gan.gov.il/.
23. Alldas.org archive of defacement of www.esale.co.il, 13 January 2001, http://defaced.alldas.org/mirror/2001/01/13/www.esale.co.il/.
24. This makes questioning the WFD, and other hackers, problematic for researchers, together with the hackers' inherent suspicion and reluctance to dialogue post-9-11. There are obvious difficulties in obtaining representative 'samples' of opinion, and indeed determining the reliability of the owner of an (often anonymous) e-mail address. It is hoped to pursue this line of enquiry in future research.
25. Alforatein, www.geocities.com/alindex_2000/.
26. Alforatein, www.geocities.com/alindex_2000/spy.htm.
27. This listing is contained on Humam's own pages, although that does not imply that Mr Linux Lover and Humam are one and the same individual. www.geocities.com/alindex_2000/linuxlover.htm.
28. Gebal, http://gebal.virtualave.net.
29. SuperHiMY, discussant, formerly known as 'Froot Loops', 2 March 2001, Madinat al-Muslimeen, archive, 'Muslim Hackers!', 1698, www. jannah.org/cgi-bin/yabb/YaBB.pl/YaBB.pl?board=ark&action= display&num=1698.
30. Ibid., Jannah, 2 March 2001.
31. Sheikh Faisal Mawlawy, vice president of the Islamic European Fatwa Council, cited in Mariam Al Than, 'Muslims Discouraged Against Hacking Israeli Sites', *Islam Online*, 17 January 2001, www.islam-online.net/ English/News/2001–01/17/article6.shtml.
32. The Internet extends the questions and challenges associated with notions of Islamic authority articulated by critics, such as the Egyptian Judge Muhammad Sa'id al-'Ashmawi in his book *al-Islam al-siyasi* (Cairo: Sinan li al-Nashr, 1992). See the discussion by Zayle G. Antrim, 'Renegotiating Islam: the Reception of al-'Ashmawi's *al-Islam al-siyasi* in

the Egyptian Press', *Bulletin of the Royal Institute of Inter-Faith Studies*, Vol. 1, No. 1, 1999. The area of self-proclaimed online authority is discussed in Gary R. Bunt, *Virtually Islamic: Computer-mediated Communication and Cyber Islamic Environment* (Cardiff: University of Wales Press, 2000), pp. 104–31.

33. iDefense report, Israeli-Palestine Cyber Conflict, Version 2.0PR, 3 January 2001, www.idefense.com/pages/ialertexcl/MidEast_010501.htm.

34. NetVision, http://wwwnew.netvision.net.il/cyber/english/.

35. Israel had 1.1 million Internet hook-ups in 2000, more than 22 Arab countries combined. Lee Hockstader, 'Pings and E-Arrows Fly in Mideast Cyber-War', *Washington Post Foreign Service*, 27 October 2000. Also see National Infrastructure Protection Center, Middle East E-mail Flooding and Denial of Service (DoS) Attacks, 26 October 2000, www.nipc.gov/warnings/assessments/2000/00–057.htm.

36. *Newsbytes*, Brian Krebs, 'Hackers Worldwide Fan Flames in Middle East Conflict', citing Ben Venzke, director of intelligence production at iDefense, *Newsbytes*.com, 25 November 2000, www.newsbytes.com.

37. Faris Muhammad al-Masri, interviewed by Giles Trendle, 'The e-Jihad against Western Business', *IT-Director*, 5 April 2002, www.it-director.com/article.php?id=2744.

38. Ibid.

39. Alldas.org archive of defacement of www.kmahler.com personal home page, 22 November 2000, http://defaced.alldas.org/mirror/2000/11/22/www.kmahler.com/.

40. Alldas.org archive of defacement of http://astronomy.org.il, 16 April 2002, http://defaced.alldas.org/mirror/2002/04/16/astronomy.org.il.

41. Agence France Presse/Mena Report, 'Hizbollah, Israel Fight Cyberwar', 6 November 2000, www.menareport.com.

42. *Newsfactor Network*, Robyn Weisman, 'Teen Hackers Crash Hizbollah ISP', 22 January 2001, www.newsfactor.com/perl/story/6880.html.

43. *BBC News Online*, 'Hamas Hit by Porn Attack', 7 March 2001, http://news.bbc.co.uk/hi/english/world/middle_east/newsid_1207000/1207551.stm. Hamas maintained an online presence on various servers, but was subject to several closures during 2003. In February 2003, the URL was http://www.palestine-info.co.uk/hamas/.

44. Pramit Pai Chaudhuri, 'What are Islamic Fundamentalists Doing in Porn Sites? The CIA Tells You', *Hindustan Times Online*, 18 February 2001, www.hvk.org/articles/0201/92.html.

45. D. Ian Hopper, 'Kashmir-minded Pakistani "Hacktivists" blitz', *CNN*, websites, 8 October 1999, www.cnn.com/TECH/computing/9910/08/pakistani.hack/.

46. Thomas C. Greene, 'Celebrity Hacktivist Joins the Mid-East cyber-war', *The Register*, 7 November 2000.

47. AIPAC, www.aipac.org.

48. Ibid.

49. For a technical breakdown of Nuker's activities, see Michael L. Jenkins, 'Hacktivism: Compromise Techniques Used by GFORCE-Pakistan', 24 October 2000, SANS Institute, http://rr.sans.org/infowar/hacktivism2.php.

50. Ian Lynch, 'Anti-US Hacker Hits World Trade Portal', VNU Net, www.vnunet.com/News/1125576, 21 September 2001.
51. Alldas.org archive of defacement of Silicon India, www.siliconindia.com, 4 June 2000, http://defaced.alldas.org/mirror/2000/06/04/www.siliconindia.com/.
52. For the full Alldas.org listing, see http://defaced.alldas.org/?attacker=PHC.
53. Thomas C. Greene, 'Mideast "Cyberwar" Veteran Indicted', *The Register*, 1 November 2001.
54. US Department of Justice, press release, 'Computer Hacker Intentionally Damages Protected Computer', 22 October 2001, www.usdoj.gov/criminal/cybercrime/khanindict.htm.
55. Brian McWilliams, 'Hacker "Doctor Nuker" Claims FBI Fingered Wrong Person', *Newsbytes*, 31 October 2001, www.newsbytes.com/news/01/171726.html.
56. Alldas.org, http://defaced.alldas.org/?attacker=Dr-Hacker.
57. Alldas.org, mirror of GFORCE defacement of U.S. Defense Test & Evaluation Processional Institute (DTEPI) http://bb.lrc.usuhs.mil, Reasons for Defacement, 6 September 2000, http://defaced.alldas.org/mirror/2000/09/06/bb.lrc.usuhs.mil/.
58. 'Web Hackers Hit US via Taiwan', *Taipei Times*, 11 January 2002, www.taipeitimes.com/news/2002/01/11/story/0000119478.
59. Jenkins, 'Hacktivism'.
60. Incidents.org ISTS Report, www.incidents.org/ists/102301.php#3, 23 October 2001, citing 'Now, Pak Hackers Wage Cyber Jihad', *The Statesman*, 22 October 2001. It was not possible to verify this report in *The Statesman*'s online archive.
61. Incidents.org ISTS Report, www.incidents.org/ists/102401.php#1, 24 October 2001, citing 'Enter al-Qaida Alliance on Cyber Battlefield', *The Statesman*, 24 October 2001. It was not possible to verify this report in *The Statesman*'s online archive.
62. Brian McWilliams, '"Bin Laden" Worm Targets ICQ, Outlook Users', *Newsbytes*, 24 October 2001, www.newsbytes.com.
63. Brian McWilliams, 'Pakistani Group Strikes U.S. Military Web Site', *Newsbytes*, www.newsbytes.com, 21 October 2001.
64. The alldas.org defacement archive database listed 212 defacements credited to GFORCE between 28 February 2000 and 27 October 2001. Alldas Defacement Archives, http://defaced.alldas.org/?attacker=GForce.
65. *Taipei Times*.
66. mi2g, 'Israel Suffers Escalating Hack Attacks', 15 April 2002, www.mi2g.com/cgi/mi2g/press/150402.php.
67. 'Middle East Tension Fuels Hacker Fury', *Mena Report*, 3 October 2002, www.menareport.com.
68. *Reuters*, cited in Security Watch, 'Political Computer Hacking Increases', 1 November, 2002, www.isn.ethz.ch (citing mi2g).
69. Khalid Hussain, 'Inside Track on Pak Hackers', *Times Computing Online*, 16 May 2001, www.timescomputing.com/20010516/nws1.html. 'Junaid' is a pseudonym.

70. US Department of State, 'U.S. Internet Watchdogs Warn of Increased Hacking Activity', 17 September 2001, http://usinfo.state.gov/topical/global/ecom/01091701.htm.
71. John Schwartz, 'Cyberspace Seen as Potential Battleground', *New York Times*, 23 November 2001, www.nytimes.com.
72. John Leyden, 'Hacking Activity Plummets', *The Register*, 10 January 2002, www.theregister.co.uk/content/55/23628.html.
73. For a useful overview on aspects of cyber-law, see Mark Rasch, 'US Assumes Global Cyber-police Authority', *The Register*, 27 November 2001, www.theregister.co.uk/content/6/23036.html.
74. Bill Goodwin, 'Cybercrime Crackdown on Pan-European Scale', *Computer Weekly*, 22 November 2001, www.cw360.com.
75. Barak Jolish, 'The Encrypted Jihad', *Salon.com*, 4 February 2002, www.salon.com/tech/feature/2002/02/04/terror_encryption.
76. For a discussion on Ramzi Yousef, see Simon Reeve, *The New Jackals* (London: André Deutsch, 1999).
77. Jolish, 'The Encrypted Jihad'.
78. Ibid.
79. Shyfile, www.shyfile.net.
80. Shyfile, 'About ShyFile', www.shyfile.net/page2.html.
81. For an overview of Carnivore, see Thomas C. Greene, 'How Carnivore Works', *The Register*, 19 December 2000, www.theregister.co.uk/content/archive/15591.html.
82. Pramit Pai Chaudhuri, 'What are Islamic Fundamentalism Doing in Porn Sites?'
83. Alan Cullison and Andrew Higgins, 'Computer in Kabul Holds Chilling Memories', *Wall Street Journal*, 31 December 2001, reproduced on MSNBC, www.msnbc.com/news.
84. Alan Cullison and Andrew Higgins, 'Spy Trip Log Matches Reid's Travels', *Wall Street Journal*, 16 January 2002, reproduced on MSNBC, www.msnbc.com/news.
85. 'Authorities Track E-mails Sent by Alleged Shoe Bomber', *CNN*, 21 January 2002, www.cnn.com/2002/WORLD/europe/01/21/inv.reid.emails/.
86. MSNBC, 'E-mail Ties Richard Reid to Pakistan', 19 January 2002, www.msnbc.com/news.
87. Robert Windrem, 'How al-Qaida Keeps in Touch', MSNBC, 6 March 2002, www.msnbc.com/news.
88. 'Talib's Anti-American E-mails', Associated Press, 7 February 2002. Reproduced by *Wired*, www.wired.com/news/politics/0,1283,50286,00.html.
89. 'Tracing the Kidnappers' e-mails', BBC News, 6 February, 2002, http://news.bbc.co.uk/hi/english/sci/tech/newsid_1805000/1805173.stm.
90. For example, see Thomas C. Greene, 'Do-it-Yourself Internet Anonymity', *The Register*, 14 November 2001, www.theregister.co.uk/content/6/22831.html.
91. Canadian Office of Critical Infrastructure Protection and Emergency Services, 'Al-Qaida Cyber Capability', 2 November 2001, www.epc-pcc.gc.ca/emergencies/other/TA01–001_E.html.

92. See the statement by Chaos Computer Club, 'CCC Condemns Attacks against Communication Systems', 13 September 2001, www.ccc.de/CRD/CRD20010913.en.html. For an overview of post-9-11 hacking issues, see Robert Lemos, 'Hackers Split over Vigilante Strikes', *ZD Net*, 18 September 2001, http://news.zdnet.co.uk.

93. Tim McDonald, 'Hackers Mobilize for War against Islamic Web Sites', *NewsFactor*, www.ecommercetimes.com, 17 September 2001.

94. Jochen Bölsche, 'Mailing-Liste gehackt', *Spiegel Online*, www.spiegel.de, 19 September 2002; Rick Perera, 'Hacker Cracks Islamist Mailing List', *NetworkWorld Fusion/IDG News Service*, 20 September 2001, www.nwfusion.com.

95. John Leyden, 'Hackers Lash out at Islamic Usenet group', *The Register*, 19 September 2001, www.theregister.co.uk/content/55/21752.html.

4   Cyber Islamic Reactions to 9-11: Mujahideen in Cyberspace

This book earlier noted that the net is applied in the dissemination of *fatwas*, the content of some of which could be interpreted as a form of e-jihad. Examples include Sheikh Hammoud al-Uqlaa ash-Shuaibi's *fatwa* in November 2000, supporting the Taliban, in response to American threats to impose new sanctions against Afghanistan for its government's failure to curb 'terrorism'.[1] This *fatwa* appeared on the Azzam site, based in London, which has been proactive in promoting military jihad across the world, notably in Chechnya and Afghanistan, and was using the Internet to solicit donations.[2]

The Azzam website (followers of bin Laden's mentor and Mujahideen supporter Shaykh Azzam) published a photo of the Pentagon after the attack under the headline 'The Monumental Struggle of Good Versus Evil'. There was a quote from George W. Bush stating that, in this struggle, 'good will prevail'; there was also a statement from Osama bin Laden: 'the terrorist act is the action of some American group. I have nothing to do with it. The United States had invited Allah's wrath because it is trying to control the entire world by force.' Below these quotes is an extensive 'study' relating to Islamic law scholarship on the struggle between truth and falsehood. It includes quotations from various commentaries of the Qur'an and comparitive analyses on the issue (based on a book by Abdul-Kareem Zaydan that was published prior to 9-11). The various sites were associated with Azzam Publications and were registered in North London. They continued to seek funding and webspace; the pages were prominently promoting militaristic jihad in Chechnya, Afghanistan and elsewhere; the site also contained a discussion on the 'permissibility of executing Russian prisoners'. Although the pages were closed during November 2001, I noted that the pages re-emerged in February 2002 under the azzam.co.uk and azzam.com URLs with a temporary front page, and through other mirror sites.[3] The most recent content appeared to be a video of Osama bin Laden expressing support for Muslims in Palestine.[4]

A number of 'Taliban' sites continued to operate after 9-11. TalibanOnline's main site was not functioning, but there were several 'mirrors' of its content, updated in many cases to reflect the Taliban's changed circumstances following the conflict in Afghanistan after 9-11. The site opened with a multi-media Flash banner, featuring the Qur'an, a map of Afghanistan, gunfire, and recitation. It noted that there was 'limited news' at the time of writing. These pages incorporate apologetics associated with the movement and its relationship with al-Qaeda:

> The Taliban requires proof that that exiled Saudi dissident Osama bin Laden has attacked:
>
> – US embassies;
> – USS Cole;
> – Egyptian tourists;
> – an Egypt airplane (The one with 38 Egyptian generals aboard);
> – WTC and perhaps other targets.
>
> Since US cannot provide one single piece of genuine proof, the US might realize that they cannot go on telling widespread lies forever but has to increase the accusations to make people even more blind to truthful counter-arguments.[5]

This is perhaps the most detailed area of the site, although there are some link pages to multi-media, and several links to other sympathetic sites.

TalibanOnline linked to the Arabic language Jehad.net, which opened with a picture of George W. Bush and Osama bin Laden facing one another.[6] This contains a substantial archive of information, regularly updated and including audio-visual materials, advice, speeches and articles. The front page incorporates links to many jihad-oriented groups, and an 'anti-American' logo. A multi-media Flash section contained 25 downloadable files on Chechnya, Afghanistan, Palestine and other conflicts – emphasising the militaristic aspects of jihad. One clip juxtaposes film of aircraft carriers and missile launches with the victims of conflict in Chechnya and elsewhere.[7] Another shows images of the attacks on the World Trade Center and the Pentagon, juxtaposed with Osama bin Laden's speech, a *jihadi nasheed* and photos of victims of conflict in Iraq, Palestine, Afghanistan and Kashmir. Jehad.net also features more 'spiritual' content in this section, relating to the Qur'an and prayer.

The site was registered in December 2001 to an Ahmad Ali, living at a Kuwait address, although the site was hosted by a Worcester (UK)-based ISP company.[8]

The presence of such material on UK- and US-based ISPs, during the height of the Afghanistan campaign in April 2002, was a curious phenomenon. The Jehad.net site is one of several actively promoting militaristic jihad online. The impact of this type of material on a wider audience is open to question. Some of the campaigns could be said to have had an underlying popularity within the 'Muslim world', notably in relation to Palestine. Is there a blurring online between 'acceptable' and 'inappropriate' jihad, and how would readers of these sites read this? These are questions which require further analyses and perhaps fieldwork in a variety of Muslim contexts, and certainly demand further observation.

A site entitled Taliban News continued to be online six months after 9-11. Registered in December 2001 to Abu Hidayaah from a company called Halal Flowers in Staten Island, New York, this well-designed and professionally organised site contained detailed news (from the Taliban's perspective) on Afghanistan, Chechnya, Palestine and other regions. The site is fully searchable and has prominent links to various Azzam-related sites and other sites, including Clearguidance.net (Chechen), myislam.info (a Philadelphia-registered site making substantial use of JavaScript) and Islamway (run by the Islamic Assembly of North America). This in itself is not necessarily reflective or an mutual endorsement. However, there are some areas which are shared, notably the 'Salafi' perspective of myislam.info and islamway.com. The Qur'an link goes directly to myislam.info, which has a substantial number of recitations in various formats. Taliban-News banners include a photo of a Talib in a tank holding a gun, with the slogan 'In Pursuit of Shariah'. The central story was the 'martyrdom' of a senior Chechen Mujahid, Ibn ul-Khattab, a Gulf Arab, whose biography was presented on the site:

Born in the Arabian Gulf, Khattab was brought up in a relatively wealthy and educated family. He grew up to be a brave and strong teenager, who was known to be daring and fearless. After mastering the English language, he obtained a place in an American High School in 1987. 1987 was the peak of the Afghan Jihad against the invading army of the (then) Soviet Union. Youngsters from all over the Muslim world were flocking to Afghanistan after responding to the calls of Jihad made by Islamic personalities such as Sheikh

Abdullah Azzam (assassinated 1989), Sheikh Tamim Adnani (died 1988) and Usama bin Ladin. Miraculous accounts of heroic feats and daring displays of valour against the World Superpower were reaching the ears of the Muslims. As the time approached for him to leave for a new life of education in the U.S., Khattab decided to follow many of his friends and relatives to Afghanistan for a short visit. Since the day he waved goodbye to his parents and family, at the end of 1987, he has never returned home since.[9]

The article goes on to list his campaigning in Afghanistan, Chechnya and Tajikistan. Elsewhere, the site details his 'martyrdom':

Ibn El-Khattab was being sent a letter from another Arab commander two weeks ago. Ibn El-Khattab sent a messenger to receive the letter, but this messenger was a hypocrite working for the Russians (who was trusted by the Mujahideen). So he put poison on the letter which was touched by and thus infected Ibn El-Khattab. It took less that five minutes for his body to leave his soul and for him to be accepted with the martyrs (Insha Allah).

After that, the youth with Ibn El-Khattab took photos and made videos of Ibn El-Khattab, and this is the video released by the Russians. However on the way to give this video to the Mujahideen Military Council, the youth carrying the videos were ambushed and in the aftermath of that ambush the videos fell into the hands of the Russians.

And this was how Ibn El-Khattab was killed and how he gained what it was he wished for.

Praise is due to Allah in all situations.[10]

This account is revealing for a number of reasons, in particular its resonance (in elements) with classical Islamic heroic accounts of other 'role models' and 'heroes', in particular events within the life of Muhammad himself.

Taliban-News links to Meem Sites.com, a web hosting company also apparently run by Halal Flowers. Taliban-News is hyperlinked to Kavkaz Center, a Chechnya-oriented site (registered in Florida), offering content in English, Russian and Turkish.[11] This is another example of a regularly updated, well-designed site, which is fully searchable. It prominently links to a number of other Islamic organisations discussed in this chapter, together with other news sources. The video section Battlefield Chechnya contained graphic Real Player and Windows Media clips, with titles such as Attacks of the Mujahideen and Evidence of War Crimes.[12]

Expressions of support for the Taliban and bin Laden were contained on several 'jihad'-oriented sites. The Kashmiri Wahhabi website Harkat-ul-Mujahideen continued to apply the Internet as a means of promoting jihad, incorporating a detailed commentary on Jihad in the Qur'an and in hadith.[13] The Jihad in Islam section (of the original site) 'analysed' issues such as martyrdom, and details of 'Mujihideen Attributes' focusing on the minutiae of detail associated with 'appropriate' military behaviour. This makes the following comment, which may have had pertinence in relation to a number of ongoing conflicts in 2002:

> Today, the prophecy of the last Rasool of Allah Salallahu-alaihi-wasallam has become true, word for word and is fully applicable to our era and situation, in which RasoolulLah Salallahu-alaihi-wasallam has mentioned about the Ummah following the leads of the Jews and the Christians. The last Rasool of Allah Salallahu-alaihiwasallam has pronounced 'You will follow the Jews and the Christians to such an extent, that if they enter into the hole of a lizard (or an iguana), then you will also follow suit and will enter the hole behind them.'[14]

Its author, Khubaib Sahib, provided material that originally featured in the Taliban Online site, and that of Jihaad ul-Kuffaari wal-Munaafiqeen.

Jihaad ul-Kuffaari wal-Munaafiqeen (Jihad against Unbelievers and Hypocrites) is an exhaustive jihad resource, drawing on international resources in order to network materials and concepts, which has a close affiliation to the ideas of Azzam (whose works are archived on the site).[15] Many militaristic jihad-oriented sites have links on this page, which is divided into sections, including The Importance of Jihad, Guidance in Attaining Allaah's Victory, Allaah's Right concerning Ourselves, our 'Leaders' and Rulers, Concerning our Rulers Specifically; From the Ideal Leader to the Imaams of Kufr, and Concerning the practical application of Jihaad today. The site's IP Whois tracked back to a server in Montana, USA.[16]

Alemarh.com was another supporter of 'Islamic Afghanistan' post 9-11, incorporating regularly updated reports from the region with religious 'commentary' on the situation, with the site still being online at the end of March 2002. There were also photographs of weaponry, such as mortars and guns, and images taken from the battlefield.[17]

A related site is produced by Khurasaan.com, which is registered to Asad Siddiquei in Lahore, although its ISP is in the UK. This focuses on Central Asian issues, including the United States' involvement in the region and its strategic implications. The site is dominated by military symbols, such as bullets, grenades, guns and bombs, which are used to highlight articles. A pistol dominates the banner on each page. The site is well organised and designed, with sections on Jihad, Faith, Qur'an and Hadith, and a Gallery. There was a feature on Amir Khattab (above) on the front page, and a number of 'jihadi' articles posted by readers, reflecting the overall ethos of the site. These included an account of angels fighting alongside the Mujahideen in Palestine, which reflects traditional accounts of the battles undertaken by Muhammad in the early years of Islam, such as the account of Badr:

> I swear with the name of Allaah, that I and my brethrens saw the Jewish soldiers running away from the battlefield like cowards, leaving the injured and their weapons behind. A few of our brothers from the Mujaahideen reported yesterday (10/4/2002) that some of the Jewish soldiers shot each other during the battle.
>
> And more strangely, the Mujaahideen didn't even fire a single shot at the Jews, but mysteriously, the Mujaahideen heard shots being fired at the Jews (none of the Mujaahids used their weapons). And then we heard a Jewish soldier who survived the battle, running and shouting, 'I saw fierce looking creatures coming towards us, to attack us. The creatures are not humans.'
>
> The incident was reported to TV ANN. The next morning, when i woke up for fajr prayers, I saw on the TV, Abu Muhammad al-Maqdisi was being interviewed. Abu Muhammad al-Maqdisi said:
>
> 'Bismillahir Rahmaani Raheem, I swear with the name of Allaah, the Most High, that have been making duah to Allaah for His Help 12 days ago and by Allaah, Allaah's help has indeed come. I swear with the name of Allaah, that I saw in my dream an army from the Heavens come down to Junain to help and fight side by side with the Mujaahideen.'[18]

This translated account of angels is highly unusual in a jihadi site of this nature. There are more conventional materials on the site too. The Stories of the Sahabah is a collection of materials about the companions of the Prophet Muhammad; the Qur'an and Hadith sections focus on 'scientific proofs' relating to the Qur'an. The Gallery indicates an element of satire, with a spoof 'BBC' page on the post-Taliban benefits in Afghan society;[19] it also includes photos from the abortive 1993 American forces mission in Somalia.[20] Multi-media incorporates clips of Osama bin Laden, and a number of Urdu *nasheed* (religious songs), some of which are satirical in nature. An example is the 'Shaykh Osama bin Laden "Nasheed"':

> When you're driving through a posh English country town ... insert your tape 'Shaykh Osama Nasheed', wind down your window and push your volume to max! I love this one. *'Islam ka hero number one, Mera shear Osama bin Laden'*.[21]

The site provides 'A Practical Guide to Dealing with Hassle from British Authorities' posted by 'our friends at azzam.com', indicating the strong links and affiliations between organisations. This offers advice on dealing with the police and legal aspects of being arrested. Its conclusion states:

> A Muslim believes that no harm can come to him except by Allah's Permission. Likewise, no-one can bring him benefit except by Allah's Permission. Therefore, the Intelligence, Police and all the authorities in the World cannot do anything to you without Allah's Will. They may be smart, but Allah is smarter than them. They may 'beat' you in this Life, but Allah will beat them in the end. If it is written for you by Allah that you will go to prison, then no-one on Earth can stop that from happening. Likewise, if Allah has written for you to be protected, all the powers in the World cannot change that. Know that whatever happens to you is a test and happens by Allah's Will. Consider the Police and Intelligence as filthy human beings in your mind and that will help you win over them. Do not feel relaxed if they bring a 'Muslim' officer or 'scholar' to question you; he is on their side, not yours. It is a trap. Islam survives on its members being firm and steadfast. Do not 'crack', waiver, falter or fail. Be firm and in the end, victory will be for you, for Islam, for Allah and His Messenger (SAWS).[22]

Given the militaristic edge on Khurasaan.com, it may be surprising if security forces did not target those readers who are overtly sympathetic. Indeed, the maintenance of the site on a UK server (at the time of writing) raises some interesting questions relating to freedom of speech and censorship. There may be sound national security reasons for such a site to be *kept* online, as a means of electronically tracking readers and sympathisers.

Khurasaan.com contains substantial and detailed content, including personal accounts of meeting (and interacting with) the Taliban. Mir Adeel Arif visited the region in 2001 and wrote a diary of his experiences, including seeing Mullah Mohammed Omar in Kandahar. He also visited the football stadium, where a police officer was due to be executed for killing a student, and gives an 'insider' account of the scene:

> A large number of the inhabitants of this town were watching all this in pin drop silence. I too was watching a healthy young person in front of me, who will very soon be executed, seemed to be having an awe inspiring deterring impact on the spectators.
>
> After the young officer finished his prayers he moved some steps further in the middle. There a man tied his hands at his back and covered his eyes with a black cloth. Then he was laid down on the ground with his head tilted towards the Ka'aba. I saw some men sitting beside me had tears in their eyes. Even though he was the killer but still a soft corner developed in our hearts for him. The sword was handed over to the deceased's father so he could chop the head off.
>
> Everyone was watching the last moments with fear and sadness overtaking their hearts. The good thing was that an order of Allah was being fulfilled and justice was being done. The father of the deceased student raised the sword up high. He was about to chop the head off with full force when suddenly he stopped and forgave the murderer.
>
> All of a sudden the whole stadium stood up in joy overwhelmed in emotions. People ran into the middle of the ground to see the father and to congratulate the officer for the new life he just got.[23]

Following this account, there is a justification for such punishments:

> The implementation of these divine punishments has eradicated all kinds of social evils from the Afghan society. This is why the corruption level is almost zero in Afghanistan and there is peace and security for a common individual.[24]

Khurasaan.com's stance was further highlighted in the Jihad section, which includes video clips of Osama bin Laden and extracts of speeches by Azzam and other activists, together with various mujahid 'diaries' and postings. One article discusses military activities in Afghanistan, questioning why bodies of martyrs smell 'sweet' in comparison with those of the opposition. The article also incorporates a critique of so-called 'moderate' Muslims:

To American [sic], riding on the horse of pride and arrogance; drunk with the wine of power and strength, this question might seem incomprehensible. But those simple people who call themselves Muslims, yet have made mortal fame and wealth their god, must ponder upon it. These Muslims upon whose eyes dollars have cast a veil, who go in mortal fear of America's power, who call the Taliban extremists and the other mujahideen terrorists; who call 'foolishness' confronting America 'lunacy' who have used all the might of their pen to malign the Taliban and point out their 'mistakes' 'defects' and 'failures'; who puff up with pride at the chance to shake hands with the American President; who out of the fear of losing America's good will avoid declaring that they are Muslims; who cry out day and night that they are 'liberals' 'moderates' and nothing else; who are afraid of death and wish to live forever; when these Muslims think about it the truth shall dawn upon them they shall realize that this world and its life are not the real thing; that we can suppress our feelings and emotions through the arguments of our pen and tongue; that we can cow others into submission but one day death will snatch away the pen from our hand and our tongue too shall be still. Then these still bodies will tell the world who was correct and who was not; who was on the Path of Right and who was walking upon the way of Batil; who was successful in the end, and who was not. But wisdom lies in learning a lesson from the present. Come, let us all think upon this question and try to find out its answer. Why is there this difference after all?[25]

The impact of such rhetoric on the Internet is difficult to determine. It can be read in conjunction with the Current Affairs section, which was presenting 'Dharb news' from military activities in Afghanistan. Dharb-i-Mumin news was previously part of the taliban.com website.

The title 'Dharb-i-Mumin' re-emerged separately online, with a regularly updated 'unofficial' site, registered to an Ohio-based management company.[26] The banner on the site states that it is produced with the 'blessing of the jurisprudent of the era, Hadhrat e Aqdas Mufti Rasheed Ahmed Ludhynavi (Rehimahullah' Ta'ala), Founder of "Darul Ifta'Wal Irshad", Nazimabad, Karachi'. Whilst this Dharb site is not necessarily *directly* associated with the previous site of the same name, the site does seek to answer criticism of the Taliban:

> Taliban's entire tenure was free from corruption and irregularities. Nobody in the world can find even a small blame against any of the ministers of Taliban. Can anybody present such a precedence?[27]

Given the stance of the Dharb, its appearance on a Tripod 'free' (advertising-supported) webpage raises some interesting contradictions: amongst the free advertising that emerged on the Dharb's page was a promotion for an American oil distributor. The site contained a Shari'ah section, with basic questions (none relating to jihad) and some Afghan news features. The Guestbook indicates a supportive readership, including appreciative messages from Argentine Christians. The Dharb-i-Mumin site in turn links to a number of other pages, including Khurasaan.com and the anti-Shi'a site Haq Char Yaar Services.[28] It is interesting to consider that not all those hyperlinked to Dharb's site would necessarily be sympathetic to one another's objectives, methodologies or perspectives, and historically there have been clashes between (and within) the related movements.[29]

There is a link on the Dharb pages to the Sipah-e-Sahaba (Army of the Companions of the Prophet) paramilitary organisation.[30] Sipah-e-Sahaba were alleged to have been connected with Ramzi Yousef, who was convicted of the 1993 World Trade Center bombing; the movement have been proactive in heightening tensions between Pakistan's Sunni and Shi'a population, as well as being implicated in an assassination attempt on Benazir Bhutto in 1993.[31] Sipah-e-Sahaba's URL is part of farooqi.com, registered by Singapore Traders in Karachi and hosted in Florida.[32]

Dharb also links to the Dar-ul-Uloom, India,[33] centre of the Deobandi modernising 'reform' movement, which was been interpreted as instrumental in influencing aspects of Taliban understanding. The Deobandi schools, with their combination of intellectual learning of Islamic sciences – particularly shari'ah – and an emphasis on the spiritual experience linked to Sufism, influenced aspects of Pakistan's Islamic development, although the Deobandis themselves did not support the Partition process.[34] Deobandi influences can be found predominantly within urban Pakistani contexts, and also amongst *muhajirs*, and Pathans in Sarhad (North West Frontier Province).[35] The Dar-ul-Uloom site itself details a brief history of the movement, and its 'anti-imperialist' roots, describing itself as follows:

> Darul-Uloom Deoband was moulded in such a way that it, on the one hand, revived the basic values of religion and on the other hand, created a dynamic force of scholars and freedom fighters who continued their sacrifices till the country was completely free.[36]

The site lists those 'who had sacrificed their whole life for the motherland',[37] and describes the courses on offer at the institution. There were links to a related Darul Uloom–Deoband site, which contains limited materials in Arabic, English, Hindi and Urdu.[38]

Dharb-i-Mumin sees it as appropriate to link to the 'quietist' Tablighi Jama'at movement, founded by Mohammed Ilyas and represented on the al-Madina 'Fazail-e-Sadaqaat' (Virtues of Charity) website.[39] The site is registered to Maulana Abdul Mannan of the Islahul Muslimeen of North America, based in a mosque in Detroit.[40] In the past, the association of the Tablighi Jama'at with such activist 'jihadi' networks might have been interpreted as atypical, so it would be interesting to determine how this relationship might be changing, at least in the zone of cyberspace. Al-Madina's more traditional Tablighi definition of 'jihad' indicates a potential conflict of interests:

> Jihad may normally mean sometimes fighting a war against oppressors and non believers. Actually however, it means spreading belief in Allah (Subhanahu wa Taala) being One and enforcing Allah (Subhanahu wa Taala)'s commandments, which is also the topmost aim of Tabligh.[41]

Al-Madina contains a pro-Taliban *fatwa*, issued by Hammoud bin Uqlaa' ash-Shuaibi in November 2000, which also featured on the Azzam website.[42] There is a disclaimer from al-Madina regarding the content of the *fatwa* on the page, although its incorporation within the substantial content of this site could imply (for some) acceptance or sympathy towards its message.

The Islahul Muslimeen of North America linkage is interesting, given its mission statement, which focuses on providing 'humanitarian assistance in its various forms to "third world" nations' and suggesting that it 'is also dedicated to provide the necessary and proper spiritual guidance to the Muslim community according to Islamic tradition on how to be law abiding, well-mannered and productive citizens of the United States'.[43] The Islahul Muslimeen of North America focuses on its Sufi heritage, and its founder was a Deobandi, demonstrating a linkage between the two religious perspectives:[44]

> The founding of Islahul Muslimeen of North America was inspired by a great scholar, elder, and saint of the Indian Subcontinent. He is known as Maulana Sayyid Asad al-Madani. Maulana Madani is a world renowned spiritual master, being a Shaikh of the Chishti Sufi Order as well as the Qadriyya, Naqshbandiyya and Suhrawardiyya.[45]

There was sustained antipathy from the Taliban to many aspects of 'Islamic mysticism' or Sufism, which makes the link between this site and al-Madina unusual. Elsewhere, it describes itself as an 'authentic' 'Ahl us Sunnah wa'al Jamaah' website (a common claim in some areas of cyberspace), presenting explanations of Sufism and extracts from a traditional guide to religious teachings (*Bihishti Zewar*, written by Maulana Ashraf 'Ali Thanawi). IMNA does not present any statements relating to jihad. It has charitable status, focuses strongly on works in Bangladesh and has undertaken 'humanitarian' work in Chechnya, Iraq, Kosovo and Palestine. There is a link to the Jamiat Ulama USA website, which posits itself as a group 'dedicated to teaching and disseminating the religion, Islam, through authentic and reliable sources of knowledge'.[46] Dharb also contains hyperlinks to KhanQah Imdadiya Ashrafiya, containing lectures and 'bayans' in audio files, which are dedicated to the memory of Ashraf 'Ali Thanawi.[47]

A UK-hosted site, Mujahideen, created a substantial archive of materials relating to 9-11, and other jihad-centred topics. Much of the material came from or was edited by 'non-Muslim' sources, such as an article entitled 'Seven of the WTC Hijackers Found Alive!'[48] The site also included an article on encryption issues, with a demonstration of how the technology works (with examples).[49]

Other reactions to events provided evidence of how relatively small organisations can utilise the web to acquire maximum publicity. Al-Muhajiroun and its mentor Omar Bakri Muhammad attracted particular attention in the UK for its statements that were broadly supportive of bin Laden and the Taliban. The impact on the wider Muslim communities, which are not necessarily supportive of the organisation, of such statements is significant, given the degree of publicity the organisation receives in the mainstream press. The Muslim Council of Britain, for example, was keen to demonstrate their opinions on Omar Bakri Muhammad and Abu Hamza (see below):

> Inayat Bunglawala, spokesman for the Muslim Council of Britain, said: 'For a long time we have felt that we must keep our heads down and let these people bring trouble on themselves.
>
> 'But if we don't speak out they will do enormous damage to our community. Through their remarks about America they are inciting hatred against Muslims. We want to put clear water between the mainstream community and these fringe groups.'[50]

Defining the 'mainstream' is perhaps beyond the scope of this book, but certainly the material contained on the Muhajiroun website (and affiliates) alienated many Muslim organisations in the UK and elsewhere.[51] Such activities may form part of Omar Bakri's publicity-driven agenda. Many of these featured on various websites. Contentious material included a *fatwa* against General Musharraf and the US, suggesting that the US has a 'dream to take the Indian Subcontinent' and that 'the USA are at war with Muslims'.[52] Punishments for Muslims allied with the *Kuffar* (unbelievers) include murder, crucifixion and mutilation.

The *fatwa* was authored by Muhammad al-Masseri and Omar Bakri Muhammad, as part of the Shari'ah Court UK section of the OBM site. On the related al-Muhajiroun section, there was a question-and-answer section relating to the attacks. It suggested that the attack was 'a crime and violation for the sanctity of Human beings which is prohibited in Islam'.[53] However, the pages suggest that the attack is a result of 'atrocities' committed by the US government against the Third World and Muslims. The site also contained an illustration of the Pentagon, with the banner 'USA The enemy of Islam'. The site also issued a *fatwa* against working for the intelligence services (who themselves were monitoring the site's output closely).

Perhaps predictably, the website became unavailable for a time in late 2001, but was restored in 2002, continuing to be proactive with speeches and posters. Examples of the headlines in March 2002 indicate the on- and off-line agenda of al-Muhajiroun:

2 Hindu Soliders Killed. Praise be to Allah! Two Hindu Soldiers were killed and an equal number injured when militants attacked a search party in Baramullah district in Jammu and Kashmir on Friday night.

16 year old sister becomes Shahid. Allahu-Akbar! A 16-year old Muslim sister became Shahid today and killed at least three Jewish occupiers in an attack at a busy supermarket in Jerusalem. 'Aaeat al Akhras' died along with another Shahid in the latest martyrdom operation.

UK Troops prepare to die ... for Jews. From the safety of their bases in the UK, 1,700 British servicemen are on their way to the mountains of death in Afghanistan, which have repeatedly become the place for *kuffar* to die at the hands of Mujahideen.

Letter from Osama Bin Laden. Praise be to Allah who says: 'O Prophet, Strive against the infidels and the hypocrites,' and peace and prayer be upon the head of the mujahideen and leader of those who on the Day of Judgement are identified by the shining emblems.[54]

Whilst al-Muhajiroun's perspective should not be seen as indicative of that of the wider Muslim communities in the United Kingdom, such pronouncements and comments do represent a specific worldview which could be interpreted as provocative and divisive. Other headlines on this front page included 'Afghanistan: Atrocities', 'Fascist State of Israel', 'Kufr Education vs. Islamic Education' (*kufr* representing 'non-believers'), and 'Iraq: Murder Continues'. Such headlines may tap into a wider audience (Muslim and other), but also cause resentment and concern which could manifest itself in prejudice against Muslim individuals and communities in the UK and elsewhere. This is particularly true when the wider media pick up on the headlines and views expressed on these websites. The site's authors have become media players themselves, aware of what kind of headline will attract attention (and readers) to their site. Parallel content was located at OBM Network, which contained an al-Muhajiroun hyperlink and banner.[55]

Al-Muhajiroun's pages after 9-11 also contained supportive correspondence from readers. One complained that Omar Bakri Muhammad failed to respond to e-mails to the related OBM Network address – the al-Muhajiroun webteam gave out his phone number for an answer.[56] Elsewhere, the perspective of the group is clarified for a reader who is not a Muslim:

> Yes we do believe the law in this country is immoral, in fact not just immoral, a better word would be 'oppressive'. Likewise the way of life in this country and ALL the countries in the world, as not a single country in the world today implements the Shari'ah, hence the oppression, bloodshed, war, etc. We have no problem with ordinary citizens, in fact, most of us grew up with non-Muslims, and have been educated here. Our problem is with the law and order, and how it brings corruption such as homosexuality, paedophilia, rape, murder, crime, etc. and the fact that the people do not wake up and remove this corrupted democracy and replace it with Islam.[57]

Perhaps more controversial in nature was the reproduction of the 'post-9-11' letter from Osama bin Laden, the provenance of which clearly was difficult to verify at this time. This letter discussed al-Qaeda's approach to jihad, and how 'US Zionist' conspiracies were combining with the Saudi government against the cause of the Palestinian people.[58]

The UK-based Islamic Observation Committee (IOC) was highlighted through its pro-bin Laden stance, and the arrest in October 2001 of its organiser Yasser Tawfiq al-Sirri. The IOC's website linked to several pro-jihad sites associated with conflicts in Kashmir, Afghanistan and Chechnya. A cache of the site in November 2001 highlighted pages on 'human rights' and detention in Egypt, linked to trials of Muslim activists associated with Egyptian Islamic Jihad, and denounced the 'regime' of President Hosseni Mubarak. It cites various reports on detention and justice issues in Egypt, including those of Amnesty International and local committees, focusing on accusations of torture.[59] The URL was subsequently adjusted and content mirrored on a site hosted in Pakistan. New material had been added.[60] The front page of the site gave no evidence of any direct linkage with content associated directly with Osama bin Laden and al-Qaeda. Close affiliation has been noted elsewhere, with the 1999 trial of members of the Egyptian Islamic Jihad (an offshoot of the Muslim Brotherhood), whose leadership included bin Laden's associate Ayman al-Zawahiri (tried *in absentia*), famously filmed alongside bin Laden during 2001. Long term, close connections were

suggested between the Egyptian Islamic Jihad and al-Qaeda – and
with various international cells. Al-Qaeda is said to have merged with
the Egyptian Islamic Jihad in 1998.[61] One report indicated that there
had been an increase in the monitoring of websites such as IOC:

> US intelligence sources said that websites like those of the IOC are
> now central to the efforts of Muslim fundamentalist groups not
> only bringing in funds but also being used to promote extremist
> opinions.
>
> As a result the US has intensified its scrutiny of websites and is
> now moving to intercept any email traffic generated by the
> websites. Western intelligence agencies are also routinely snooping
> on visitors to extremist Muslim websites.
>
> ... 'For an investigator with no evidence to go on, the Internet
> is providing square one,' said an intelligence source. 'By picking up
> individuals on websites you can get direct evidence of association.
> What is happening is that these portals are being used to attract
> people and funds. Once a sympathiser has been identified their
> details are taken and they are approached off-line of donations.'
> The source added that the US operation was building up a database
> of visitors to Muslim sites.[62]

As part of a related tracking operation, the British Intelligence Service
MI5 placed messages on Muslim web chat rooms under a pseudonym,
with a contact number for those able to provide intelligence.[63]

Certain Islamist sites continued to contain information on weapons
training and manufacture in 2002. However, the closure of a number
of Islamist websites is another result of 9-11. A number of sites were
hacked/cracked. Internet service providers took others off-line.
Examples in the UK include the Sakina Security Services, which offered
the 'Ultimate Jihad Challenge', involving firearms training and live
ammunition drills, together with militaristic activities/services, under
the title of 'Islamic Threat Management'.[64] The pages detailed the
programme, which concluded with the statement:

> Students will receive The Sakina Instructors Certificate and Oath
> Of Loyalty to the Ummah of Allah Divine Religion of Submission.[65]

The Sakina site was shut down in October 2001, apparently
following intervention by British security forces, although there had
been concern over the organisation for at least 18 months before

9-11.[66] Run by a British-born Muslim, Mohammed Jameel, Sakina was associated with al-Muhajiroun's Omar Bakri Muhammad and the Supporters of Shariah's Abu Hamza al-Masri (discussed below).[67] Sakina's 'amir' or leader, Sulayman Bilal Zain-ul-abidin, was arrested in October 2001 under the Prevention of Terrorism Act. There were allegations that some of the jihad training may have been in the United States.[68] One report suggested that a search of Zain-ul-abidin's house had revealed replica firearms and documentation linking Sakina to al-Qaeda.[69] However, in August 2002, he was declared innocent at the Old Bailey:

> In fact, the Old Bailey jury learnt that the only person found to have taken such a course was a security guard from a London branch of Sainsburys [the supermarket chain].
>   Scotland Yard issued a statement saying:
>   'Officers from the Anti-Terrorist Branch believe the prosecution was properly brought before the court. The case was meticulously prepared in liaison with the CPS and Treasury Counsel. All of the available evidence was presented to the court.'[70]

The Supporters of Shariah (SOS) were prominent and vocal supporters of the Taliban, and promoters of jihad activity under Abu Hamza, who was based at a mosque in North London. He was arrested in 1999 under the Prevention of Terrorism Act, but subsequently released. The SOS website had been the focus of attention for its statements relating to Chechnya and other conflicts.[71] Initially, they also lost their webspace after making statements supporting the Taliban and applauding the 9-11 attacks. However, the site re-emerged in 2002, with a new supportersof shariah.com URL, and a UK-based host.[72] Abu Hamza was suspended in April 2002 by the Charity Commission from his post in the mosque (the mosque being a registered charity), following an injunction in the High Court primarily based on alleged inflammatory statements made during sermons; however, he continued to preach, and incorporated Real Audio sermons onto his website in the Downloads section. There were over 50 sermons, with titles such as Exposing State Control of Mosques, Islam's Weapons of Mass Destruction, The West Against all Religion, The Reality of Bin Laden's Video, The Victory of Bin Laden and The World Trade Center Plot. The selection of books was primarily titles by Abu Hamza, supplemented by *Defence of Muslim Lands* by Abdullah Azzam.[73]

Tapes of sermons and lectures were also listed for purchase, through mail order or telephone. The al-Jihaad Online Islamic News Magazine continued to be published on the site (running to 13 issues and an archive), focusing on Qur'anic analysis of concepts surrounding jihad.[74] There was a direct link to azzam.com on the Islamic Emirate page. Charitable projects were emphasised, including an educational development programme for women in Afghanistan and a food distribution programme.[75] The site featured similar material in Arabic. Film of Abu Hamza subsequently emerged on the site al-Qaida Exposed, including statements recorded in Finsbury Park Mosque.[76]

It is significant that a number of different articulations of the jihadi message emerged in cyberspace, from a number of different contexts and representing diverse Muslim viewpoints. Some were to emerge from traditionally quietist sources and locations, notably the minority context of Singapore. In September 2001, an e-mail was posted on the Fateha website in Singapore, promoting militaristic 'jihad' in Afghanistan and suggesting that 'Muslims get to know "members of the Tabligh movement promoting Prophet Muhammad's teachings in the mosque" if they wanted to join a jihad or "holy war" in Afghanistan'.[77] Mosque leaders were critical of the e-mail (partly in response to governmental pressures) because it was seen as presenting a negative impression of Muslim communities in Singapore, especially as the e-mail had remained on-site despite sustained criticism.[78] Coincidentally, it was during December 2001 that a number of Muslims based in Singapore were arrested because of alleged connections with a conspiracy to attack US military establishments and personnel. Reuters subsequently reported that the government had 'ordered a Muslim group to register its Internet portal as a political Web site after its leader said the government had prompted local Muslim terror plots by aligning itself with the United States and Israel'.[79]

Fateha.com continued to be online at the time of writing, with content primarily in English, including extensive coverage of events in Palestine. It continued to contain some statements that might be defined as 'ambiguous' relating to 9-11. The statements are in response to a question sent to the site on 25 September 2001. The central question was 'What is our position in the acts of terrorism and announcement of Jihad?' In it, the questioner ('Siti') notes her sadness at the events of 9-11, and the ways in which 'many of my older muslim friends believed that this trajedy [sic] is due to oppression in the Arabic countries and that we should support fellow

Muslims. As an educated muslim, I find this morally wrong.' Amongst the questions are 'Is it wrong for me to show my support for the victims families?' 'What is our position on Jihad? Isn't Jihad a "war on words" in the spread of Islam? Isn't holy war only in defence for the right to practise Islam peacefully? ... Is Osama Bin Laden a muslim [*sic*] leader or just a political figure defending his prowess?' Siti also questions the appropriate Islamic response to perceived 'degradation of Muslim women and children in Afghanistan'.[80]

The response (which had not been updated since being written in September 2001) suggested, 'There is no proof to show that the attack was done by Muslims. Therefore, we hope you are not sad on that particular account ... There is proof that the investigators were being led by parties who wish to implicate Arabs and Muslims.' Fateha.com goes on to launch a defence of Osama bin Laden, which focuses on jihad in some detail:

What is obvious though, is that the United States has a bone to grind with Osama ben laden. Within 2 hours, before there was any investigation into the attacks, CNN reported that Osama is the prime suspect.

And now, Colin Powell claimed that there are evidence to show Osama is responsible but these evidence are classified.

That is too convenient. If they apprehend him, will they declassify the 'evidence'? If yes, why don't they do so now? ...

1. Islam does not forbid us to show sympathy for those who are in distress, regardless of their religion.
2. Jihad takes many forms. In its totality, it is to struggle or to strive for Allah. We should then, jihad in the context of the situation.

As individuals, our jihad is to gain Allah's grace. As a community, we should strive to be the best in every sense, whether educationally, economically, morally, etc.

Therefore, when a Muslim country is attacked, then it is also required for us to strive to ensure their protection. This is especially true when they are attacked for being Muslims ...

However, we do recognise that some individuals have taken matters into their own hands ...

There are individuals who may have done so. This usually happens when they lack the knowledge. What we should focus on, is the punishment of the individuals who perform the assault and educate the public on acting with wisdom.

4. As for Osama ben Laden, if he is a political leader protecting his prowess, he would have been better served as a wealthy businessman in Saudi Arabia.

From reported accounts of his life and character, Osama ben laden is a practising Muslim and he requires the same of his followers and family members. His family follow Islam as best they could. This is better than some of the supposed Malay leaders in Singapura [Singapore].

Is he a Muslim leader? He leads some Muslims. The extent of this is anyone's guess.[81]

Elsewhere, it attacks the criticism of Afghanistan made from 'Jewish' and 'feminist' sources. This apologist response makes implicit criticism of 'mainstream' (government-supported) Muslim leadership in Singapore, suggests a conspiracy against Islam, and highlights appropriate 'jihad in the context of the situation'. Such statements are perhaps surprising, given that Singaporean society is highly regulated in relation to criticism of state organisations (such as the Singaporean Islamic Council – MUIS). The Reuters' report noted that Fateha's chief executive, Zulfikar Mohamad Shariff, had effectively been silenced, at least for a short period:

Zulfikar could not be reached for comment on Friday as he was recently called up for several weeks of national military service and has been barred from speaking to the media till he completes his reservist duty.[82]

The site continued to be updated during 2002, although it was being monitored closely. Coincidentally, in January 2002, a hard disk was recovered from one of the detained suspects that was said to prove links between the Singaporean Jemaah Islamiah group and al-Qaeda, even though much of the data on the disk had been erased (a proportion was recovered).[83]

NOTES

1. Azzam, 'Fatwa of Sheikh Hammoud al-Uqlaa' on the Taliban', 29 November 2000, www.azzam.com.

2. The Azzam name comes from Dr Sheikh Abdullah Azzam, a Palestinian scholar instrumental in reviving jihad in the twentieth century. He was assassinated, allegedly in a joint plot by the CIA and KGB, in Peshawar in 1989. Azzam, FAQ, 'Where does the name "Azzam Publications" come from?', www.azzam.com.

3. For example, see Azzam, http://66.197.135.110/~azzam/ (active April 2002), which mirrored the entire Azzam site.

4. This was a link to a copy of a CNN film clip. http://66.197.135.110/~azzam/html/newsoblvideo.htm#230601.

5. Mirror site of Taliban OnLine, http://muntaqim.web1000.com/text/taliban/911.htm#Osama.

6. Jehad.net, www.jehad.net/.

7. Jehad.net, www.jehad.net/flash.htm. A good example, showing film from Chechnya, was www.jehad.net/snkhod.swf.

8. Whois entry.

9. Taliban-News, Profile, Ameer Ibn ul-Khattab, 29 April 2002, www.taliban-news.com/article.php?sid=281.

10. Taliban-News, Mujahideen Military Command Council Confirms The Martyrdom of Ibn El-Khattab, 28 April 2002, www.taliban-news.com/article.php?sid=278.

11. Kavkaz, www.kavkaz.org.

12. Kavkaz, Battlefield Chechnya, www.kavkaz.org/eng/video.

13. Harkat-ul-Mujahideen, www.harkatulmujahideen.org. The Harkat site functioned until March 2002, when its URL registration lapsed. The site was 'taken over' by an American journalist, Brian McWilliams, who registered the site and retained its original content (based on a mirror image of the original Harkat organisation's site placed on the Pakistan Ummah.net server www.ummah.net.pk/harkat) in order to see how the site functioned as a 'recruiting tool' for 'terrorists'. McWilliams also staged (and was exposed for) the fake 'hacking' of his Harkat site. Leaving aside the issue of journalistic 'integrity' (which some might perceive as an oxymoron), this raised concerns associated with the 'authenticity' of specific websites and their contents. Faking a site by using 'authentic materials' from other sites would be a relatively easy exercise. McWilliams claimed that he was contacted by a number of terrorist 'affiliates' and that the FBI was convinced as to the authenticity of his site. See 'American Journalist Poses as Terrorist Group, Fools US Gov', 2600 News, 9 February 2003, http://www.2600.com/news/view/article/1526, and CBS News, Journalist Perpetrates Internet Hoax, 7 February 2003, http://www.cbsnews.com/stories/2003/02/07/tech/main539900.shtml.

14. Harkat-ul-Mujahideen, Mufti Khubaib Sahib, 'Attributes of the Mujahideen: Compliance with the Sunnah', www.ummah.net.pk/harkat/jihad/attribut.htm.

15. Jihaad ul-Kuffaari wal-Munaafiqeen, http://jihaadulkuffaarin.jeeran.com/.

16. IP Whois/Traceroute via UXN of http://jihaadulkuffaarin.jeeran.com, 2 May 2002.

17. Alemarh, 'America in Afghanistan', 30 March 2002, www.alemarh.com (Arabic language site).

18. Khurasaan.com, 'Angels fight along with Mujaahideen in Palestine', www.khurasaan.com/s_content.php?id=2002–04–26–5113.
19. Khurasaan.com, Afghan Women Find New Freedom, www.khurasaan.com/s_content.php?id=2002–03–29–2201.
20. Khurasaan.com, 'Somalia Lions', www.khurasaan.com/s_content.php?id=2002–02–25–5723.
21. Khusanaan.com, Multimedia, quote from main Multi-media page, hyperlink is to RealPlayer files, www.khurasaan.com/s_content.php?id=2002–04–06–2916.
22. Khurasaan.com, 'A Practical Guide to Dealing with Hassle from British Authorities', www.khurasaan.com/s_content.php?id=2002–03–03–2119.
23. Khurasaan.com, Mir Adeel Arif, 'My 12-day Visit to Afghanistan', www.khurasaan.com/s_content.php?id=2002–04–08–2905.
24. Ibid.
25. Khurasaan.com, Qari Mansoor Ahmed, 'Why the Difference?', www.khurasaan.com/s_content.php?id=2002–04–15–3602.
26. Dharb-i-Mumin, www.dharb-i-mumin.cjb.net.
27. Dharb-i-Mumin, Mulla Jeewan, 'Remembering the Past, A Befitting Reply!', http://abuusman03.tripod.com/abu1.htm.
28. Haq Char Yaar, www.kr-hcy.com.
29. See Gary R. Bunt, *Virtually Islamic* (Cardiff: University of Wales Press, 2000), pp. 68–9.
30. Sipah-e-Sahaba, www.farooqi.com/ssp.
31. For a perspective on Sipah-e-Sahaba, see Simon Reeve, *The New Jackals: Ramzi Yousef, Osama bin Laden and the Future of Terrorism* (London: André Deutsch, 1999), pp. 50–1.
32. Whois entry, 2 May 2002.
33. Deoband Online, www.deobandonline.com.
34. Discussed in Ahmed Rashid, *Taliban: Islam, Oil and the New Great Game in Central Asia* (London: IB Tauris, 2000), pp. 88–90. An overview of the Deobandi movement's historical roots can be found in Barbara Daly Metcalf, *Islamic Revival in British India: Deoband, 1860–1900* (Princeton, NJ: Princeton University Press, 1982).
35. Hamza Alavi, 'Ethnicity, Muslim Society, and the Pakistan Ideology', in Anita M. Weiss (ed.), *Islamic Reassertion in Pakistan: The Application of Islamic Laws in a Modern State* (New York: Syracuse University Press, 1986), pp. 30–2.
36. Deoband Online, www.deobandonline.com/darululoom.htm.
37. Ibid.
38. Darul Uloom, http://darululoom-deoband.com.
39. Al-Madina, www.almadinah.org.
40. Whois entry, 2 May 2002, April 2002.
41. Al-Madina, Fazail-e-Aamaal, 'Muslim Degeneration and Remedy', www.almadinah.org/FazailAamaal/MuslimDeProcedureForTabligh.htm.
42. Al-Madina, Hammoud bin Uqlaa' ash-Shuaibi, *Fatwa on the Shariah Implementation of the Taliban Government in Afghanistan,* 29 November 2000, www.almadinah.org/DawaLinks/talebanfatwa.htm.
43. Islahul Muslimeen of North America, 'Mission Statement of Islahul Muslimeen', http://chishti.net/mission_statement.htm.

44. An Ahmadiyya site discusses how various religious authorities had fatwas issued against them, including Madani. Lahore Ahmadiyya Movement, Fatwas against individual leaders, http://tariq.bitshop.com/misconcep tions/fatwas/individual.htm.
45. Islahul Muslimeen of North America, 'The Spiritual Foundation of IMNA', http://chishti.net/chishti_lineage.htm.
46. Jamiat USA, 'History of Jamiat USA', http://jamiatusa.org/historyjusa.html.
47. KhanQah Imdadiya Ashrafiya, www.khanqah.org.
48. Mujahideen, 'Seven of the WTC Hijackers Found Alive!', www.mujahideen.fsnet.co.uk/wtc/wtc-hijackers.htm.
49. Mujahideen, Encrypted Messages Hidden in Images, www.mujahideen.fsnet.co.uk/hidden-messages.htm.
50. Richard Alleyne, 'UK Muslims Disown "Lunatic Fringe"', *Daily Telegraph*, 20 September 2001, http://news.telegraph.co.uk.
51. For an earlier discussion on this, see Gary Bunt, '*islam@britain.net*: "British Muslim" Identities in Cyberspace', *Islam and Christian–Muslim Relations*, No. 10 (1999), pp. 353–63.
52. Al-Muhajiroun, 'Fatwa or Divine Decree against General Musharraf-USA', 16 September 2001, www.al-muhajiroun.com.
53. Al-Muhajiroun, 'America under Attack', 20 September 2001, www.al-muhajiroun.com.
54. Al-Muhajiroun, www.al-muhajiroun.com, 30 March 2002. The URL was not always functional during 2002.
55. OBM Network, www.obm.clara.net.
56. Al-Muhajiroun, 30 March 2002, www.al-muhajiroun.com/letters.
57. Al-Muhajiroun, 28 March 2002, www.al-muhajiroun.com/letters.
58. Al-Muhajiroun, 'Letter from Bin Laden', 30 March 2002 www.al-muhajiroun.com/lnews/29–03–02.php.
59. Google cache of Islamic Observation Committee, 28 November 2001, www.ummah.org.uk/ioc/egindex.htm. Neither the cache nor the original site was available at the time of writing.
60. IOC, www.ummah.net.pk/ioc/egindex.htm. Coincidentally, the ummah.net.pk domain also houses the Muslim Brotherhood's pages.
61. 'Egyptian Physician with a $5 million Price on His Head', *CNN*, n.d., www.cnn.com/CNN/Programs/people/shows/zawahiri/profile.html.
62. Chris Blackhurst, 'Bin Laden Web Link Registered in Suffolk', *The Independent*, 28 October 2001, www.independent.co.uk/story.jsp?story=101895.
63. 'British Security Chiefs Launch Web Terror Hunt', *Reuters*, 25 October 2001, www.reuters.com.
64. Sakina Security Services, 'Ultimate Jihad Challenge', 20 September 2001, www.sakinasecurity.com. URL deleted.
65. Sakina Security Services.
66. '"Holy Wars" Website is Shut Down', *The Times*, 4 October 2001.
67. 'British Muslims Join "Holy War"', *BBC News Online*, 26 June 2000, http://news.bbc.co.uk/hi/english/uk/newsid_806000/806422.stm, Nigel Rosser, 'British Muslims Training Fighters for "Holy War"', *Evening Standard/This is London*, 21 September 2001, www.thisislondon.co.uk.

68. Mike Brunker, 'Did "Jihad" Arms Course Visit U.S.?', *MSNBC*, 27 December 2001, www.msnbc.com/news.
69. Steve Gold, 'Alleged Jihad Internet Terrorist Pleads not Guilty', *Computeruser*, 15 October 2001 (citing *Reuters* source), www.computeruser.com/mews/01.10/15/news2.html.
70. *Channel 4 News*, '"Jihad" Chef Cleared', 9 August 2002, www.channel4.com/news.
71. Discussed in Bunt, 'islam@britain.net'.
72. Supporters of Shariah (SOS), http://supportersofshariah.com. The host ISP was located through an Opus One Trace Route analysis. UXN, http://combat.uxn.com, 2 May 2002 (in 2003, this site relocated to www.shareeah.com).
73. Supporters of Shariah (SOS), Downloads, http://supportersofshariah.com/Eng/download.html.
74. SOS, Al-Jihaad Online Islamic News Magazine, 2 May 2002, http://supportersofshariah.com/Eng/aj/ajindex.html.
75. http://supportersofshariah.com/Eng/project.html.
76. Al-Qaida Exposed, http://johnathangaltfilmscom.powweb.com/movie.html.
77. Ahmad Osman, 'Mosque Raps Fateha for "sign up for Jihad" E-mail', *Straits Times*, http://straitstimes.asia1.com.sg/usattack/story/0,1870,98429–1011823140,00.html.
78. Bunt, *Virtually Islamic*, pp. 88–9, 91.
79. Amy Tan, 'Singapore Tightens Grip on Vocal Muslim Web Site', *Reuters/Singapore Window*, 25 January 2002, www.singapore-window.org/sw02/020125re.htm.
80. 'Siti' (questioner), on Fateha.com, 'What is our position in the acts of terrorism and announcement of Jihad?' www.fateha.com/cgi-bin/newspro/qa/fullnews.cgi?newsid1001413396,19170, 25 September 2001. The page remained online in April 2002.
81. Ibid.
82. Tan, 'Singapore Tightens Grip'.
83. 'ISD Finds Videotape Linking S'pore Terror Group to Al-Qaeda, *Straits Times*, http://straitstimes.asia1.com.sg/usattack/story/0,1870,98907,00.html. It should be noted here that, during 2001–2, the *Straits Times* was condemned by some Muslims in Singapore for its 'anti-Muslim' stance, and that this was the subject of some debate, including on the Fateha.com website.

5   Cyber Islamic Reactions to 9-11: The 'Inter-fada' and Global E-jihad

Whilst 9-11 may initially have detracted from the Cyber Islamic focus on Palestinian issues in 2001, a synthesis of themes relating to Palestine and 9-11, in association with an escalation in conflict in the region, meant a sustained increase in activity online. A growing interest in Islam internationally following 9-11 also impacted on the type of content that appeared online in Palestinian-related sites. It has to be stressed that some of these sites emerged from outside the region, and that Palestinian issues comprised part of a wider global activist agenda (both prior to and following 9-11). As discussed elsewhere, Palestine-related activists have taken advantage of the medium for several years to promote diverse agendas, and were well equipped to offer technologically sophisticated and widely accessed responses to the crisis.[1] Some groups took advantage of the situation to facilitate their own political and religious propaganda agendas in different ways.

The Palestine Information Center (PIC, which also hosts Hamas pages) suggested that Israel was guilty of attacking New York and Washington. On 13 September 2001, under a photograph of the burning twin towers of the World Trade Center (adjacent to a photo of Mohammad ad-Durra moments before his death) was the question:

> Who could be behind an atrocity on such a scale ... could it be the same entity behind the bombing and destruction of USS Liberty in 1967 to widen the conflict?[2]

Elsewhere, the PIC site had photos and statements indicating 'Terror is our common enemy', with suggestions that Palestinians empathised with the United States, 'despite their criticism of U.S. support for Israel during the Palestinian uprising'. PIC also claimed that:

> Israeli, Jewish and Zionist media have embarked on a malicious campaign of vilification against Islam and Muslims around the world, taking advantage of tragic events in the United States.[3]

With the escalation of the 'second Intifada', the PIC site regularly reported on activities within Israel and the occupied territories by the Qassam Brigades and other associated organisations. For example, on 27 March 2002, a suicide bomber killed at least 29 people in a hotel in Netanya, Israel. The PIC website quickly issued a statement, commencing with a portion from the Qur'an:[4]

In the name of Allah the most Gracious the most Merciful
Qassam Brigades
Military communiqué
It is not ye who slew them; it was Allah: when thou threwest it was not thy act, but Allah's.

Fight them, and Allah will punish them by your hands, cover them with shame, help you (to victory) over them, heal the breasts of Believers.

Zionists would not enjoy security before our people enjoy it in practice.

Our Mujahid Palestinian people ... our great Arab and Islamic Ummah.

With the grace of Allah the martyr hero:

Abdul Baset Mohammed Qassem Odeh, 25, from the steadfast city of Tulkarm ... was able to penetrate all Zionist security lines to arrive at Barak Hotel at 7.25 PM on Wednesday 13th Muharram 1423H – 27/3/2002AD in the city of Um Khaled called Netanya established on our occupied lands in 1948. He blasted his pure body amidst a gathering of Jewish settlers who usurped our cities and villages.[5]

The statement continues, thanking Allah for its success and describing the operation as 'one in a series' against the 'terrorist Sharon and his Nazi government':

what the Zionist entity and its ally America call 'innocent civilians' are called in our Brigades and our Palestinian people's lexicon settlers and usurpers of our lands. They will only receive death and displacement and if they wish to save their lives they have to pack up and leave before they regret it ...

... our operation, [which] coincided with the Arab summit in Beirut, is a clear message to our Arab rulers that our Mujahid people have chosen their road and know how to regain lands and rights in

full depending on Allah only. Our people do not accept other than Jihad and resistance as the main path to regain usurped rights …
And it is a Jihad until either victory or martyrdom.[6]

The Palestine-Info site lost its .com status, to be replaced by a dot.co.uk domain, in October 2002.[7] This was following pressure from a number of online activist organisations, including the Simoky Fed 'Haganah' site operated by the Jewish Federation of Southern Illinois, Southeast Missouri and Western Kentucky. This started monitoring 'anti-Israeli' and 'terrorist' platforms in August 2002, launching concerted efforts to pressurise Internet Service Providers to close pages associated with Hamas, al-Qaeda and related organisations.[8]

A pattern emerged of domains closing and resurfacing, or organisations applying new URLs in order to continue circulating information, and to maintain their web presence. The al-Neda site, operated by al-Qaeda supporters, was allegedly 'hijacked' in August 2002, and replaced by a pro-American message:[9]

US sources believe Alneda is al-Qa'ida's media mouthpiece because it has been the only source to report news of Usama Bin Ladin over the past months. The most recent of these reports is an audio recording of al-Qa'ida official spokesman Sulayman Abu-Ghayth declaring the network's responsibility for the Tunisia blast that killed 21 people, including 14 German tourists. The announcement of Alneda's return online came in an e-mail that al-Sharq al-Awsat received a copy of yesterday through the Jihad Online website, which is the most updated fundamental site on the World Wide Web.

Abd-al-Rahman al-Rashid, a Gulf fundamentalist and general supervisor of Jihad Online, congratulated the brothers on the return of the Islamic Studies and Research website to the web. The website is still in its original location – www.alneda.com. The most prominent topics on the website include a series of analyses under the title 'America's Rise To the Abyss,' which is a four-part series on the reasons behind US globalization, the reasons for the disputes between United States and its allies, which limited its ability to continue its expansionist track, as well as the reasons behind America's declared war on Islamists online. The analysis adds: 'Islamists must be prepared to have their websites shut down in any minute, but must search for alternatives online, the most important of which being email lists that Islamists can create and use to disseminate news'.[10]

The extent to which the al-Neda site represented bin Laden 'officially' is perhaps open to question, given that his whereabouts or existence was difficult to ascertain during 2002. Al-Neda content also featured on the drasat.com URL, and operated using a 'Centre for Islamic Studies and Research' banner. This 'centre' had no academic affiliation (particularly with this writer's own Centre for Islamic Studies!), but featured a wide range of materials in diverse media formats promoting its interpretation of jihad. It included articles condemning America, including material written by Sulaiman bu Ghaith, an al-Qaeda 'spokesperson'.[11] In December 2002, a substantial proportion of the original al-Neda site reappeared on a site that had been 'occupied' by al-Qaeda supporters. It included a small amount of English-language content, alongside Arabic materials such as news and guidance on jihad and warfare. It reproduced a statement attributed to Osama bin Laden, which appeared in other parts of cyberspace, which made reference to attacks made by al-Qaeda in Bali in November 2002, and a siege of a Moscow theatre by Chechens in October 2002:

> From god's servant Osama ben Laden to the peoples of the countries allied with the American government; Peace on those who follow guidance.
>
> The path of security begins with the ending of aggression. It is equitable to mete equal treatment. The events taking place since the New York and Washington conquests up to the present – like of the killing of Germans in Tunisia and the French in Karachi, the explosion in the giant French tanker in Yemen, the killing of the marines in Faylaka, the killing of the British and Australians in the Bali explosions, the recent Moscow operation, and some dispersed operations here and there – are all reactions and treatment in kind dealt by the zealous sons of Islam in defence of their religion and in response to the order of their god and prophet, peace be upon him.
>
> The action of the pharoah of the age, Bush, in killing our sons in Iraq and the actions of America's ally, Israel, in bombing houses in Palestine on the heads of the old men, women, and children in them using American aircraft were all sufficient cause for the wisemen and for your rulers to distance themselves from this

criminal gang. Our people in Palestine are being killed and tortured for a century almost. Now, if we defend our people in Palestine, the whole world rises up to band together against the Muslims under the lying and deceitful banner or combating terrorism ...

... If you are dismayed by seeing the male dead of yours and your allies in Tunisia, Karachi, Faylaka, and Yemen remember our children dying every day in Palestine and Iraq remember our people deliberately killed in the wedding parties in Afghanistan. If you are dismayed by looking at your dead in Moscow remember our dead in Chechnia.

Till when will murder, destruction, homelessness, orphans, and widows be our preserve alone leaving you with security, stability and happiness to be your own preserve?

This is an unjust division. It is now time to get equal in the goods. Just as you kill you will get killed and just as you shell you will get shelled. Await then what will dismay you.

...

Finally, I ask God to provide us with help from Him to enable us to uphold his religion and keep fighting for his cause until we meet Him pleased with us He is well capable of that.

The last thing we say in our prayer is Praise be to God the lord of creation.[12]

The (re-) emergence of this statement on the Centre for Islamic Studies and Research website represented a 'temporary' measure, as it was likely to be removed by the ISP when the site's owner became aware of its presence. Its provenance was difficult to determine at the time of writing, as was the veracity of the origins of 'Osama bin Laden's' statement – its ideological affiliations would give no doubt to its author's support of al-Qaeda. Versions of this statement appeared on various sites and chat rooms, as well as in media sources unaffiliated with al-Qaeda.

The levels of 'authority' of such 'official' al-Qaeda websites are also a moot point, and their links to effective 'operational information' may be tenuous. They are seen as an effective propagation tool and a channel for information, in the same way as 'non-Islamic' news channels such as al-Jazeera. Consideration should also be given to whether al-Neda and related sites represent an 'Islamic' identity online, and how that manifests itself through symbolism, language, strategy and other reference points. The content of al-Neda was reproduced and featured substantially on other jihadi-oriented sites discussed in this chapter. The al-Neda URL was frequently not functioning at the time of writing, but related e-mail listings were difficult for the various authorities to close and other sites contained associated content. Sophisticated 'cat-and-mouse' tactics and web-tracking systems were applied on all sides. Whether this had a real impact is open to question. It may be that such closures were simply a temporary inconvenience for dedicated readers and supporters, with mirror sites quickly establishing themselves in safe (or occupied) servers, and news of new URLs rapidly circulating through e-mail listings and chat rooms. As mentioned earlier, they may also be more effective for intelligence communities and organisations when they remain open, and covertly monitored, rather than simply shut down. The sheer number of these online elements made them difficult for the 'authorities' to monitor effectively, despite a substantial intelligence and technology investment. The blurring of Internet agendas online, between al-Qaeda and other interests (for example, in relation to Palestine), ensured some cohesion of resources and strategies, even though not all Muslims associated with the Palestinian cause welcomed the affiliation:

> Shaykh Salman al-Oadah, for instance, who was admired by Bin Laden as one of the two religious leaders of Saudi Arabia's opposition movement in the mid-1990s, condemned the September 11 attacks for killing civilians. In April, he coordinated an open letter by 150 Saudi intellectuals entitled How We Can Coexist, calling for a dialogue with the west. Muntasser al-Zayyat, a lawyer for Egypt's radical Islamic Group, part of which merged with al-Qaida in the 90s, criticised al-Qaida for releasing a video featuring one of the September 11 hijackers explaining his motives for martyrdom at a time when Israeli-Palestinian violence was at its peak in April. He said the video, broadcast by al-Jazeera, diverted attention from the Palestinian issue and risked alienating potential supporters of the Palestinian cause in the west.[13]

However, the analogy of al-Qaeda having a cell-like structure, with various elements not always being aware of one another, also played out on the Internet, with a profusion of online support (and similar content) even though there was discontent from a number of other perspectives.

These are complex ideological affiliations and relationships, and it is understandable that some Palestinian perspectives were concerned that their viewpoint was being subsumed or that they were the renewed focus of Internet attack post-9-11. It is likely – even if the events of 9-11 had *not* occurred – that there would have been considerable (and continued) cyber activity associated with the Palestinian jihadi cause. It is not proposed to speculate on how that might have played out or how the history of the Palestinian cause inexorably changed after 9-11. In cyberspace, Palestinian Muslim activists continued to appear or reconfigure their previous output: the Qassam brigade emerged with a new site representing their interests, hosted in Houston.[14] The brigade has had a long-standing presence online, with an early example of a martyrs' gallery,[15] and continued the tradition of an online martyrs page – 'new' *shahid* quickly appeared on the site, with a photograph, personal details and information about their 'operation'.[16] The Kataeb Ezzeldeen Arabic language site had a banner with a 'jihadi' combatant dressed in white (with the Ezzeldeen logo on his chest). The pages included a list of prisoners held in Israeli jails.[17] The news section, on the front page, was updated daily with 'operational' information.

The site linked directly to Palestine Info and other jihadi sites, such as Samidoon ('Resistance'); this had a banner prominently displaying Sheikh Yassin's (and Yusuf Qaradawi's) photo. This connection is an interesting one, reconciling Hamas and Qaradawi, who is seen to present himself as a voice of 'reformist' Islam. Qaradawi is discussed elsewhere in this book, where his role as a 'moderating force' and authority is considered. The Samidoon site contained diverse online forums, discussion areas and guest speakers drawn from activist platforms, and is one worthy of detailed long-term analysis and future research.[18] The 'religious identity' manifests itself in these discussions, and also tangibly in the section of *nasheeds* (religious music) on offer.[19]

Jihad Online, a high-profile, Arabic-language, Palestinian jihad-oriented site, synthesised Islamic Jihad and pro-Palestinian ideologies. The printing and circulation of posters of *shahid* suicide bombers has been a notable development in recent years. The online equivalent can be found on this site, which is a development of 'memorial' pages discussed by this writer elsewhere, and was updated on a regular basis in 2002. The site was created in January 2002 and was registered to Haissam Abou-Ghezlan, at a Beirut address.[20]

Neda al-Quds established their Arabic-English website with a specific role to 'bond' the forces of uprising or revival together, in order to facilitate the 'liberation' of al-Quds (Jerusalem). The site represented the Islamic Jihad Movement in Palestine; the Arabic content was more detailed than the English content. The site's administrative contact's e-mail address resolved to an address registered in Tehran, although no address was given; the site's technical contact address was in Dulles, Virginia.[21] The site opens with a sound file and features militaristic music and an invocation to fight for 'history' in the name of Islam. The site's banner contains a collage of pictures, including the death of Muhammad al-Durra, a dead infant, the Palestinian flag and an image of the Dome of the Rock mosque. The front page included a regular source of news about Palestine, focusing on the Palestinian victims of conflict, but also showing evidence of attacks on Israelis; for example, in October 2002, there was coverage of a 'martyrdom operation' that killed over 20 Israelis in a bus. The site's content makes frequent references to 'jihad', and discusses the activities of those killed in suicide attacks. There are also sections on Islamic interpretation. One of the most interesting pages is the one discussing the role of the Internet within Neda al-Quds' activities.

> Our Arab and Islamic nation has encountered all kinds of wars and thereby encountered all forms of lies. Lies, deception and manoeuvres are the political instrument, which colonized us, disunited us and disunited our Palestine. We lost Palestine because we believed the enemy and thereby we lost ourselves after we had lost God's assistance.
>
> When our enemy became our exemplar we started following his examples. We began to lie on ourselves before lying on others. Ignorance, folly and dishonesty became virtues. Science, knowledge and sincerity became tribulation. We didn't realize that lying, which serves the enemy, is the core of his nature, ethics, values and satanic objectives. We didn't conceive that our victorious weapon is that of the prophets, the weapon of faith, patience, perseverance, truth and knowledge and how to put things on their right track.
>
> With this view, we are on this website that we want it to be a contract and a memorizer, a contract between who and whom? And a memorizer for whom?
>
> First, it is a contract between us and a memorizer for all of us. This website is for those who watch the past, present and future with (Quds' eyes). By Quds' eyes we mean the word in all its dimensions. Al-Quds is a spirit and a doctrine Al-Quds is a land

and a nation. Al-Quds is the visible and the invisible; the mujahed (freedom fighter) and the martyr.

Al-Quds is in our doctrine and contract, in our memory, in our day and night and in our dreams and future. It is one of the stations of reckoning and examination of conscience. Reckoning by God and examining by people and oneself. Be it good or evil, victory or defeat, winning or losing.

We want this website to be one of our fields of action to deliver the truth, the good word, the useful information, the wealthy experience, the engaged thinking and the sound opinion.

This website is from you and for you.

We want this website to be a bond joining us together and eliminating many of the damages inflicted by our enemy, at the head of which is disuniting us as a nation, an entity and an education. We want this website to be a book or an encyclopedia from and for our nation, to the whole world. We want this website to be a website for freedom of our people and friends.[22]

The effectiveness of this mission statement is open to question. However, given the resources that have been integrated into the site, it is clear that it is seen as part of an overall strategy of dissemination, primarily for Arabic-speaking supporters, of the 'Islamic jihad' message. At the time of writing, the site also contained a substantial amount of online dialogue between supporters in the chat room, the majority from 'anonymous' Hotmail addresses; it would be interesting to determine whether this dialogue is from a dedicated core of users or from a broad range of users. The anonymity of the e-mail accounts, and the unlikelihood that users would respond to questions from researchers, leave this an open question at present. On the site itself, religious themes are utilised, although there is no specific 'Qur'an' section of the site. Religious imagery is a part of the sound and video section, featuring downloadable files with poems, music, chants and speeches. The *nasheed Allah-hu-Akbar*, for example, eulogises the role of jihad and martyrs.[23]

Support for Palestinian causes takes many forms and can be more subtle in nature. An example is contained on the AlMinbar site, which is hosted in Mecca, and at the time of writing was being populated with content. There was a substantial archive in place, primarily translations from Arabic of sermons by prominent scholars and authorities. It illustrates, perhaps, that there is a fine line between notions surrounding *fatwas* and sermons. The information contained within this sermon site is responsive to contemporary concerns and situations. Viewed prior to Ramadan, the site was gearing up to provide materials on a variety of topics. The motivation behind the site was to provide 'thousands of Khutbahs translated into English and a variety of material to help you prepare for Islamic talks and Khutbahs'.[24] AlMinbar offers a searchable database, together with folders containing contemporary topics, and a sidebar illustrating recent sermons. Options included sermons from Mecca, Medina and al-Aqsa – often described as the three most important mosques. The al-Aqsa sermon section highlighted a sermon from Shaikh Abu Sunaynah, summarised under themes including 'The pathetic state of the Muslims and how their enemies conspire against them', 'The enmity of the USA, the UK and Russia against Islaam and the Muslims' and 'The betrayal of the Muslims in failing to support Palestine'. The sermon synthesised quotations from the Qur'an and hadith with political statements:

Slaves of Allaah! The nature of this issue is different from other issue. It is a central Islamic issue that concerns the entire Muslim Ummah, and Israel is trying to change this fact and make it a Palestinian–Israeli issue.

Israel backed the United States to launch this dirty war against Muslims and the Islamic movement world wide. The United States used the most destructive bombs against Afghanistan, and raised close to thirty-seven billion dollars in the war against Islaam. The United States vetoes any decision at the United Nations related to helping the Palestinians, so how can we expect the United States to help us and be fair with us?

Britain (the state behind the criminal entity (Israel) which occupies Palestine) is ordering the Palestinian forces to eradicate the Islamic movements. They seem to forget that they themselves are at the top of the list of terrorism – terrorism against Islaam and the Muslims. As for Russia, they are trying to fortify themselves from the Islamic movements within their territory, which is why they are defending Israel.

O Muslims! This pressure on the Palestinians to stop their uprising coincides with a shameful betrayal from the Arab leaders. The Israelis and the Zionist media worldwide are playing up the issue of attacking Iraq, Syria, and Iran with the claim that they are countries that endanger the security of Israel.[25]

This sermon is integrated into the database of other materials relating to Islamic issues, including mundane topics such as the World Cup, and serious social concerns such as the use of drugs. It should not necessarily be a great surprise that this religious-political message forms part of a user-friendly interface for sermons, designed specifically for circulation and reproduction within global mosque contexts. The collection of sermons, within a searchable format on a single site, also 'enhanced' by sermons from Mecca and Medina, gives (further) credibility to various Islamic organisations active in Palestine and highlights (if that is necessary) the importance of the issue to Muslim networks and individuals. It would be interesting to measure the impact of such sermons in mosque contexts, in terms of how or whether they are downloaded and applied. AlMinbar was soliciting donations via its pages, in order to expand its service:

> The English site requires your generous support in order to be fully functional. We have more than two-thousand carefully selected khutbas ready to translate; we therefore need to hire more translators, editors, and data entry personnel to continue bringing you professional articles.
>
> We remind you that the Prophet Sallallahu aalaihi wa sallam said: 'Charity does not decrease wealth'.[26]

The impact of such expansion is worthy of future monitoring.

One significant question that emerges is whether there is a pattern to the use of these sites by supporters of various organisations (in terms of frequency of readings), where the majority of their readers are located, and whether supporters cluster round and visit a set pattern of sites associated with a cause. It is the writer's personal experience that simply visiting several of these sites and reading *new* content on a daily basis is a time-consuming task, which can (depending on what is in the news) take several hours a day. The expansion of Arabic-language Internet sites has made the task even more exhaustive. Add to the cluster of activist sites the necessity of reading various news feeds (whether connected directly to a 'cause' or not), and perhaps one might wonder whether the dedicated reader would have any time to physically pursue an activist agenda. The digests of materials available on various e-mail listings and websites may become even more important to supporters of various activist causes, especially given the fluidity of affiliations. There are indications that the traffic to sites is substantial, although this is difficult to verify without an inside track to sensitive information, which is unlikely to be disclosed to a researcher; and if it were, it would be difficult to scientifically verify.

Despite these issues relating to the sheer quantity of materials available online, the Internet has become a means through which Muslim 'dissident' (however that term is defined or justified) voices can articulate their views, and it is also a growing medium of protest. For Palestinians living in the West Bank, Gaza and in refugee camps in the Lebanon, the use of e-mail, chat rooms and the web have been seen as a form of 'online intifada', as expressed in this extract from an article in the *Daily Star*, Lebanon:

> While borders around the towns remained sealed, locals took refuge in one road that could not be blocked off: the Internet. And as they sent their accounts through cyberspace, the Palestinian refugees who received them fought back in their own way. Forwarding them onto list servers, distributing news throughout refugee caps, and flooding the Internet with letters of protest and support, they made it clear that throwing stones wasn't the only way of resisting.[27]

The article discusses how computer servers were destroyed in arson attacks, and how those in refugee camps use a small computer terminal centre to find out news from the West Bank. The effectiveness allowed the experiences of Palestinians (Muslims and Christians) to reach the wider world:

> the Internet increasingly gives names, faces and voices to those involved in the intifada ... Last week as the city of Beit Jala fell under siege, local Palestinian biologist Ihab Lulas posted a letter online. 'Even the birds have gone, my mother told me this morning.' Days later, those words became the title to a piece published in the 'Israeli' daily *Haaretz* by Gideon Levy, who quoted the entire letter in an article regarding the sieges on Bethlehem and Beit Jala. The next day, Palestinian-American activist Muna Hamzeh distributed that article online to people in America, the West Bank and Lebanon. For anyone who doesn't know, this is what is happening in this Holy Land.

And while Lulas may be one voice, collectively these voices are making an impact. Ali Abunimah, media activist and vice-president of the Arab American Action network, recently wrote that 'For the first time in decades, Palestinians in the Occupied Territories, Palestinians in "Israel" and Palestinian refugees (especially in Lebanon) are all protesting simultaneously.'[28]

Online expressions of support for jihad in Palestine linked into other campaigns in which jihad was a cipher. Such linkage may be one reflection of how some Muslim global networks have been operating and affiliating with one another. Linkage was frequently drawn between campaigns in Palestine, Afghanistan, Chechnya and Kashmir. For example, expressions of support for the Taliban and Osama bin Laden were contained on the Kashmiri website Harkat-ul-Mujahdeen (banned in the United Kingdom) and continued to apply the Internet as a means of soliciting funds.[29] Campaigns in support of a Muslim Kashmiri state also featured on the website of the Lashker-e-Taiba, or 'Army of the Righteous' – the paramilitary arm of the Pakistani organisation Markaz ud-Da'wah ('Propagation Centre').[30] The Markaz ud-Da'wah website included provocative statements relating to the future evacuation of London and suggestions of future conflict. Abu Johar Musa of the Department of Super Computing and Defence Automation registered the site itself in 2000 in Kabul.[31] The front page in Urdu includes a Markaz symbol, featuring a submachine gun over an open Qur'an, a flag with a sword and extracts from the Qur'an. The site contained detailed Urdu and English news headlines, with an Indian subcontinent focus, and regularly updated. There is a series of articles, some of which respond to the post-9-11 situation. Particularly illuminating is an article entitled 'The Excuses and Pretexts against Jihad' by Hafiz Abdussalam bin Muhammah.[32] This provides a refutation of the reasons given by some Muslim organisations and individuals as to why jihad cannot take place. These include:

Jihad cannot be carried out without a Khaleefah ...

First of all we are to strive against our own baser selves, then against the Devil, then against worldly desires and materialistic pursuits on our part, and finally, if these efforts of ours meet with success, only then are we to wage Jihad against the enemy ...

It is not permissible to seek help from the disbelievers in the course of fighting ...

[In Relation to the jihad in Kashmir] We should stop helping the Kashmiris, beside to help them we must fight alongside the Pakistan government; who are Taaghoot ...

[In Relation to the jihad in Kashmir] Because of the activities of the Mujahideen, Muslim women are raped in Kashmir. The Mujahideen hit Indians and then run away. But the Hindu forces, in retaliation, crack down on the Muslim population, killing the youths and molesting the womenfolk ...[33]

The refutation is based on 'scholarly' research, particularly based on Qur'an and hadith sources, together with accounts from biographical and historical sources associated with the life of Muhammad. It also cites Ibn Taymiyya's 'Enjoining Right, and Forbidding Wrong', a title (based on a Qur'anic expression) which has been influential on many 'reform'-centred movements, and similarly reflects a 'Wahhabi'-influenced agenda through its denunciation of Sufism.

The Markaz ud-Da'wah has been connected to al-Qaeda and related organisations. Other features in the site illustrate the networking potential for the medium, and the ways in which the information contained on the site can have an influence far wider than the Indian subcontinent, with contributions from writers in Europe, and an Arabic section (down at the time of writing). Some of the Urdu pages were not functioning at the time of writing, including the donations and jihad pages. The site also incorporated an English-language translation/interpretation of the meaning of the Qur'an, which appears to reproduce the Saudi Arabian publication by Muhammad Taqi-ud-Din al-Hilali and Muhammad Muhsin Khan.[34]

Other regional conflicts also provoked online jihadi responses. Laskar Jihad, based in Jakarta, Indonesia, was allegedly connected with al-Qaeda, and proactively applied the Internet as a means of disseminating its ideology (in Indonesian and English). The site was regularly updated, with news, articles and photographs. Prominent on its front page were details of its bank accounts, in order that donations could be sent to further its aims.[35] The site contains details of the organisation's paramilitary activities in the Moluccan Islands (Maluku Islands) against (elements of) the Christian population. Two thousand jihadis were said to have arrived there in June 2000, promoting an interpretation of 'holy war'. It sought to justify this activity through answers to various e-mail enquiries, such as 'Does Laskar Jihad fight against neutral Christians?'[36] The photo-gallery contains over 40 graphic images of *Muslim* victims of conflict in the region.[37] The site contains substantial news updates and also promotes its own Laskar Jihad Indonesian language magazine. The watermark on several pages in the site uses the symbolism of a Qur'an and two intersected swords. The front page contains a banner with a bullet, and the phrases 'Victory or Martyrdom' and 'Jihad in Ambon'.

One way in which various jihadi perspectives were linked together was through a 'web-ring'. Yahoo contained one ring, with 55 members (October 2001), linking organisations including the GIA (Algeria), Sakina Security Services, Dharb-i-Mumin, Islamic Kuqiat and Laskar Jihad with more 'mainstream' *da'wa*-related sites. This ring was down at the time of writing. However, other Islam-related rings continued to function, including a Jihad WebRing with several members, organised on the WebRing site.[38]

One member of this webring was Hezb-e-Mughalstan (Party of Mughalstan), seeking 'the restoration of Mughalstan – the historical homeland of the Mughal-Muslims stretching from Kashmir to Bangladesh to Sindh and which has existed for more than 1000 years'. It was sponsored by the Hindu Dalit and Dravidian Organisation, which sought to 'DEFEAT BRAHMIN And UPPER-CASTE PARTIES (Congress, BJP), which have exterminated 70,000 innocent Muslim men, women and children and demolished the sacred Babri Masjid. Muslims must vote in order to defeat the Brahmin and upper-caste candidates in every single constituency.'[39] Although (at the time of writing) the site had not been updated since October 2000, it contained various reports on human rights issues, associated with the Indian subcontinent's Muslim populations. Elsewhere, it contained an article reproduced from *India Today*, which noted that 'Bin Laden plans restoration of Mughalstan'.[40] In relation to the Internet, the site is proactive in using electronic campaigning to distribute its message, suggesting that (South Asian Muslim) readers 'Join the Cyber-Army of Mughalstan', although its methodology is perhaps idealistic at times:

YOU are at RISK ! – You may think that because you are not a practising Muslim, have Hindu friends or are a 'secular' Muslim, that you are out of danger. Think again ! ... You have been born a Muslim, and no matter what some Hindus might say, there is no way you can ever become a Hindu – that is strictly prohibited as per their religion. A Hindu can only be born a Hindu. Hence you are automatically a target. You will also be cleansed and your family exterminated when the time comes. Whether Bangladeshi, Sikh, Mohajir, Punjabi, Pakistani, Sindhi, Dakhini, Navayat, Moplah, Shiah, Sunni, Ahmediya, or Kabirpanthi, whoever has the slightest resemblance to a Muslim is a target for this Hindutva program of ethnically cleansing Muslims.

What YOU can do – You may think that you won't make a difference. The point is: you can. The immense power of the Internet is at your fingertips. With this new weapon, a single person can mould the minds of millions of men. Gone are the days when the only voice heard was the Brahmin-controlled Indian mass media – now your articles immediately reach millions. The power of public opinion has been enough to influence entire nations everywhere. Let us remember that it was public opinion that stopped the war in Vietnam. We have to stop this Hindutva war on the Internet. Our people, our civilization, our future and every single ideal we stand for is at stake![41]

Hezb-e-Mughalstan suggests that e-mail should be applied as a means of protest, especially to lobby ISPs of 'anti-Muslim material', whilst chat rooms and newsgroups should be utilised in order to present pro-Mughalstan opinion. It highlights the application of anonymous e-mail, and encourages websites to be set up in support of the campaigns, detailing free hosts available and providing basic instructions on website promotion. Hacking is advocated for those who are 'experienced', with the following caveat:

This is highly dangerous, and not advisable for the ordinary person. Only do this if you are an expert in computers. The enemy is using chemical, nuclear and biological weapons against Muslims. Attacking Hindutva-run Indian Union computers is relatively safe if you are outside the Indian Union. If you are experienced at such exploits, you can learn more from major Mughalstan websites linked to in this email. Do not try this if you are inside the Union, or are inexperienced.[42]

The site advises that it is possible to adopt another identity on the Internet, in order to impersonate other Indian ethnic, religious and/or cultural groups:

It is easy to take on another identity on the Internet. You can pretend that you are a Dalit Sena member, a Tamil separatist,

Bengali secessionist, or whatever you want. This is a very powerful weapon. Using this, you can split the much-vaunted 'Hindu Unity'. By pretending to be a militant Tamil separatist, you can disrupt the Hindutva unity on an entire forum, demolishing Hinduism from inside.[43]

Information is given as to which 'friendly' ideologies could be supported through this method. It recommends that personal identities should not be divulged at any cost. Perhaps this site is a good example of an 'e-jihad', through which the technology can be applied in different ways to achieve political-religious objectives. There is certainly evidence of a belief on this site that the Internet can be a transformational tool for Muslim political and religious change. The linkage with non-Muslim agendas and platforms is unusual (although not unique). The success of such online campaigning is difficult to quantify, and it is perhaps telling that the material on the site was not updated frequently.[44]

In the months following 9-11, other sites continued to promote variations of the jihadi message. Last Flight to Paradise or Hell, a German-based Islamic site, continued to be available despite its allusions to paradise and its cost, and its photos of jet planes. It contained a page entitled 'Bin Laden or Bin America?', which had been online prior to 9-11.[45] The site underwent a major redesign in 2002, with the statement 'This site does not support terrorists' dominating the pages. However, there were links to 'mujahideen' sites, Azzam and bin Laden quotes and anti-Israeli materials.

Other sites still available in October 2001 included instructions on militaristic action and the production of explosives. A Mujahideen page offered video files of martyrs, a photo album of operations in Chechnya and information relating to the creation of explosives. It was pointed out that the ingredients were the same as those found on 'Anarchy' pages. The page suggested that this was 'serious stuff that is meant for mature muslimeen (especially living in troubled areas who would like to defend their faith, themselves, their honor and their property)'.[46] The site was subsequently removed from the server.

Jihad Unspun, registed in Canada to Bev Kennedy, sought to provide 'objective' reporting in relation to post-9-11 contexts:[47]

Jihad Unspun is an open information source dedicated to under-standing the issues behind the US war on 'terrorism'. We publish mainstream and uncensored news, articles, and opinions without influence of any government, corporation, or association.

Our mandate is to provide a platform where facts and viewpoints that address the issues at the heart of this 'jihad' can be considered, devoid of the constraints of mainstream media. Our goal is to encourage debate, discussion and collaboration among ethnic, religious and political stakeholders so that you, the viewer, can come to an informed understanding of these events that are challenging freedom, democracy and human life.[48]

Its content included statements from Osama bin Laden, including video clips and a statement marking the first 'anniversary' of 9-11, which included film that had not been shown in other contexts.[49] There was also a transcript of a recording said to be by Ayman al-Zawahiri.[50] A video 'store' included some pay-for-view materials, and other content derived from al-Jazeera, such as 'The Nineteen Martyrs', which included audio material of bin Laden praising the 9-11 suicide attackers:

There is not enough time to adequately acknowledge the lives of these men and what they have accomplished, the pen is unable to write all of their good deeds and the success of their blessed attacks however we will try to mention some of them for whoever doesn't know them, will not dignify these martyrs enough.[51]

The site contained regularly updated news, including materials copied from other news sites. Its articles dated back to April 2002, including an account of Yusuf Qaradawi's sermon 'I Am a Terrorist':

He considered jihad to be an individual obligation on every Muslim (fard 'ayn) and not only a collective obligation (fard kifaayah) on the Palestinians alone, and he called on Arabs and their leaders at the Summit to oppose the attack on Iraq and not support the U.S. in that regard.

... If everyone who defends his land, and dies defending his sacred symbols is considered a terrorist, then I wish to be at the forefront of the terrorists. And I pray to Allah if that is terrorism, then O Allah make me live as a terrorist, die as a terrorist, and be raised up with the terrorists.[52]

This included a commentary by Qaradawi 'justifying' 'martyrdom' operations, which (according to this account) he did not classify as suicide.

The implications of the Jihad Unspun site as a channel of reportage present interesting issues relating to 'freedom of information', especially as the site remained open during 2002. In places, its content appears to have a pacifist agenda, but at the same time it includes statements (in video and other formats) advocating warfare against 'the West'. Its physical location in British Columbia, Canada, seemingly had left it immune, raising questions about its 'authenticity' in some quarters. It was actively soliciting for translators in order to further populate its site with content. The design and information is professionally edited and presented. Since its inception, the site had been hyperlinked by a number of jihadi organisations, including Azzam Publications. There is a certain ambiguity in its content, in terms of whether Jihad Unspun represents information-gathering or a conduit for jihadi rhetoric, and whether it is motivated by 'jihad for war' or 'jihad for peace'.

NOTES

1. Gary R. Bunt, *Virtually Islamic: Computer-mediated Communication of Cyber Islamic Environments* (Cardiff: University of Wales Press, 2000), pp. 95–6, 99.
2. Palestine Information Center, 'Today's News', www.palestine-info.com, 13 September 2001.
3. Ibid.
4. The first paragraph of the communiqué's text cites *Surah al-Anfal* (The Spoils of War), 8:17, and the second *Surah at-Tauba* (Repentance), 9:14.
5. Palestine Information Center, Hamas, 'Qassam communique 270302', www.palestine-info.com/hamas/communiques, 27 March 2002.
6. Ibid.
7. This was tracked down to being registered in Sweden, October 2002.
8. Simoky Fed, www.simokyfed.com/mt/haganah/index.php. In November 2002, the URL moved to an Israeli domain, http://haganah.org.il.
9. The URL was www.alneda.com. 'Man hijacks Al-Qaida website', *Washington Post*, 20 July 2002, www.washingtonpost.com/wp-dyn/articles/A21548–2002Jul30.html. Variations of the URL appeared subsequently as representing a pornographic site.
10. FBIS, Foreign Broadcast Information Service, 'Al-Qa'ida Affiliated Website Back Online; Taliban Official's Statements Reported', 19 July 2002, trans. from *al-Sharq al-Awsat*, http://cryptome.org/alneda-up.htm (accessed October 2002).
11. For a detailed discussion on al-Qaeda and the Internet, with particular emphasis on Palestinian issues (from an Israeli perspective), see Reuven

Paz's article, 'Qaidat al-Jihad', 7 May 2002, reproduced on Free Republic, www.freerepublic.com/focus/news/763378/posts. It is hoped to explore this issue in greater depth in future research. Paz's institution is the International Policy Institute for Counter-Terrorism, based in Israel. www.ict.org.il.

12. Centre for Islamic Studies and Research, 'From God's servant Osama ben Laden to the peoples of the countries allied with the American government', accessed 19 December 2002 on www.cambuur.net/cocI/indexe.php?subject=2&rec=8. Some editing for typographical errors.

13. Paul Eedle, 'Terrorism.com', *Guardian*, 17 July 2002, www.guardian.co.uk/g2/story/0,3604,756498,00.html.

14. Whois entry, 23 October 2002.

15. Discussed in Bunt, *Virtually Islamic*, p. 99.

16. For example, see Kataeb Ezzeldeen, 'Karim Mohammed Abu-Abyad', www.kataeb-ezzeldeen.com/shohda2/shaheed.asp?ShaheedID=340. The organisation also uses the www.kataebq.com URL.

17. Kataeb Ezzeldeen, 'Prisoners', www.kataeb-ezzeldeen.com/prisoners/index.asp.

18. Samidoon, www.samidoon.com/.

19. Samidoon, 'Nasheed', www.samidoon.com/general/nasheed/nasheed.html.

20. Whois entry, January 2002. Jihad Online was off-line in October 2002. www.jihad-online.net.

21. Whois entry, 23 October 2002.

22. Neda al-Quds, 'About Us', [spellings corrected by writer], October 2002, www.qudsway.com/Links/English_Neda/AboutUs/Link_AboutUs.htm.

23. Neda al-Quds, Sound and Vedio [*sic*], www.qudsway.com/Links/SoundAndVedio/Link_S&V.htm.

24. AlMinbar.com, www.alminbar.com.

25. AlMinbar.com, Abu Sunaynah, 'Islaam, between the Enemies Plans & the Muslim's Betrayal', Khutbah 2284, www.alminbar.com/khutbaheng/2284.htm.

26. AlMinbar.com, 'Support Us', www.alminbar.com/supportus.asp.

27. 'Palestinians are Taking the Intifada Online', *Daily Star*, Lebanon, 2 November, 2001, reproduced on Hizbullah's Moqama website: www.moqawama.org/articles/doc_2001/taking.htm.

28. *Daily Star*, 'Palestinians'.

29. Harzat-ul-Mujahdeen, www.ummah.net.pk/harkat/.

30. This involvement of militaristic jihadis from outside Kashmir was in contrast to what are perceived as the quietist Sufi influenced beliefs of 'traditional' Kashmir.

31. Whois entry, 2 May 2002.

32. Hafiz Abdussalam bin Muhammah, 'The Excuses and Pretexts against Jihad', www.markazdawa.org/englishweb/islami-articles/200204/excuses.htm.

33. Ibid.

34. Muhammad Taqi-ud-Din al-Hilali and Muhammad Muhsin Khan, *Interpretations of the Meaning of the Holy Qur'an in the English Language*

(Riyadh: Maktba Dar-us-Salam, 1993). Discussed in Bunt, *Virtually Islamic*, p. 24.

35. Laskar Jihad, www.laskarjihad.or.id.
36. Laskar Jihad, 'Does Laskar Jihad fight against Neutral Christians?', 22 March 2001, www.laskarjihad.or.id/english/qa/eqa0103/eqa010322.htm.
37. Laskar Jihad, www.laskarjihad.or.id. Click on Gallery>Slaughtering Tragedy.
38. Jihad WebRing, http://i.webring.com/webring?ring=jihadring;list.
39. Hezb-e-Mughalstan, www.dalitstan.org/mughalstan/.
40. Hezb-e-Mughalstan, www.dalitstan.org/mughalstan/laden/targetin.html, reproducing 'Now We Should Target India', *India Today*, 4 October 1999.
41. Hezb-e-Mughalstan, 'Join the Cyber-Army of Mughalstan', www.dalitstan.org/mughalstan/azad/joincybr.html.
42. Ibid.
43. Ibid.
44. It also raises another issue of the veracity and origins of 'Islamic' websites and how they can be sued to 'detract' from the message of Islam, or even to gather information about people visiting them.
45. 'Last Flight to Paradise or Hell', www.haus-des-islam.de/flight, 17 September 2001. Site retitled Haus des Islam in 2002.
46. Mujahideen, 'I Take Refuge ...', www.expage.com/page/mujahideen, October 2001, page subsequently deleted.
47. Jihad Unspun, www.jihadunspun.net, Sam Spade DNS tracking.
48. Jihad Unspun, www.jihadunspun.net/aboutJUS.php.
49. Jihad Unspun, www.jihadunspun.net/articles/10152002-To.The.Islamic.Ummah/.
50. Jihad Unspun, 'Al-Zawahiri on the Invasion of Iraq', www.jihadunspun.net/BinLadensNetwork/statements/azotioi.cfm, 8 October 2002.
51. Jihad Unspun, Osama bin Laden, 'The Nineteen Martrys', www.jihadunspun.net/BinLadensNetwork/articles/19martyrs.cfm.
52. Jihad Unspun, Hasan Ali Daba, 'Sheikh Qaradawi's Jumu'ah Khutbah, "I Am a Terrorist"', www.jihadunspun.net/IslamUnderAttack/articles/iaat.cfm.

6 Cyber Islamic Reactions to 9-11: Jihad for Peace

Both e-jihad and the online *fatwa* demonstrate the significance of computer-mediated communication on sectors within Muslim societies, and as such should form part of a growing area of relevance in the study of contemporary Islamic thought and expression, as well as being relevant within the study of 'cyber-society' and the application of religious identities in Internet frameworks.

Statements issued by various platforms illustrate the complexity of definitions and allegiances associated with military activity and Islam. An example of this is the Algerian Front Islamique du Salut (FIS), which many governments would represent as a 'terrorist' organisation, but expressed condemnation for the 9-11 attacks. There may be significant strategic and political reasons for this, both relating to the FIS relationship with other Muslim platforms, as well as their domestic and international positions. FIS owns a website based in Lausanne, Switzerland, featuring Arabic, French and English material.[1] There is a forum and chat room for discussion, and a selection of audio clips from leaders. A quote in Arabic associates FIS with jihad, Islam and Muhammad, but a brief survey of existing content in different language zones suggested that there was little in the way of what could be described as direct religious propagation or symbolism (a proportion of the site was 'down' at the time of writing). The FIS 'jihad' against the army and government in Algeria is couched in political symbolism and language, emphasising the massacres that have taken place in the country and how 'democratic' rights have not been observed. The 'El Minbar' (The Pulpit) section featured political analysis and discussion, rather than sermons. There is broad-ranging news coverage, however, especially in relation to Palestine, including analysis, articles and an archive. The site also released a statement on 18 September 2001, condemning the 9-11 attacks:

Muslims throughout the world have spoken unambiguously and without hesitation. What happened on 11 September 2001 is a reprehensible crime against humanity. The ruling of Islam is very clear in this matter. No soul shall bear the burden of another soul.

Muslims feel shocked, aggrieved and saddened that acts which defy reason and humanity can be undertaken by persons who claim to act on their behalf. One should add that we still do not know who carried out the attacks against the World Trade Center and other targets but the presumption has already fallen on so-called Islamic extremists.[2]

The site also discusses 'the opportunism of certain totalitarian Arabic regimes, the Algerian putschist generals being at the forefront, which have tried taking advantage of these events by using them as a means to attack their opponents.'[3] Determining where to position FIS in any analysis is up to the individual reader. There may be cynicism at the FIS statements against 9-11, and fingers could be pointed at para-militaristic activities in France and elsewhere which allegedly have been the handiwork of FIS. The FIS link page connects to Chechen groups such as qoqaz (associated with Azzam) and Salafi.net, as well as 'mainstream' sites on human rights issues.

The Islam for Today pages presented a specific section responding to 9-11, as part of their overall site content, which focused on 'converts' to Islam. It contains an extensive series of articles and links seeking to 'promote a positive image of the *religion* of Islam today'. In October 2001, the Muslims Against Terrorism section contained quotations from the Qur'an and other sources relating to 9-11, headed by the following hadith:

'By God, he is not a true believer, from whose mischief his neighbors do not feel secure.' Prophet Muhammad (Bukhari, Muslim)[4]

The page then contained an extract from *Surah al-Zihal* (The Earthquake):

Whoever does good equal to the weight of an atom shall see it and whoever does evil equal to the weight of an atom shall see it.[5]

The page contained photographs of the attacks on New York, and President George W. Bush (showing his reaction on receiving the news of the initial attack). There were quotations from Muslims, including Muhammad Ali and members of the US Armed Forces. Links were given to articles in which 'Prominent American Muslims denounce terror committed in the name of Islam' (a transcript of a CBS television programme), and various statements from North

American Muslim organisations and academics. These include *fatwas* against the events of 9-11 from Muslim scholars and authorities. Amongst the illustrations of the attacks, there were also photos of demonstrations for and against the United States. The page noted that Islam for Today had only one photo supporting the stand against 'terrorism', and 'umpteen' of people demonstrating against the United States. This was during the initial phase of the Allied attacks on Afghanistan, so the hyperlink to the Islam for Today section on the Plight of the Women of Afghanistan was particularly pertinent: it contained a representative sample of academic and journalistic articles documenting the treatment of women by the Taliban. Some of the material is violently graphic in nature and links to the extensive site produced by the Revolutionary Association of the Women in Afghanistan (RAWA).[6] These pages incorporate digital photographs secretly taken to document the deprivations of the region, and to comment on how RAWA has endeavoured to provide health care and education in the face of adversity.

By April 2002, the page was headed the image of a Qur'an, a dove and a graphic image file (gif) of Osama bin Laden and his deputy Ayman al-Zawahri above the previously quoted hadith. Further statements against the attacks were reproduced from a variety of senior Sunni scholars and prominent Muslims, including Shaykh Abdul Aziz al-Ashaikh, Grand Mufti of Saudi Arabia and Chairman of the Senior Ulama, Shaykh Yusuf al-Qaradawi, 'Grand Islamic Scholar and Chairman of the Sunna and Sira Council, Qatar', and various Syrian, Egyptian, African, Pakistani, North American and European 'authorities'. As well as linking to media articles, the site focuses on the statements of American Muslim writers and scholars, in particular prominent converts to Islam. The site's authors were able to find two more photos protesting against terrorism.[7]

The emphasis on the front page of the site had shifted, suggesting it was focused on 'Westerners seeking a knowledge and understanding of Islam'. Amongst the articles highlighted on the front page were pieces by the controversial pro-Shariah Sudanese government minister Hassan al-Turabi;[8] Sudan, incidentally, was known to be harbouring al-Qaeda members during the 1990s, including Osama bin Laden. On the same index page was a link to an Islam for Today page containing 'Islamically argued' denunciations of the Taliban.[9] Similar 'conflicts of interest' appear elsewhere on the page: there was a link to the Markfield Institute of Higher Education, part of the Islamic Foundation in the UK, which has strong ideological ties with the Muslim political party Jama'at-i-Islami Pakistan (which itself had links to the Taliban).[10]

Jamaat-e-Islami's leader, Qazi Husain Ahmad, issued a statement on September 11 condemning the attacks as 'blatant terrorism'; it noted that Muslims lived in the attacked areas, 'therefore these centers could not be targeted by Muslims', and that the US government should not 'fall prey to the mischief of biased media hype' when determining who was responsible.[11] Husain Ahmad was arrested by the Pakistan government in November 2001 and charged with sedition after encouraging the army to overthrow President Musharraf.

Islam Online, strongly linked to the influential Shaykh Yusuf al-Qaradawi, contained extensive analysis of and reactions to 9-11 and its aftermath. These include statements and *fatwas* from Qaradawi, such as his speech at a Christian-Muslim summit in October 2001:

> I would like here to stress that I have issued a declaration denouncing the September 11th attacks on the United States. Many other Muslims scholars have also strongly condemned the killers of innocent civilians regardless of their religion, race or nationality.[12]

The 9-11 page linked heavily into its extensive online *fatwa* section (discussed separately in this book). This had reacted quickly to the crisis, producing a response on 12 September 2001 to a question on the attacks, seeking an appropriate 'Islamic response'. It is useful to survey Qaradawi's own response, which was incorporated into the answer:

> Truly, our hearts bleed for the attacks that have targeted the World Trade Center (WTC) as well as other institutions in the United States despite our strong opposition to the American-biased policy towards Israel on the military, political and economic fronts.
>
> Islam, the religion of tolerance, holds the human soul in high esteem, and considers an attack against innocent human beings a grave sin. This is backed by the Qur'anic verse which reads: 'Whosoever kills a human being for other than manslaughter or corruption in the earth, it shall be as if he had killed all mankind, and whosoever saves the life of one, it shall be as if he had: saved the life of all mankind' (Al-Ma'idah: 32) ...

Haphazard killing where the rough is taken with the smooth and where innocents are killed along with the wrongdoers is totally forbidden in Islam. No one, as far as Islam is concerned, is held responsible for the actions of others. Upon seeing a woman killed in the battlefield, the Prophet, peace and blessings be upon him, renounced the act and said: 'That woman shouldn't have been killed anyway!'

Even at times of war Muslims are not allowed to kill anybody save the one who is indulged in face-to-face confrontation with them. They are not allowed to kill women, elderly, children, or even a monk in his religious seclusion.

That is why killing hundreds of helpless civilians who have nothing to do with the decision-making process and are striving hard to earn their daily bread, such as the victims of the latest explosions (in the U.S.) is a heinous crime in Islam. The Prophet, peace and blessings be upon him, is reported to have stated that a woman was qualified to enter Hell because of the cat she locked up and starved to death.

We Arab Muslims are the most affected by the grave consequences of hostile attack on man and life. We share the suffering experienced by innocent Palestinians at the hands of the tyrannical Israeli entity who raze the Palestinian homes to the ground, set fire to their land, kill them in cold [blood], and leave innocent orphans wailing behind.

...

I categorically go against any committed Muslim embarking on such attacks. Islam never allows a Muslim to kill the innocent and the helpless.

If such attacks were carried out by a Muslim – as some biased groups claim – then we, in the name of our religion, renounce the act and incriminate the perpetrator. We do confirm that the aggressor deserves the deterrent punishment irrespective of his religion, race or gender.

What we warn against – even if it becomes a reality – is to hold a whole nation accountable for a crime that was carried out by a small group of people, or to characterize a certain religion as one that supports violence and terrorism.

When the well-known Oklahoma incident was carried out by a Christian American who was driven by personal interests, neither Christianity, America or even the Christian world were accused of the attack because a Christian masterminded it.

I have been asked several questions on television and on public lectures about the martyr operations outside the Palestinian territories, and I always answer: 'I do agree with those who do not allow such martyr operations to be carried outside the Palestinian territories. Instead we should concentrate on facing the occupying enemy directly. It is not permissible, as far as Islam is concerned, to shift confrontation outside the Palestinian territories. This is backed by the Qur'anic verse that reads: "Fight in the way of Allah against those who fight against you, but begin not hostilities. Lo! Allah loves not, aggressors."'[13]

The immediacy of this online response is significant, given the popularity of both the Cyber Islamic site and the scholar's own interest in information technology as a means of disseminating religious opinion.[14] Islam Online also published statements condemning the attacks from Muslim scholars in North America.[15]

The references to the Palestinian situation, and also to the Oklahoma bombing, are perhaps pre-emptive. It should be seen in the light of its point of writing, which was prior to the campaign in Afghanistan. When that commenced, the Islam Online service faced a new series of questions, relating to whether it was appropriate for Muslims to serve in the armed forces. This was answered by the 'Islam Online Fatwa Committee, which cited Qaradawi (as 'chairman of the European Council for Fatwa and Research') together with Sheikh Faysal Mawlawi (vice-chairman) and Taha Jaber al-'Alwani, 'President of the Graduate School of Islamic and Social Sciences and President of the Fiqh Council'.

The status of these organisations and their officials is perhaps open to question; they do not have any 'official' meaning or remit, even though they may publish edicts and other materials, and meet regularly. That is not always clear to the uninitiated surfer, although they are happy to pronounce on these issues. Professors at al-Azhar University in Cairo, and a Moroccan professor of Shari'ah provide other statements. It is not the purpose here to be critical of these individuals' status, just to note that the significance of their statements (or status) is not indicated or hyperlinked on the specific *fatwa* page.

Qaradawi is perhaps the most prominent of this online quorum. Here, he quotes various hadith as part of his argument prohibiting Muslims fighting Muslims, and then notes the dilemma when faced with the following question:

what about a Muslim recruited in the army of a non-Muslim country that is at war with Muslims? Such [a] helpless Muslim soldier has no choice but to yield to the orders of his army commanders and he has no right to say 'No' or 'Why?' This is a well-known military system worldwide.

...

The Muslim soldier may resort to this form of limited participation in order to avoid harm to himself as well as to the Muslim community of whom he is part and parcel. Without this [limited participation] the Muslim as well as the Muslim community may be accused of high treason. Such an accusation may pose a threat to the Muslim minority and this may also disrupt the course of Da'wa that has been in full swing since tens of years ago, and has started to reap fruits.

...

Muslim individuals should not set their conscience at ease and refuse to participate in the war, if this will endanger the whole Muslim community. This is based on the juristic rule, which states that the lesser harm may be borne to prevent a greater harm, the private harm may be borne to prevent a general one and the right of the group takes precedence over that of the individual. Such juristic rulings are part of an important part of Fiqh, which I call 'Fiqh Al-Muwazanaat' or applying a juristic preference to strike a balance in order to weigh the pros and cons of a certain thing in view of an existing situation. Many Muslims lack this kind of Fiqh nowadays. They should not consider the opinion of the general public who lack juristic preference to justify certain apparent situations allowing them to take precedence over the main objectives of Shari'ah.[16]

The presentation of such 'fiqh' online is particularly interesting, especially given the statements presented elsewhere on the web from Muslims serving in the US military (such as those on the Islam for Today site). The impact of such pronouncements is impossible to measure, but certain factors are ignored. For example, they do not reflect the precedents of other military campaigns in recent history, where Muslim fought Muslim, or the status of individuals classifying themselves as 'Muslim' who fight regimes or individuals who they interpret as being 'un-Islamic'. Perhaps these are questions for other fatwas. There is certainly a case for these pronouncements, and their effects, to be studied and observed in greater detail.

Al-Islam.org, produced by the Ahlul Bayt Digital Islamic Library Project, is (in terms of volume of content) one of the most prolific English-language Shi'a websites in cyberspace.[17] By 20 September 2001, al-Islam had produced a detailed 'categorical and unequivocal condemnation of crimes against humanity'. This incorporated broad Shi'a perspectives and a 'pan-Islamic' understanding:

We at Al-Islam.org condemn the cowardly, terrorist acts committed in New York City, Washington, DC, and Pennsylvania on September 11, 2001. We are deeply saddened and outraged by the loss of innocent lives resulting from these gratuitous displays of violence, and we offer our heartfelt condolences to all those who will no longer see their loved ones come home. We pray to the Almighty for a speedy recovery of those who have been injured – physically and emotionally – as a result of these senseless acts of terror. And we urge American and international law enforcement agencies to help bring the perpetrators of these heinous crimes to justice.[18]

The page continued with a quote from the Qur'an, and links to photos of 'Muslim leaders' condemning the 9-11 attacks. It also sought to encourage visitors to the site to explore al-Islam.org:

In this time of difficulty and uncertainty following the tragic events that took place in America, we encourage all of our visitors to embrace rational thinking and to avoid an attitude of ignorance and racism that seeks to blame entire nations or an entire religion for the deplorable acts of a handful of people. These difficult times have brought to the fore the need to remove the dark, ugly clouds of ignorance, bigotry, and hate; we invite you to explore Al-Islam.org and learn more about Muslims and the teachings of Islam, the religion of peace.[19]

The site's authors note that they had received a sustained correspondence from visitors to their site following 9-11:

Despite our unequivocal and categorical condemnation of terrorism, many of these emails have been filled with ignorance and virulent hate, and they have caused us to wonder in dismay whether we Americans will live up to the test that has been placed before us – a test of tolerance, understanding, love of fellow neighbors, and the very principles that make up the cultural, moral, and religious mosaic of the American society. However, correspondence we have received from others has assured us that there is hope.[20]

This is a pattern reproduced on other sites, such as the Muslim Council of Britain (discussed below), although al-Islam.org reproduce only the 'positive' correspondence received. The apologetic stance continues, with 'FAQs' (Frequently Asked Questions) about Islam and jihad. There were then links to an anti-sanctions site (Iraq Action Coalition) and a pro-Palestinian site (Palestine Media Watch), followed by links to articles about 'the realities of Middle Eastern politics'. Unlike Islam for Today (above), al-Islam *were* able to find photos associated with condemnations of the attacks, including images from a variety of mosques. There were also statements from senior Shi'a and Sunni scholars, and photographs of President George W. Bush in the company of a prominent American imam. There were also photos from a broad range of 'ecumenical' religious services commemorating the victims of 9-11 (in North America, and in other Muslim majority and minority contexts). These photos were primarily from Associated Press sources, and did not specifically reflect a Shi'a perspective or Shi'a participants. There was a specific 'Palestine' section, notably illustrated by a photo of a banner stating 'We deplore all acts of terror'. This allusion to the conflict between Palestine and Israel was significant, but did not dominate or intrude on the reflections contained on this page. Finally, the page (which is all one document) contains statements and photos relating to 'Prejudice and Intolerance against Muslim and Arab-Americans'. The content of the page had not changed six months after it went online on 20 September 2001.

The Muslim Council of Britain was proactive in seeking to represent the interests of Muslim communities in the United Kingdom. Its site includes a statement made by 'British Imams and Scholars', defining 'terrorism' and discussing the implications of 9-11 for Muslims living in the UK.[21] There is also an archive containing the e-mails (negative and otherwise) sent to the Council after the attacks. Some were abusive, but were still published online. In March 2002, there were 105 pages of correspondence. The MCB also linked to the UK Islamic Mission site,[22] which itself contained hyperlinks to Jamaat-e-Islami, vocal supporters of the Taliban in Pakistan.[23]

'Unofficial' media channels linked to activist agendas also became a significant source of information. The Movement for Islamic Reform in Arabia (MIRA) is a good example of an Arabic-English website applying the Internet as an effective means of mobilising political opposition. MIRA's campaigning against the Saudi royal family had previously used faxes and videotapes to disseminate its message, but has found e-mail and webpages more effective. MIRA's founder, Saad al-Fagih, lectures in Arabic on the site through the net, and its audience has substantially increased despite efforts at censorship by the Saudi authorities. The MIRA Internet site's address is frequently adjusted in order to prevent its being blocked, with new site address notifications being forwarded automatically on request via e-mail. Its site incorporates chapters on 'Islamists and the American-Saudi Propaganda Machine' and 'The American Phenomenon and The Bin Laden Phenomenon'. In a substantial analysis, which incorporates other themes from the MIRA perspective relating to US influence in Arabia, it described bin Laden as:

> a good warrior, faithful to his cause and willing to sacrifice self and property for it. He can plan and execute operations against his enemies. All this is true. But that alone does not explain his success. The truth is that the reality of the situation in which he emerged, together with all the historical, social and political cir-cumstances, contains the ingredients that makes him the unique tool that naturally and automatically turn these ingredient into a complete enterprise.
>
> There was a man who forsook a life of luxury and put self and property in the service of a cause he sincerely believed in. He fought in the far Muslim land of Afghanistan by choice, then decided to fight the American although it meant a life of destitution, hunted from one country to another.[24]

MIRA is based in London and has acquired a high profile through its Internet pronouncements. As a channel for discussion and alternative perspectives relating to Islam, it has been the focus of some attention, especially following 9-11 – but has remained open, despite pressure and censorship efforts from Saudi Arabia.

E-JIHAD: CONCLUDING COMMENTS

The consequences of the events of 11 September 2001 manifested themselves in a number of ways on the World Wide Web, both in the general sense in the way that the medium was applied to disseminate and obtain information, and in the way that it was applied within diverse Cyber Islamic Environments. At the time of writing, the proximity to the events and their impact on the world mean that it is not possible to provide anything but a sketch of how Cyber Islamic Environments were affected; it will only be with the further passage of time that a more developed analysis can be provided. What can be interpreted now reflects different notions of so-called 'e-jihad' and its consequences, and indicates that varied and sophisticated notions of jihadi symbolism – based in part on traditional interpretations of the concept – are now articulated in cyberspace.

The extent to which they represent a 'digital sword' is open to question, but there is no doubt that they are an important (if unquantifiable) indicator of elements of contemporary Muslim beliefs, whilst also being conceptually similar to notions of jihad that would have been familiar to Muhammad and the earliest followers of Islam. The problems associated with 'censorship' mean that state agencies in Muslim majority contexts may have very limited controls over what their populations read online, especially those educated, multilingual elites with personal net access who are *au fait* with the technology and sympathetic to the broad objectives of the various jihadi organisations represented online. It may be that governmental agencies in 'western' contexts will be closely monitoring the statements from the articulators of e-jihad, whose messages often originate (through the geographical location of ISPs and/or author origins) from within Muslim minority contexts, and that they remain 'open channels' because they represent a useful means of intelligence-gathering.

The articulation of jihad in the modern era is limited only by knowledge of Internet technology and relatively low levels of access within Muslim majority contexts: the impact of this in the twenty-first century (or the fifteenth Islamic century) may represent a shift in models of Muslim propagation as dramatic as that of the widespread use of print media in the nineteenth century, and as pervasive as broadcasting media in the twentieth century. Jihad has now truly 'gone global'.

NOTES

1. Front Islamique du Salut – Conseil de Coordination, www.ccfis.org.
2. Front Islamique du Salut, 'Claims of Vindication on the Back of a Tragedy', 18 September 2001, www.ccfis.org.

3. Front Islamique du Salut, 'PR30: The Events in the USA and the Vile Opportunists of Algeria', www.ccfis.org.
4. Islam for Today, 'Muslims against Terrorism', 25 October 2001, www.islamfortoday.com/terrorism.htm. Bukhari and Muslim are the hadith sources, from which this hadith (saying of the Prophet Muhammad) was taken.
5. Islam for Today, 'Muslims against Terrorism', citing *Surah al-Zihal* (The Earthquake), Surah 99: 7–8.
6. Gary R. Bunt, *Virtually Islamic: Computer-mediated Communication and Cyber Islamic Environments* (Cardiff: University of Wales Press, 2000), pp. 71–3.
7. 'Muslims against Terrorism', Islam for Today, accessed 22 April 2002, www.islamfortoday.com/terrorism.htm.
8. Hassan al-Turabi, 'On the Position of Women in Islam and in Islamic Society', Islam for Today, www.islamfortoday.com/turabi01.htm.
9. 'The Taliban of Afghanistan', Islam for Today, www.islamfortoday.com/taliban.htm.
10. Islamic Foundation, www.islamic-foundation.org.uk.
11. 'Qazi Condemns US Attacks', Jamaat-e-Islami Pakistan, 14 September 2001, www.jamaat.org/news.
12. Yusuf al-Qaradawi, 'Why Muslim and Christian Scholars Come Together', Islam Online, www.islamonline.org/English/contemporary/qpolitic-17/qpolitic1.shtml.
13. Ask the Scholar, Yusuf Qaradawi, Islam Online, Response to question from 'Shoukry, Australia', 'Islamic View on the Latest Attacks on America', 12 September 2001. Edited version. Qur'an quotes were originally in bold type. www.islamonline.net/fatwaapplication/englishdisplay.asp?hFatwaID=49349.
14. Bunt, *Virtually Islamic*, pp. 115–16.
15. 'U.S. Muslim Scholars Condemn Attacks', Islam Online, 12 September 2001, www.islam-online.net/English/News/2001–09/13/article1.shtml.
16. Ask the Scholar, Yusuf Qaradawi, Islam Online, Response to question from 'Zainab, Canada', 'Ulama's Fatwas on American Muslim Participating in US Military Campaign', 16 October 2001, www.islamonline.net/fatwaapplication/english/display.asp?hFatwaID=52014.
17. Al-Islam, www.al-islam.org. Al-Islam.org is discussed in Bunt, *Virtually Islamic*, pp. 30, 49, 110–14; Gary Bunt, *The Good Web Guide to World Religions* (London: The Good Web Guide, 2001), pp. 64–5; Gary R. Bunt, 'Surfing Islam', in J.K. Hadden and D.E. Cowan (eds.), *Religion on the Internet: Research Prospects and Promises* (New York: Elsevier Science, 2000), pp. 140–41.
18. Al-Islam, www.al-islam.org/dilp_statement.html.
19. Ibid.
20. Ibid.
21. Muslim Council of Britain, www.mcb.org.uk.
22. UK Islamic Mission, www.ukim.org.
23. Jamaat-e-Islami, www.jamaat.org/news/pr092101.html.
24. 'The American Phenomenon and The Bin Laden Phenomenon', MIRA, www.miraserve.com/pressrev/ARTICLE1.htm.

7 Islamic Decision-Making and Advice Online

O Ye who believe! Obey God, and obey the Apostle, and those charged with authority among you. (The Qur'an)[1]

The following chapters investigate decision-making processes in Cyber Islamic Environments, and the challenges faced by online communities and individuals seeking to reconcile or balance (if they feel it necessary or relevant) the practice of Islamic beliefs, and living within contemporary societies. It cannot be assumed that there is a conflict between these two elements, and indeed many meeting points can be found (on- and off-line). The central factor is to ascertain (if not measure) the online discourse that occurs in Islamic decision-making, whether in the form of *fatwas*, *ijtihad*, or other notions surrounding Islamic religious authority. With these points in mind, Chapters 8 and 9, 'Sunni Religious Authority on the Internet I and II', explore online authority primarily from a (so-called) 'orthodox' Sunni perspective. (The term *fatwa* is used in its singular, 'Islamic English' form throughout, rather than its technically correct translated plural *fatâwâ*.) The discussion includes a *fatwa*-producing Sufi-oriented site, because it is possible to be 'Sunni' and Sufi in orientation, and many people could be described as falling into this category. It is certainly not the purpose of this book to determine who is 'qualified' to be 'orthodox' or not. It is categorically not the purpose of this book to challenge an authority's categorisation of a *fatwa*, or to dispute the authority of an individual or an organisation to issue an edict or opinion (however that is labelled). Chapter 10, 'The Online Mujtahid: Islamic Diversity and Authority Online', focuses on Shi'a worldviews, but also refers to other elements of Muslim identity (which may or may not affiliate with Shi'ism and/or Sunni Islam).

Defining who is a highly qualified scholar is a contentious issue in both Sunni and Shi'a interpretations of Islam. This is represented in cyberspace, whilst determining levels of authority and qualifications should necessitate the surfer to exercise caution – although whether such caution is actually applied is open to question.

These categories are not necessarily rigid, holistic or distinct for those who fall within them. Some may see them as artificial barriers to the concept of a 'global *ummah*' or single community of Muslims, whilst other critics might suggest that such a typology is divisive, especially when put in place by an 'external' academic. However, these are common labels within academic and religious discourse, and go some way to help in unpicking the fabric of Muslim societies in real and virtual contexts. It will be seen that there is much that is shared, but also much that is distinct, within the main routes and back alleys of Cyber Islamic Environments.

DEFINING ISLAMIC AUTHORITY ONLINE

Is it possible to live 'Islamically' within a contemporary society? What informs online decision-making and ensures that activities retain a 'Muslim' nature? In what ways does Islam influence everyday life for millions of Muslims across the world? Themes that emerge in this discussion are broad-ranging and indicative of how Muslim activists, scholars and individuals have attempted to introduce Islamic approaches to a variety of concerns. Some of these relate to ethical issues that are common outside the 'Muslim world'. *In vitro* fertilisation, genetic engineering and organ transplantation can be significant issues for Muslims, who demand to know the appropriate 'Islamic' approaches to key associated questions. Others petition (or besiege) 'scholars' and 'authorities' on topics such as nuclear power, the impact of the Internet and the influence of soap operas on children. This is in addition to dialogues and questions on longer-standing issues, such as beliefs, family relationships and finance. This book demonstrates that these issues are being vigorously debated online and that the search for Islamic 'remedies' – in the Divinely Revealed Qur'an or in other sources – is not just the preserve of traditionally trained Muslim scholars. Others from outside the traditional scholarly paradigm believe they are qualified to interpret pragmatically sources according to their own abilities, without recourse to an authority that they may perceive as being 'out of touch' with the modern world and contemporary concerns. Some of these themes have been introduced in the writer's earlier work on Islam and the Internet.[2]

A number of key issues are addressed in this book, which have broad implications not just for the 'Muslim world', but for those individuals and institutions (insiders and outsiders) engaging with

Muslims in local, national and global contexts. Studying the application of Islamic sources within decision-making processes in different Cyber Islamic Environments has a distinct bearing on the nature of Muslim societies. Understanding the nature of authority within Islamic contexts informs approaches towards the wider impact of decision-making processes in such areas as personal law, economics, technology, education and medicine. Knowledge of the diversity of 'Islamic values' enhances the ability to see beyond the homogenised perspectives presented in some media and academic sources relating to Islam. An interest in human interaction and intellectual thought is informed by awareness of how Muslims reconcile the dynamics of varied Islamic beliefs with life in secularising and/or modernising societies, and to what extent 'extra-Islamic' socio-political and religious interests aid or abet the decision-making processes.

This book's analysis incorporates a subtext on interpretations of Islam. One underlying theme is the frequently articulated understanding that solutions for all issues can be located in the divinely revealed text of the Qur'an:

> And no question do they bring to thee but We reveal to thee the truth and the best explanation (thereof).[3]

What are the questions being brought for 'the best explanation' within Cyber Islamic Environments? How do online Islamic 'authorities' approach 'new' issues of practical concern to Muslims? Who is qualified to make a decision or provide an opinion, based upon interpretation of Islamic sources? Can this individual be identified as a *mujtahid*? Can these sources be utilised to tackle the different pressures on contemporary Islamic societies? Exploration of these questions may be of practical value to non-Muslims seeking to comprehend Islam more fully, and to Muslims interested in alternate approaches towards the practical concerns of living life as a Muslim – however that is defined.

The discussions in this book are influenced by diverse work in numerous fields and do not draw from a single 'school' or body of literature. Extensive literature exists on what could be described as the 'mechanics' of decision-making processes within Islam. Discussion on the nature of authority and decision-making processes dates back to the time of the Prophet Muhammad (570–632), and this informed the development of subsequent Muslim communities. Islamic written sources range from the Qur'an to vast collections of hadith and sunna (sayings and actions of Muhammad), sources based on oral transmission which were subsequently assembled, analysed and systemised within various written collections. The lines can blur between definitions of these concepts, with different stresses being placed on the normative practices of the Prophet, his Companions and their successors.[4] Biographies of the Prophet Muhammad and histories of Islam also informed the development of decision-making. Substantial works attributed to different Schools of Islamic law, philosophy, and other individual and collective Muslim scholarship from a variety of Muslim perspectives, also adds to the corpus of knowledge. These works (or selections from them) have in turn informed the training of various Muslim authorities throughout the generations, and in contemporary contexts their influence is felt in sermons, academic discourse, dialogue and diverse media – ranging from print sources through to the Internet.

These works have also informed the writer's approach to this book. The emphasis is less on the semantic and lexicographic nuances of Islamic terminology, although selected key terms are incorporated in the discussion; instead, the focus is on how Islamic understanding can have a direct impact upon people 'at ground floor level'. The discussion has been informed by existing studies on Islamic terminology and concepts relating to Islamic decision-making in contemporary contexts. In particular, an understanding of *ijtihad*, a term often (but not exclusively) associated with a striving for the pragmatic interpretation of Islamic primary sources in the light of contemporary conditions, has been a key to examining in detail the processes associated with decision-making. The word *ijtihad* can be synonymous with 'renewal' and 'reform' within certain Islamic contexts – although 're-evaluation' and 're-alignment' may be appropriate alternatives. These terms have entered Muslim discourses in several languages, and can be referred to within dialogues without explanation: the terms have several levels of meaning and relevance, depending on context.

It will be seen that some Cyber Islamic Environments frequently refer to the term, whilst others ignore it and related concepts altogether. It cannot be assumed that all Muslim societies apply *ijtihad*, but the term can have some currency within analysis of 'Islamic law' and its historical development, especially in relation to understandings of the Qur'an and the scholarship surrounding various significant Islamic sources – such as the collections of hadith, and/or analysis of the practices of Muhammad, his contemporaneous society, and subsequent Muslim communities throughout the world.

Idealised models of Islamic societies, influenced by historical and contemporary 'renewers' and 'reformers', have through time filtered through to the realities of everyday existence. Conceptual framework transmission has pulsed through communities and continents, specific reference points often emerged in circumstances shared by their originators. A loose, paradigmatic model can be constructed, with *ijtihad* as one possible reference point in understanding re-appraisals of 'Islamic ways of life'. The advocates of change in understanding and interpreting Islam have been motivated by a variety of factors – political, philosophical, social, economic and/or religious in character. Frequently, reform was sought in response to a shift in historical circumstances: invasion, expansion, colonialism and emigration have all stimulated reappraisals of Islamic interpretation. The stimulus might incorporate a need to return to the examples of the first Muslim community, to see how Muhammad and the early Muslim community dealt with analogous situations, perhaps through examination of the Qur'an and hadith. Similar paradigms might be sought through studying other ideological, historical and religious influences. The expansion of Islam saw an integration of pre-Islamic customs and practices within new Islamic frameworks, raising new questions for which a fresh perspective and a new precedent were sought. Knowledge of the sources, often reflecting intense training within an academy, may be required in order that *fiqh* or 'jurisprudence' in 'Islamic law' – based on interpretation and comprehension of Islamic primary sources – can be applied. Dissatisfaction with the status quo, where a deterioration or stagnation in society was blamed on failure to interpret Islam 'correctly', or the need for more complete or refined understanding, has led in some contexts to attempts at *ijtihad*.

There may be a desire to follow the 'straight path', or even relocate it amidst the maze of alternatives generated through history. It is not necessarily true that the advocates of change agree with one another. The recognition and understanding of *ijtihad* (if seen as viable or part of an individual or community 'worldview') can be linked to forms of Islam practice, and reliance on different post-Qur'anic sources of interpretation and legislation. There are varied understandings of who is entitled to apply *ijtihad*, whether an 'appropriately qualified' *mujtahid* is required, and if the decision is binding on individuals, a community or the Islamic world. A *mujtahid* is a person (invariably male) who is appropriately qualified to exercise judgement on issues of interpretation, utilising authoritative sources (which can vary according to the individual's perspective), but are likely to include the Qur'an. This opinion may be articulated in the form of a *fatwa*; the term which historically has reflected a legalistic statement, 'opinion' or 'edict', but can possess an inherent flexibility in Islamic discourse – especially on the Internet – referring to a variety of 'authoritative' statements and declarations. A *fatwa* does not need to incorporate contemporary *ijtihad* by an interpreter in order to be effective or relevant, especially if an 'authority' is drawing on the opinions of earlier scholars and sources.

Over the centuries, various Muslim contexts have been occupied with the issue of qualification and authority: Muslim 'reformers' in the twentieth century presented their own views on the qualities for such interpretation, often seeking to take authority away from the traditional scholars and sources of understanding, in order to construct a new paradigm for contemporary societies. This meant that the term *ijtihad* itself acquired a new currency, amidst discussions as to whether the 'doors of interpretation' had been closed during the period of classical Muslim scholarship. Within such considerations, perhaps it should also be noted that all did not necessarily follow the complex quasi-legalistic discourse. This includes some whose focus on Islamic spirituality had a more esoteric edge, although it has to be stressed that some legal scholars were also Sufis, and that legalistic interpretations also pervade the esoteric dimensions of Shi'a discourse. Such textured and textual disputation was primarily a concern of an educated male elite, rather than the average person 'on the street', in the field, in seclusion or in the mosque.

'Reforms' have been articulated in various forms (oral, written, printed, broadcast and now electronically), and may be ignored by many, seen as a threat by other authorities or imposed upon an unwilling population. There may or may not be an element of consensus and the reasoning behind reforms may disguise ulterior political agendas, which may or may not equate with sincerely held Muslim beliefs (this depends in some cases on the level of cynicism of an observer). There is no single paradigm of 'reform': it could range from ultra-conservative Sunni 'orthodox' through to modernising reforms integrating Islamic thought with elements considered by others as 'secular' or 'un-Islamic'. Diverse 'mystical' interpretations have endeavoured to bring new (not always welcome) perspectives to understandings of Islam, which have in turn been linked to reform-centred influences and endeavours. Some Muslims see this as a challenge to their model of how pragmatic and viable the Qur'an is in all situations. They may well ask why there should be any reliance on subsequent texts and new interpretations of Islam, when Muhammad was understood to be the Final Prophet, and everything can be learnt from the Qur'an. Some might suggest that it was Muhammad's practice, and its articulation in his Companions and Successors' communities, that provided clarity of understanding of the Qur'an, especially those dimensions which were not fully articulated in its verses. Others, especially from within Shi'a contexts, place emphasis on 'successors' to Muhammad as represented in different lines of infallible and divinely inspired imams.

It has been said that critics emphasise the disunity, rather than any unity of Islam. However, the pragmatic recognition of difference has been a feature of Islamic interpretations from the time of the first Medina community. There is a danger of critics attacking Islam and Muslims for something that was never sought, and attempting to squeeze Islam into confines Muslims themselves feel are narrow and restrictive, what certain interpreters would then describe as 'fundamentalist'. It is possible to conclude that the mechanisms within Islam, revealed and interpreted esoterically and exoterically, were intended to accommodate a basic flexibility of viewpoints in certain matters. If the sayings and actions of Muhammad, recorded in hadith and sunna sources, are brought into the equation, then here we have a body of material drawn together through diverse sources and channels. The dependence on the exactitude of the sources is reflected in the provision of, on occasion, several different versions of an event or saying, whereas the Qur'an provides one definitive Divinely Revealed text. However, depending on the verse, several different commentaries (not necessarily complementary) may be applied, drawing on different interpretational techniques and dependent on the personal situation, background and qualifications of the interpreter(s). This variation plays a significant role in forming the basis of 'reform-centred' movements, for example, if the layers of understanding are believed to obscure the 'true' meaning of the text. There can be a dichotomy between the literal and implied readings of the Qur'an, which may lead to a conflict of interests.

Transformation of ideals into reality requires a common platform of intent, coupled with a realistic intellectual and educational strategy. There has been a tendency amongst some so-called reformers to suggest that *ijtihad* could provide a key to any transformation

process, incorporating a casting off of selective, 'anachronistic' interpretations of Islam, and invoking instead a recognition of certain
interpretations of Islamic principles, deemed as 'purifying' existing
belief-frameworks within Muslim communities.

The roots of Islamic decision-making can be found in the chapters
of the Qur'an, which have been interpreted as being pragmatic and
evolutionary in form. The demands on the early Muslim community
became progressively more rigid, demonstrated in the differences
between early and later Revelations. As the community developed,
the exhortation-centred verses were augmented or superseded by
Revelation providing clear instructions and commands, adapting to
the conditions and issues facing the developing Muslim state of
Medina. The extent to which there is continuity between this 'golden
era' and today, linked by *ijtihad* and reform-centred approaches to
Islam, is a key issue discussed online.

Decision-making also forms part of the 'postmodernist' equation
on globalisation, and the impact of the juxtaposition of Islam and
modern contexts and technologies.[5] There is no intention of
engaging here in the semantics of postmodernism and its validity
(or not), although it may be true that elements of this postmodernist
interest – in their wider sense – fall within this book's remit. In a
more general sense, the fact that this book was produced during the
(post-) 'postmodernist' era, utilising a variety of sources and
disciplines, inevitably influences the outcome of the research, and it
could be said that postmodernism has affected the methodology of
the present book.

Grappling with these theoretical considerations can obscure the
fact that the features of Muslim landscapes are changing (and have
changed) rapidly. Edward Said's description is particularly apt in this
book's discussion of Cyber Islamic Environments:

> new alignments made across borders, types, nations and essences
> [which] are rapidly coming into view, and it is those new
> alignments that now provoke and challenge the fundamentally
> static notion of identity that has been the core of cultural thought
> during the era of imperialism.[6]

These new alignments form a component of any discussion on
reform-centred or modernising Muslim individuals, or discussions
of Islam in cyberspace. New notions of Muslim authority and identity
transcend traditional cultural and religious frameworks by going

online. What kind of Islamic opinions are sought, and by whom? What are the qualities of an online *fatwa*? How does it differ from 'conventional' authority and sources? Does the Internet represent a transformation in the transmission of Islamic knowledge? This electronic authority, sometimes qualified by users with the term *ijtihad* (and related terms), can also influence political networking and activism by mobilising the immediacy of the Internet to promote specific worldviews and agendas.

Cyber Islamic Environments can be linked to an organisation or platform, but potentially can be equally effective and verbose when produced by an individual seeking to present her/his worldview. The substantial financial investment in the Internet by various Islamic organisations and platforms represents attempts to secure online ideological advantages. Theoretically, an individual's home page on Islam can carry the same weight and interest to a 'neutral' surfer. This is particularly apparent when approaching issues relating to decision-making and interpretation of Islam, and the 'qualifications' (if any, and if relevant) of those making pronouncements and providing online advice to Muslims (and others). It may be difficult to determine the credentials of an online Islamic 'authority', and this introduces a significant contemporary issue relating to Islam.

Within a Sunni 'orthodox' context, in particular, it can present concerns associated with the formulation of *fatwas* or legal opinions produced by religious scholars and authorities.[7] In various Shia contexts, authorities are also strategically investing time and resources to present their own online conceptual approaches towards interpretation to a global audience. The first section in this book focuses on what could be described as 'Sunni-centred' decision-making and advice resources.[8] When exploring such 'orthodox' Sunni models, there is a need to determine the types of issues deemed significant and to consider whether they constitute part of the traditional and contemporary manifestations of *ijtihad*, and associated interpretative decision-making processes.

Within this discussion, 'Sunni' Islam is an umbrella term for a variety of cultural, historical, political, legalistic, religious and socio-logical perspectives, not always in agreement with one another, but focused on the notion that religious authority and interpretation emanates from the Prophet Muhammad and his followers (including, for some perspective, elected *caliphs*) – and is contained in a variety of sources, including various legal interpretations, as well as (in varying degrees, depending on the perspective) collections of Muhammad's sayings and actions. In contrast, Shi'i Islam is an umbrella term for a separate, but interrelated, variety of cultural, historical, political, legalistic, religious and sociological perspectives, not always in agreement with one another, but focused on the notion that religious authority and interpretation emanates from the Prophet Muhammad and his descendants, including the various lines of spiritual leaders or Imams.

The term *ijtihad* has been defined and utilised in many ways by the varying perspectives, and a number of these different shades of opinion relating to the definition emerge on the Internet. The *Encyclopedia of Islam* described *ijtihad* as 'lit[erally] effort; in law, the use of individual reasoning; exerting oneself to form an opinion in a case or as to a rule of law, achieved by applying analogy to the Qur'an and the custom of the Prophet'.[9] The twentieth-century Muslim commentator Kemal Faruki described *ijtihad* as 'exerting oneself to the utmost degree to understand shariah through disciplined judgement',[10] the frequently used and abused term *shari'ah* being seen as divine law, as articulated in the Qur'an, and interpreted by human beings to contribute to 'Islamic law' or jurisprudence (*fiqh*).

NOTES

1. The Qur'an, *Surah al-Nisa'* (Surah 4:49), Yusuf Ali translation.
2. See Gary R. Bunt, *Virtually Islamic* (Cardiff: University of Wales Press, 2000), pp. 104–31, which discusses notions of online Islamic authority, including *fatwa* resources.
3. The Qur'an, *Surah al-Furqan* (Surah 25:33), Yusuf Ali translation.
4. For a discussion on the conceptual frameworks surrounding 'amal, sunna and hadith, see Yasin Dutton, *The Origins of Islamic Law: The Qur'an, the Muwatta' and Madinan 'Amal* (London: RoutledgeCurzon, 2nd edn. 2002).
5. Akbar S. Ahmed and Hastings Donnan, 'Islam in the Age of Postmodernity', in Akbar S. Ahmed and Hastings Donnan (eds.), *Islam, Globalization and Postmodernity* (London: Routledge, 1994), pp. 1–19.
6. Edward Said, *Culture and Imperialism* (London: Grafton Books, 1993), p. xxviii.
7. The transliterated plural of *fatwa* is *fatawa*. *Fatwa* will be applied in the remainder of this chapter as a singular, and in a plural with an -s when appropriate.
8. Significant materials exist in Shia and Sufi contexts. It is not intended to suggest a polarity between these sectors, or that one sector has priority

over others. See Gary R. Bunt, 'Surfing Islam', in J.K Hadden and D.E. Cowan (eds.), *Religion on the Internet* (New York: Elsevier Science, 2000), pp. 127–51.

9. *Encyclopaedia of Islam CD-ROM Edition 1.0*, 'Glossary and Index of Terms', *idjtihad* (Leiden: E.J. Brill, 1999).

10. Kemal A. Faruki, *Islamic Jurisprudence* (Karachi: Pakistan Publishing House, 1962), p. 288.

8   Sunni Religious Authority on the Internet I: Muslim Majority Contexts

The Internet brings *ijtihad*-related issues into sharp focus, when any individuals can proclaim themselves as 'authorities' on Islam qualified to make pronouncements, exercise *ijtihad*, provide 'Islamic advice' and/or issue *fatwas*. Their 'qualifications' for this activity may not be scholarly. They could ignore the traditional Islamic models endorsed by al-Azhar and other institutions. Some critics do not necessarily perceive such academic study as appropriate or relevant within Islamic decision-making, preferring to present alternative models, which they still describe as *ijtihad*. Status markers such as family connections, political authority, religiosity and/or levels of education can also potentially contribute to the power of an individual to exercise *ijtihad*. The debate on Islamic decision-making issues has now transcended traditional contexts, to emerge within cyberspace, acquiring a global dimension in the process.

On the Internet, there is a new audience for alternative Islamic opinion and interpretation, as well as the traditional articulation of religious values and understandings. Electronic *ijtihad*, or e-*ijtihad*, and/or electronic *fatwas* not only reproduce conventional processes of interpretation and reasoning to reach decisions or opinions; they are also created especially for the medium. There can be a blurring between the two digital and 'conventional' sources. There is evidence of a transition from the newspaper archives of *fatwas* that have been placed online (and columns written by 'scholars'), to the introduction of especially created online *fatwa* resources (some may run in parallel with newspaper columns). Advice on a key issue might be solicited on different websites: this may be through searching database archives of *fatwas*, edicts, opinions, questions and answers – or by e-mailing a site with a question. One advantage for petitioners (and the curious) is that use of the Internet can be anonymous. Whilst this factor has perhaps been overemphasised in cyber-studies in general, in relation to Cyber Islamic Environments some specific and unique themes are raised. These include issues linked to whether an online opinion is binding or not, and the moral implications on the person making the petition or asking the question. Should an opinion solicited by e-mail be followed? Are the moral and ethical dimensions the same as receiving an opinion from a scholar in non-electronic contexts? There is evidence that 'authorities' are approaching some of these issues. In the related area of the authority of SMS text messages on mobile phones, a 'Dubai court validated the divorce of a husband who sent his wife her marching orders by text message on his mobile phone'.[1]

There may be benefits to be gained from the study of online decision-making resources, which can act as indicators to contemporary needs of (sectors of) Muslim communities, providing personal insights into the concerns of individuals, as well as being one symbolic focus of Muslim authority in cyberspace. They also provide insight into the processes of decision-making applied by diverse authorities, indicating the language, sources and methodological approaches of *fatwa*-issuing bodies. One proviso may be that a website can look 'official', 'Islamic' and contain substantial content, whilst not being 'representative' of majority opinion. This proclaimed authority has its critics, but in terms of academic analysis does provide insight into contemporary Islamic diversity and a representation of opinion that may be difficult to locate within other source materials. Important new issues, with no immediate basis in traditional sources, can be discussed. Opinions can be disseminated rapidly, but are not necessarily observed or followed by readers, who may visit another site to solicit an opinion more in line with their personal requirements. This reflects a pattern observed by the writer in 'real-world' fieldwork exploring decision-making concerns and notions of religious authority, where in some cases several scholars noted that petitioners would shop around for an opinion that matched their expectations.[2]

Islamic websites often present *fatwas* in searchable databases, such as Fatwa-Online, Ask-Imam and Islam Q&A.[3] Opinions can also be integrated into 'sermon' content, a prevalent content theme in Sunni cyberspace. Some feature versions of newspaper columns, for example, Islamicity's Ask the Imam reproduces material from Jeddah's Arab News.[4] Those living in environments hostile to their religious worldview may find comfort, advice and inspiration through the content of web pages, whilst others might appreciate the perspectives of other dimensions of interpretation and understanding. The influence of scholars and others giving advice based on Islamic principles can extend from their own (micro-) communities to be placed before a global audience. The observation and recording of developments such as the online *fatwa* in Cyber Islamic Environments represent a significant research area in themselves.

The substantial growth in the number of Muslim religious 'authorities' making the Internet a primary channel for the pronouncement of their edicts and opinions is a significant contemporary phenomenon, requiring detailed observation, analysis and recording. 'Questions' submitted to online authorities might be 'genuine' and represent 'real' readers, but conceivably could be hypothetical questions providing authorities with an opportunity to present a religious edict to address a specific concern. When viewing such sites, it is pertinent to consider that some authorities increasingly respond to various forms of 'crises' and situations – be they moral, cultural, legalistic, spiritual and/or political in nature – primarily through the Internet. As with other areas of the medium, determining the impact of these materials on Muslim readers and popular opinion is open to question. Some sites focus on specific communities and audiences, whilst others appear intended for 'general Muslim consumption' (dependent on access).

The extent to which a Muslim surfer will apply the knowledge acquired in cyberspace regarding Islam, and be influenced by pronouncements, is difficult to quantify. Issues which could be considered dangerous or embarrassing to raise within a domestic framework can be presented to an 'authority', locally or globally, or indeed from a different cultural-religious outlook. However, local knowledge is also significant when decision-making processes are considered. The Internet can be accessed by only a small (but increasing) proportion of the world's Muslim population. The sites discussed in this book may represent one foundation for religious authority, when access levels to the medium increase. They have been chosen because they represent different online models of authority, can be innovative in nature and often appear to be relatively popular within their own theological, legalistic, cultural and/or political frameworks. Given the appropriate resources, it would be possible to analyse hundreds of such sites and make scientific consideration of the geographical locations of petitioners (questioners), the typologies of questions and the influences on responses. Many of the following sites would be worthy of detailed analysis of this nature, but for the purposes of this section it is intended to provide introductory sketches of key sites and their content. Significant issues to consider are the sites' 'Islamic' identities and perspectives, and the emphases on particular issues and interpretative considerations.

For ease of reading, the key sites have been divided between those operating in Muslim majority (in the next section) and Muslim minority (Chapter 9) contexts; in effect, this division can represent a grey area, as sites may have contributors from both contexts, or authored in one and hosted by an ISP in another. All sites are in the English language, although some operate Arabic and other channels; the extent to which this influences content is a subject for further investigation.

ANALYSIS OF SUNNI WEBSITES – MAJORITY CONTEXTS

Islam Q&A

Islam Q&A represents one model of online fatwa *provision, centred on a single Sunni scholar in a 'majority' context, who seems to provide the majority of the site's outputs. The content suggests awareness of the medium, built up from several years' experience of providing decisions and opinions online, and diversification into materials in languages other than English and Arabic.*

Islam Q&A site was founded by Shaykh Muhammad Saalih al-Munajjid from Saudi Arabia in 1997, which in Internet terms makes it one of the long-standing *fatwa*/question sites in a web format.[5] In August 2002, it was registered to al-Munajjid, at an address in al-Khobar, Saudi Arabia, and hosted by a company in Florida. The site has sections in Arabic, English, French, Indonesian and Japanese. The latter is particularly unusual in the context of online Islamic *fatwa* formulation (the Japanese section requires navigation via an English interface, before a selection of Japanese titles can be accessed). Elsewhere, there are lectures, sermons, a mailing list and Holy Quran Radio. There is an external link to the Chechen qoqaz.net (see Chapter 6).

The Q&A section of the site consists of a regularly updated database of subject areas, which is also fully searchable by date, question number or topic. E-mail questions can be posted to the site. Pages contain printable versions, and they can be e-mailed within the site to other e-mail addresses. In August 2002, the English-language section of the site contained approximately 3,975 answers (an increase from 2,700 in March 2001), clearly categorised under broad headings.[6] The largest area was Jurisprudence and Islamic Rulings (2,434), in which Acts of Worship (1,201) and Transactions (841) dominated:

> All questions and answers on this site have been prepared, approved, revised, edited, amended or annotated by Shaykh Muhammad Saalih al-Munajid, the supervisor of this site.[7]

The site has the following agenda:

- 'to teach and familiarize Muslims with various aspects of their religion';
- 'to be a source for guiding people to Islam';
- 'to respond to users questions and inquiries to the best of our resources and capabilities';
- 'to assist in solving the social and personal problems of the Muslims in an Islamic context'.[8]

Al-Munajjid was trained by Shaykh 'Abd al-'Azeez ibn 'Abd-Allaah ibn Baaz, the influential Saudi Arabian theologian and scholar (discussed below), to whom al-Munajid attributes his knowledge of *fatwas*. As with many 'traditional' scholars, al-Munajid presents full details of his education, including his teachers. He also provides information on the places where he has subsequently taught and details of the courses. This offers a detailed picture of the types of influences that inform Islam Q&A.

The site offers personal replies, as well as replies posted onto the server. At the time of writing, the Submit Questions facility was open only once a week (for 24 hours) due to high demand. There are broad ranges of issues covered within the decisions, including questions associated with the Internet. Twenty-three entries were located when the term 'Internet' was entered. Al-Munajid even recommends the net as a source of knowledge about Islam when other materials are unavailable.[9] Amongst other questions deemed significant regarding the Internet are:

- ruling on condemning people on the Internet;[10]
- benefits of the Internet in spreading knowledge;[11]

- men and women talking to one another on the Internet within the limits of good manners;[12]
- picture of Internet fiancée;[13]
- contact with a fiancée via the Internet;[14]
- ruling on transactions made via modern means of communication;[15]
- warning about Internet sites that distort the Qur'an;[16]
- investing in Internet services;[17]
- if the owner of an Islamic website takes payment for advertisements, will that detract from his reward?[18]
- advice to those who visit chat rooms.[19]

One question tackles the theme of pornography on the Internet:

Some of my friends have introduced the Internet into their homes, where their children and wives have access to it in this permissive land in which we have the misfortune of living, and they do not have any control over their children's computers. I need some statistics and numbers that I can use to convince these brothers who perhaps cannot be convinced except through numbers. I hope that you can help me in this matter. May Allaah reward you with good.

Answer:
Praise be to Allaah.
It was narrated from the Prophet (peace and blessings of Allaah be upon him) that among the Signs of the Hour is that *zina* (unlawful sexual relationships) will become widespread. (Narrated by al-Bukhaari, 1/178). According to a report narrated by al-Haakim, 'immorality will become widespread'. During the Internet age in which we are living, this hadeeth has become true, and we see the reality of the events foretold by the Prophet (peace and blessings of Allaah be upon him). No one can deny this except one who is arrogant. The kaafirs recognized the seriousness of the matter before the Muslims did. Now on the Internet there are half a million pornographic sites displaying immorality, and another 100 new sites are added every day, spreading nakedness and immorality in the world.[20]

The discussion digresses into an analysis of Internet impressions (or hits) on prominent pornographic sites. It is interesting to note that the discussion incorporates hadith source material, and an indication that the pornography sector of the net is a 'Sign' of immorality foretold by Muhammad. It also features the complex issue of Internet access and how usage can be monitored (if that is desired). Al-Munajjid is critical that *kafirs* (a derogatory term for people who are not Muslims) recognised the 'problem's' depth before Muslims. Al-Munajjid is criticised by other Muslim websites, including those who define themselves as 'pure Salafi'. Labels associated with Islam, including 'Salafi' and 'Ahl al-Sunnah wa'l Jam'aa', encompass a broad range of definitions, agendas and perspectives. They may all assert, in the words of the Qur'an, that Muslims should 'hold fast, all of you, and do not fall apart'. There are a number of broad and different definitions associated with the term 'Salafi' (*Salafiya*), including association with reform-centred movements, and also 'fundamentalism'; the Islamic practices of the 'pious ancestors' (*al-salaf as-salih*), the generation after Muhammad, are also described as Salafi. '*Ahl al-Sunnah wa'l Jam'aa*' can refer to 'the People of Custom and Community', a traditional name for people adhering to the practices of the Prophet Muhammad. Groups using these terms are not necessarily affiliated or associated within an organisational hierarchy. Surfing the Internet can highlight that dialogues about the status and classification of different Islamic groups (or 'sects') is an ongoing and frequently heated subject of discussion in Muslim contexts.

This discussion is reflected in relation to al-Munajjid; in a publication by the Salafi Society of North America, there is an allusion to him being a 'Qutubi', that is one whose perspective is presented as a follower of 'Ahl-i-Sunnah', whereas his thought is negatively deemed to be associated with the Egyptian 'reformer' and Muslim Brotherhood ideologue, Sayyid Qutb

So I do not know from this man (Saalih al-Munajjid) that he is a Salafee. Rather, his implications and indications show us that he is not Salafee. In fact, there are implications that indicate that he is a Qutubi Suroori. Either he is just like that or in the least of conditions he inclines towards them and agrees with them in their methodology, even if he isn't affiliated with them in a party. And Allaah is most High and knows best.

... So some people have good thoughts about Saalih Al-Munajjid because they think that he is one of the scholars of Saudi Arabia and that he is on the way of the Salafee scholars of Saudi. However, this man is not from Saudi Arabia, rather he is Syrian. Many people that listen to his tapes think that he is Saudi, so therefore they have good thoughts about him. But the man is a Syrian living in the Kingdom of Saudi Arabia for a while now. So it is thought that he is Saudi, but that is not so, for he is Syrian. And the reality is that Syrians are overwhelmed by the *Ikhwanis* [Muslim Brotherhood] and overcome with influence from the *Hizbee* [factional] methodologies and by the way of the Qutubis and the Surooris [followers of Muhammad Suroor], except for those whom Allaah has mercy on – and how few they are. So this is a fact and a clarification of the reality – that his homeland is not originally Saudi Arabia, and we ask help from Allaah.[21]

Muhammad Suroor is accused in a related publication of being a disciple of Qutubism, and an advocate of the 'qutubi strategem [which] … calls to civil strife and unrest, unnecessary commotion, calls for open rejection …'[22] This quotation appears on the Allaahuakbar.net site, which emphasises the teachings of Muhammad ibn Abd al-Wahhab and his 'reformation', but is strongly critical of pseudo-'Wahhabis' or those who 'make the false claim to be Ahl us Sunnah wal Jam'aah'. Such criticisms go both ways on the Internet: for example, *some* of the 'True Scholars' endorsed in Allaahuakbar.net (such as al-Albani and al-Shawkani) have been heavily criticised elsewhere on the Internet (and in Islamic literature) for having poor reputations as Islamic scholars, and for their 'neo-Salafi', 'divisive' outlook.

The argument in relation to Salafi identity is a pervasive one in Sunni cyberspace, and is returned to later in this chapter, in particular in relation to Yusuf al-Qaradawi. Some varied perspectives on Salafi Islam are also presented. It is interesting to note this divergence within 'orthodox' Islam is not always observed by commentators, whilst drawing attention to it can lead to accusations that academics are presenting 'Islam' as divisive.

Fatwa-Online

Fatwa-Online represents a model of a well-developed Sunni-oriented Internet platform, based around the output of a number of contemporary and historical scholars on a broad range of issues. At present, the focus is on the English speaking 'market' or audience.

Several Islamic websites present a searchable listing of *fatwas*, and a key word search should bring the surfer to the subject of interest within the site. The influence of Saudi Arabian scholars (or scholars located in Saudi Arabia) is evident on Fatwa-Online. If success can be measured in the growth of content, then Fatwa-Online has proved to be popular, with new content being added to the site on a regular basis. The domain is registered to an address in Medina. Its pages incorporate content obtained from at least 18 scholarly sources (from Ibn Taymiyyah through to the *fatwas* of Shaykh Ibn Baz and his former students) well connected to the Saudi Arabian Permanent Committee for Islamic Research and Fatawa (Ibn Baz is eulogised in a specific section of the site, with anecdotes about his life).[23]

The Fatwa-Online site is searchable, with an interface containing ample user assistance, whose navigation has been improved through a drop-down menu. Features that had been added during 2002 included an Arabic Language Syllabus (as studied at the Islamic University of Medina), 'Learning to Read Arabic for Beginners' and a *Hajj* Guide.[24] All the materials are in English, and there are no 'Islamic' images or graphic image files (GIFs) on the site – conforming to some Muslim perspectives on 'images', as well as accelerating its download time (a very important factor for surfers with slow Internet connections). Readers can be updated of new topics on the Fatwa-Online site via an e-mailing list. Fatwa-Online's emphasis is on translating scholarly opinion from Arabic resources. Despite a request that no *fatwa*-seeking questions be sent to them, the site's authors (some of whom are based in Medina) were inundated with questions that require translation and placing with Shaykhs for a response.[25]

During the 'second intifada' in 2002, there was a great deal of advice on Palestine-related issues, including a *fatwa* on boycotting American products, software for connections to the PalTalk webcast system, and a speech against Israel.

> The Shaykh explained that: 'the enemies of Islaam offer a false culture and civilisation which (negatively) differentiates between mankind, and nullifies (all) agreements, offering all types of weaponry to destroy mankind.'
>
> ... The Shaykh expressed 'that which has befallen the *Ummah* today is as a result of sins and weakness of *eemaan* (faith) in addition to the presence of partisanship (*tahazzub*) and (much) differing in the religion; and the last of the *Ummah* will never be corrected except by that which corrected the first of the *Ummah*.'[26]

This indicates an enthusiastic audience for online *fatwas*, and that significant questions are not answered satisfactorily off-line. The *fatwa* archive is divided into nine primary categories: Buying and Selling, Creed, Innovations, Marriage, Women's Issues, Worship, Miscellaneous, Muslim minorities and New Muslims. These are further divided into subsections. For example, Women's Issues includes sections on Beautification, Clothing, Breastfeeding, *Hijaab*, *Mahram*, Menstruation, (Idda) and Worship; Marriage features sections on Sexual Relations, Divorce and Annulment, Interview and Proposal, *Mahar*, *Mahram*, Marital Relations, Polygamy and Wedding; Worship is one of the most substantial on the entire Fatwa-Online site, with ten subsections on the 'primary duties' in Islam, and at least 45 sub-subsections.

The breadth of topics included on the site is indicated in the New Muslims section.[27] The range of questions features answers drawn from a variety of sources, including scholarly texts and classical sources, and indicates the concerns of the site's readers. A selection includes:

- 'Circumcision is obligatory so long as it does not create an aversion to Islaam.'
- 'Changing one's name after embracing Islaam.'
- 'When a disbeliever accepts Islaam during the daytime in Ramadhaan.'
- 'The ruling concerning the *salaah* of one whose clothes are polluted by pork, lard, etc.'
- 'Does a new Muslim have to separate from his wife?'
- 'A non-Muslim touching a translation of the Qur'aan.'
- 'The uncleanliness of a disbeliever is of an abstract nature.'
- 'A Christian woman married to a Muslim dies while pregnant; should she be buried with the Muslims?'
- 'Is it permissible for a non-Muslim to enter a masjid if there is hope that he might become Muslim.'[28]

The pages have strong views on a number of subjects, including relations with non-Muslims, which are condemned in the response to the question: 'I am living in Jordan in a place where most of the residents are Christian brothers. We eat and drink together. Is my *salaah* [prayer] invalid? Is my living among them impermissible?'

The response condemns the notion of 'Christian brothers':

There can be no brotherhood between a believer and a disbeliever, ever, rather it is mandatory for a believer not to take a disbeliever as a *walee* [friend].

The response, from Ibn Uthaymeen cites further from the Qur'an, before concluding:

It befits you to avoid constant mixing with non-Muslims, because constant mixing with them will obliterate the attitude of vigil and care for the religion from your heart, and may possibly lead you to love them.[29]

Ibn Uthaymeen's opinions on other subjects are also reproduced on Fatwa-Online, via his published works, including the subject of jihad. The site's subsection on jihad (incorporated into the Worship section) incorporates four *fatwas* on suicide bombings, 'Concerning suicide bombings', 'Attacking the enemy by blowing oneself up', 'Attacking the enemy by blowing oneself up in a car' and 'Committing suicide'. 'Concerning suicide bombings' reproduces an opinion from a translated published work on the subject, which is negative, and determines that suicide represents 'faulty' *ijtihad* (albeit with an 'appropriate' motive):

so when one of the Palestinian blows himself up and kills six or seven people, then in retaliation they take sixty or more. So this does not produce any benefit for the Muslims, and does not benefit those amongst whose ranks explosives are detonated.

So what we hold is that those people who perform these suicide (bombings) have wrongfully committed suicide, and that this necessitates entry into Hell-Fire, and Allaah's refuge is sought and that this person is not a martyr (*shaheed*).

However if a person has done this based upon misinterpretation, thinking that it is permissible, then we hope that he will be saved from sin, but as for martyrdom being written for him, then no, since he has not taken the path of martyrdom.

But whoever performs *ijtihaad* and errs will receive a single reward (if he is a person qualified to make *ijtihaad*).[30]

This *fatwa*, from the prominent twentieth-century religious authority Shaykh Muhammad Ibn Saalih Ibn 'Uthaymeen (1926–2001), introduces questions associated with the nature of decision-making and qualifications for making *ijtihad*, together with critical questions associated with notions of martyrdom in relation to Palestine.[31]

During 2002, the site expanded its section of Bibliographies of prominent scholars. Contemporary scholars dominate: 19 are listed from the fifteenth century in the Islamic calendar, six from the fourteenth century, and one – ibn Taymiyyah – from the seventh–eighth Islamic century. Other centuries were blank at the time of writing.

The site also incorporates a section on five 'deviant' groups, which are seen as going outside Fatwa-Online's Sunni Ahl-i-Sunna wa'l Jamaat perspective:

In this category, we shall endeavour to list short 'biographies' of deviant groups and individuals of past and present who have stained the name of Islaam, preferring to adhere to their own cocktail of whims and desires, far from the Qur.aan and the authentic Sunnah as understood by the best of generations, namely the Sahaabah, the Taabi'oon and the Atbaa' at-Taabi'een, in short, the pious predecessors, inshaa.-Allaah.[32]

This category includes 15 *fatwas*, on subjects such as the Ahmadiyya, Braylwiyya (Barelwi), Jama'at at-Tabligh and Khawaarij Muslims. One example illustrates the tone of the site. The Barelwi, a Sufi-oriented group originating in the nineteenth century, are condemned in an online *fatwa* produced by the Permanent Committee for Islamic Research and Fatwa:[33]

Whoever has these characteristics and attributes, then it is not permissible to offer your *salaah* [prayer] behind them (their imaam), and whoever knows of their condition, then their *salaah* is not correct. This is because most of their characteristics and attributes are of *kufr* [non-belief] and *bid'ah* [innovation] which negate the *tawheed* (oneness) with which Allaah had sent His messenger and revealed in His Book, and that which conflicts with the Qur.aan, such as His (Subhaanahu wa Ta'aala) saying:

'Verily, you [Muhammad] will die and verily, they [too] will die' [Soorah az-Zumar, Aayah 30].

And His saying:

'And the mosques are for Allaah [alone], so invoke not anyone along with Allaah' [Soorah al-Jinn, Aayah 18].

And their *bid'ah* which they practice should be detested with good manners, and if they accept (and leave these practices) then all praise is for Allaah (alone).

The 'soorah' (surah) quotations are from translations of the meaning of the Qur'an by Muhammad Taqi-ud-Din al-Hilali and Muhammad Muhsin Khan.[34] Elsewhere in the statement, in an extensive list of 'faults', the Barelwis are condemned for their 'innovative' practices, the form of their veneration of Muhammad, worship of 'saints' and their ritual practices. Themes contained within this online denunciation reflect elements of the thought of Ibn 'Abd al-Wahhab (1703–92) and his 'school', the influence of which having spread far beyond its Arabian origins in the two centuries after his death, and perhaps now accelerating from contemporary religious organisations in Saudi Arabia and their global subsidiaries via the Internet. The content of Fatwa-Online would not be well received in all Sunni circles, as there are parallels with the underlying ideology of Islam Q&A (above). This is a theme returned to in other sectors of cyberspace explored in this chapter.

Islam-Online

Islam-Online is an example of a substantial fatwa *resource, operating in a Muslim majority context, but reflecting the expertise from authorities and counsellors from a broad range of minority and majority contexts. The key scholar is the Qatar-based Yusuf al-Qaradawi, who also has an 'official' Arabic language website.*[35] *There can be a contextual blurring, so the location of an Internet server or* madrassah *becomes insignificant, such as the case of Islam-Online, registered in Doha, Qatar, and staffed by 100 people based in Cairo – including students and graduates from Al Azhar University.*[36]

Islam-Online's material is available in Arabic and English, although not all aspects of the site's content are paralleled in both languages. (The following discussion primarily reflects the English-language content of the site.) Islam-Online invested heavily in the notion of the online *fatwa* as part of its site content, and claimed to receive a million hits a day in 2000.[37] There are major sections for Cyber Counselling, submission of questions via Ask the Scholar, and real-time Live *Fatwa* dialogues between scholars and site visitors, in which questions can be submitted to an 'expert' and a response immediately posted back. These Live *Fatwa* are advertised on the main page of the site, with dates and times, and often provide an interesting commentary on popular opinion in relation to contemporary events.

'Scholars' utilise their knowledge on a broad range of questions which have been sent in by surfers. Scholars appear to have a wide range of backgrounds from within a set of parameters sympathetic to Qaradawi's worldview (Ebrahim Desai of Ask-Imam, discussed above, is one of the scholars listed in the database). 'Qualified practitioners' provide the counselling. Cyber counselling incorporates conventional counselling models, which might not be deemed conventionally 'Islamic' in other contexts, together with other forms of 'professional help' integrated with an Islamic ethos. There is cross-referencing between the counselling and *fatwa* zones of the Islam-Online site. Both represent indicators of contemporary issues, from petitioners across the world. Some breakdown of petitioners' gender and location may be required in further research.

It is difficult to determine the origins of petitioners, given that conditions of anonymity apply, and it is feasible that a petitioner can state that she or he comes from any country in the *fatwa* application form. In rare cases, full names have been given, but this is highly unusual, especially given the nature of the questions' content. Perusal of *fatwa* and cyber counselling areas indicate that there is a clear demand for information on Islamic issues. This may indicate a shortfall of available information, or a desire for supplementary information; the extreme nature of some of the questions would suggest that these are some issues that individuals do not wish to discuss or cannot discuss with family or local religious authorities.

Questions can be very detailed in nature, despite anonymity, and it may be possible for individuals to divulge information that could allude to their location or personal circumstances, enabling them to be 'recognised' by other visitors to the site. This is a very public domain, unlike traditional ('Islamic' and other) counselling. Given the nature of some of the questions, issues emerge as to whether some topics should be made such a public process (archives being accessible and searchable on the site), or whether greater editorial input (for example, in the editing of questions) is required.

There are parallels with newspaper question-and-answer facilities on Islamic issues, although these resources may be more conscious and experienced in ensuring total anonymity for a petitioner. Unless a petitioner uses anonymous e-mail, there is always a danger that such personal information could fall into the wrong hands. It is feasible that, if other family members have access to the petitioner's computer and e-mail account, this information could be acquired through this channel. In the case of Islam-Online, they do not divulge e-mail contact details, and many petitioners are represented by a first name and location. They do not provide any advice on anonymous e-mail or computer security. In the *fatwa* form, it is compulsory to place e-mail details; other categories, such as name, age, marital status, education, and country of origin are optional.

There are important questions to be addressed relating to the application of the 'language' of Islam within a counselling context. Professional advice is often linked to information provided by imams and 'authorities' elsewhere on the Islam-Online site. This may be a new articulation of a traditional message about Islam, but it is difficult to determine the impact, in terms of whether it is transforming approaches on personal and community levels towards 'appropriate' Islamic interpretation of issues. The 'Islamic' component of this counselling may incorporate phrases such as 'Allah knows best', religious terminology and links to specific interpretations of the Qur'an, hadith and sunna. Assumptions are made regarding the validity of *fatwas*, and the role and status of Islamic jurisprudence. References are made to forms of off-line help available, for example within mosques and local counselling organisations (Muslim and other).

The Islam-Online Cyber Counsellor section covers a broad range of issues, some of which would not be out of place in the 'problem pages' of a magazine or the content of a television exposé programme. One would not wish to over-sensationalise this listing, because clearly it involved real-life issues, which are filtered through a specific Islamic counselling matrix. The following select list is indicative of the range of topics (approaching 1,000 in August 2002) that the counsellors have had to deal with:

- 'In love with a Muslim man, who is unhappily married to a non-Muslim woman with two children.'
- 'Sexually abused when I was young, and am suffering from a lack of self-esteem and self-worth.'
- 'Good brain, a healthy athletic body, over 40 and looking to get married.'
- 'Want to marry a Muslim brother but his family won't let me as I am a white revert.'
- 'Hindu boy I met on the net is just perfect.'

- 'Slept with a woman for the first time, and now I am so sad and depressed.'
- 'Homosexual tendencies are hurting me and my marriage, are there Muslim counsellors?'
- 'Abused by the husband of my maternal aunt, and now I am unsure about marriage.'
- 'Gave up my Internet boyfriend, now he has found someone else, and I feel so hurt.'
- 'Told my husband about my past near-*zina* [adultery] experience and now he verbally and physically abuses me.'
- 'Divorced Catholic woman about to marry a Moroccan Muslim man, what should I expect?'
- 'Virtual friend turned out to be a non-Muslim man.'
- 'Spanish Catholic man interested in becoming Muslim; is it possible to be Muslim in secret.'
- 'Muslim boyfriend is pressuring me to have sex; I am non-religious and he says sex before marriage is OK in Islam these days.'
- 'Is there any help for Muslims with HIV?'
- 'Porn-addicted husband and his generally far from Islam family are making me quite depressed.'
- 'Met a man online from another country, we had sex, and now I want to marry him.'
- 'Pornography addiction is causing me to be depressed.'
- 'Feelings of guilt are killing me because I had an abortion when I was sixteen.'
- 'My online friend wants to keep me company on 'eid day and I don't want to come between him and his family.'
- 'Met a man on online matrimonial service, now he says he won't marry me.'
- 'What about using the Internet to get married?'
- 'Dad was into drugs and I never knew him, but his death has left me in pain.'
- 'I am a German, married to a Somali, and serving time in Peru – please help.'
- 'Pregnant and stressed out over husband visiting pornographic sites on the Internet.'
- 'Feeling regretful for lying to parents about an Internet friend.'
- 'Falling in love on the Internet and inter-racial/cultural marriages.'[38]

Examples of the type of advice and questions that appear on the site (drawn from the Counselling section of Islam-Online) are discussed below, in order to approach the counselling methodology and type of language applied by petitioner and counsellor.

In the first case, a 'new Muslim' woman in an American city was concerned about having been approached by an Iraqi Muslim man in a grocery store, and being asked to meet him unsupervised in a restaurant, with him claiming that this was permissible under Islam:

> Q *Melanie United States*: A man from Iraq, age 34 approached me at a Halal grocery store. I told him that I was a new Muslim and he wanted to exchange email addresses. After chatting online, he wanted me to call him, so I did. He tells me that he is looking for a wife and wants me to meet him at a restaurant. He also wants to see my apartment. I told him that is forbidden in Islam. He said that nowhere in the Quran does it state supervision is required for a meeting between a man and a woman. He said that it is only a social rule that is different for each country. Help me because he is pushy and I do not want to meet him alone ....[39]

The answer from Islam-Online urged the woman not to contact the man, especially as he was (in their eyes) misinterpreting the Qur'an on this issue. Their response included an appropriate saying from Muhammad and advice to the woman on learning more about Islam (which included contacting the local imam):

> A: May Allah (swt) protect you and strengthen your *Iman* [religious faith].
> A: 'Under no circumstances should you allow him to enter your apartment or know where you live. Please do not meet him at any restaurant either. We urge you not to continue this relationship with this man. If he is this forward and outgoing with you, why should you trust that he has not also asked other sisters for their emails, or their telephone numbers, or to see their apartments? You need not feel obligated to respond to his emails or his phone calls ...
>
> In addition, he is misinterpreting both the Quran and the hadith regarding proper interaction between unmarried males and females. This is not about culture, it is about a direct saying of the Prophet Muhammad (peace be upon him) that *shaytan* [Satan] is always the third person when a man and woman are alone.

If there is a chance that you like him, then we strongly suggest that you get the local Imam involved. Tell your Iraqi friend to contact the Imam if he wants to see you or speak to you about marriage. You cannot afford to repeat the mistakes of sisters before you who were new and vulnerable and were taken advantage of. We do not know this specific person and cannot judge him, but we are advising you to proceed with caution ...

Make *du'a* [prayer] to Allah (swt) to guide you, to protect you and to strengthen your Iman.

Keep in touch. And Allah (swt) knows best.[40]

This particular extract raises a number of contemporary issues associated with converts to Islam, knowledge of religious duties and Internet chatting. The formula in the answer is one based on pragmatism, warning of the 'mistakes' of others in relationships, and advising contact with a local Imam (not just his cyber-equivalent), together with making prayer (*du'a*) to God.

The harsh realities of family relationships and the issue of child abuse/sexual assault are brought into another stark question on the Islam-Online site: a young woman had been 'abused' by her uncle, having been made uncomfortable by his behaviour in the past, and had e-mailed the site for advice. The young woman was concerned about the implications of having to maintain dialogue with this errant family member (which she was reluctant to do), and about the psychological impact on her in terms of future relationships with men:

3. *Muslima* My problem is my uncle! I did not grow up with him and I did not know much about him. The first time I saw him was when I was a young girl and all I remember is that I did not feel comfortable around him. I did not know why. When I grew up I met him again and I told my mum that I did not like him. She felt sad about that and told me that I should try to get to know him because after all he is my uncle and he loves me and I should love him back ...

One day, he did something to me and I was so shocked. I did not know what to do. I felt very dirty and sad. I got depressed and could not talk to anyone at first, but after a while I told my mom. She confronted him with it and he denied it. My mom did not believe him and told him to stay away from me and he did.

My problem is that he is married and has children. I hear that as a Muslim I should not cut off relations with my family. He is family and his children too. What should I do? Do I have to keep in contact with them? And if yes, what can I do about my feelings towards him?

A: It is not clear from your message, but we are assuming that you are referring to being sexually abused by your uncle only because you have referred to feeling uncomfortable by the way he 'touched' you. You also felt 'shocked' and 'dirty' after he did something to you.[41]

Islam-Online invokes Allah's protection on the young woman and her mother (who had offered some constructive help), whilst stating that the uncle required 'professional help'. The site suggested that the young woman obtains professional counselling:

May Allah (swt) protect you and guide you. You have handled the situation extremely well by reporting the abuse to your mother. May Allah (swt) bless your mother for believing you and for taking some action. Your uncle needs professional help so that he does not repeat such behavior ...

We are very concerned that you have not really processed your feelings since the occurrence of the abuse. If you have not yet done so, please seek professional help so that you can come to terms with what has happened. Your uncle is entirely at fault and you are not to blame yourself for his behavior. In addition, you are not 'dirty' for what your uncle did to you. You are the victim of abuse and you need to seek help from a counselor so that you can begin the process of healing ...

Seek the help of Allah (swt) so that *insha'allah* [God willing] with His protection and guidance, you will be comfortable in being with and trusting your future husband.

Make *du'a* to Allah (swt) to protect you and also seek forgiveness for your uncle.

Should you feel you would like to address this issue further, you may write directly to our counselors at cybercounselor@islam-online.net.

We look forward to hearing from you. And Allah (swt) knows best.[42]

In some settings the reporting of such an assault would demand the intervention of the police, and it is perhaps surprising that this suggestion is not incorporated into Islam-Online's professional advice. The notion that the uncle might remain tolerated and 'undiscovered' within the family sphere might be abhorrent to many readers (from whatever cultural, ethical or religious background). The online Islamic counselling model may incorporate anonymity and confidentiality, but it also raises some important ethical issues, which also have importance in other contexts.

Not having access to the petitioners, it is difficult for this writer to gauge the impact of the advice provided by Islam-Online. It is a comprehensive and regularly augmented resource, covering a broad range of questions. Consideration might have to be given to the legal implications of such advice being placed online, and the ways in which the information is accessed and processed by the respondent. This would require the establishment of monitored reader groups and is a subject that could be the focus of future research.

One hundred and thirty-four new answers to questions (not necessarily deemed '*fatwas*') appeared in the Ask the Scholar section during July 2002 on contemporary and 'traditional' themes. Each issue is a substantive one in its own right, as indicated by this random selection of titles:

- Has the Bible been tampered with?
- A husband refusing intimacy with his wife.
- Immunisation: does it contravene belief in the *ghayb* [unseen]?
- Islamic workable measures to overcome AIDS.
- Is body piercing permissible in Islam?
- Is liposuction permissible in Islam?
- Islamic remedy for procrastination and laziness.
- How Islam views cremation.
- Hymen repair surgery.
- Placing American flags on Islamic centres in the States.
- Arab-centric religion makes me upset, I want to stop feeling like a fraud.[43]

Questions transcend the 'Islamic issues' that one might find in contemporary collections of *fatwas* elsewhere, including child abuse, physical violence, fraud, subterfuge, drug and alcohol abuse, and criminal acts. Issues of sexuality and relationships appear to dominate the listings. The impact of personal information being circulated has serious implications, given that the forms of judgement and opinion often found in conventional Muslim frameworks of petition are suspended. This can be very much a raw, real-world experience, rather than the ideals of Muslim societies expressed in other contexts (on- and off-line).

Islam-Online also contains several *fatwas* associated with Internet behaviour. Internet 'chatting', especially between the sexes, raises cultural and religious concerns associated with 'appropriate' behaviour. There is evidence of online 'relationships' being conducted and subsequent meetings taking place, together with offers of marriage. Some of these are inter-continental, electronic 'dangerous liaisons'. Such activities and issues are not exclusive to the Muslim sphere, although there are particular religious and cultural concerns which may be specific to diverse Muslim interests, in particular how such behaviour might contradict forms of religiously sanctioned relationships and appropriate Islamic conduct. These issues are also not necessarily exclusive to the Internet, as they reflect concerns that are being faced by individuals, families and communities throughout the 'Muslim world', and indeed they can reflect historical precedence. The electronic dimension is added to traditional and cultural questions of interpretation and behaviour, whilst the formal parameters of control have, in some cases, been transcended.

Two examples of *fatwas*, representing the online formulation of petition and response, are provided below. The first, a good example of a contemporary issue relating to the Internet, and seeking a solution via an electronic *fatwa*, comes from a Jordanian reader on the subject of marriage through the Internet:

I want to know your opinion about the following issue of mine. My story began when I knew a man through Internet chatting. He is a good Muslim and I think he is the right and suitable man for me. He is living in USA. Is this wrong? Be assured that my intention is good and this is the same for that man. He said he would not leave me and he would try to come to Jordan to get engaged to me. He tried before that but he couldn't. So he sent some friends from Syria to meet my father, but my father refused, and said what I am doing is wrong and not right. I really want your advice. I think the Internet is a new way for communication; so if you think that I am not doing anything wrong, please advise me on what can I do and how can I convince my father …

A: 'In principle, conversation between males and females is lawful, so long as both of them observe the Islamic rules and manners of talking to members of the opposite sex. If the conversation is decent and abides by the rules of Islam, then it is permissible; however, if it is indecent and is only sought to exchange love and emotions, it is absolutely Haraam and rejected by Islam.

Internet chatting is very similar to writing letters or talking to someone on the phone. Actually it is a combination of both. Muslims have to observe the same rules as they observe in writing letters or making telephone calls. Islam forbids love letters or intimate conversations between males and females who are not married to each other. In all our correspondence and conversations we must be decent and observe a high sense of bashfulness. It is unacceptable for a non-mahram Muslim male and female to indulge in long conversations with each other unless it is necessary for purpose of education, business, *Daw'ah* etc. All conversation must be decent.

As for chatting which does not have any goal or purpose and just sought for the purpose of socialisation and passing time, it is blameworthy and should be avoided …

Therefore, Internet chat is *Halaal* so long as the words used are decent and customarily accepted, but it may become Haraam if it contains something which contradicts the rules of Islam or is customarily held as indecent.

Your father should talk to the man, ask about him, and if he finds out that he is a good Muslim and of high morals, he should accept him as your lifetime partner. It does not matter if this man has come through the Internet or anywhere else.[44]

This response is particularly interesting, as it provides some parameters for Internet activities, including the appropriate application of chat technology and its use to acquire marriage partners. The response integrates quotations from the Qur'an (the title of individual surahs being placed in brackets after a quote). Such activities are not unique to Muslim Internet sites, and it would perhaps be naïve to consider that they should be 'banned' from use, or even if a ban could possibly be effective. The following response is one of several pertaining to the 'appropriate' application of the Internet on Islam-Online (other responses have condemned the use of chat room technology altogether):

Q: Is Internet chat allowed in Islam or not? Because when you chat on net you don't know whether the person you are talking [to is a] him/her or what is his actual age …

A: Salaamu Alaikum Sister. We must always be very cautious about making something haram that has not been made explicitly unlawful by Allah. Chat rooms, chat forums and emails are all tools for communication. Communication itself is not wrong or haram, even between men and women. However, what is being communicated and under which circumstances information is being communicated, are factors that could determine the lawfulness or the unlawfulness of chat forums and chat rooms. I am not a scholar and will not make any rulings …

Allah knows best, but I would say the answer to your question is 'no'. Public forums (like this one) can be a wonderful place to discuss topics of concern or relay helpful knowledge to others … If modesty and a business-like/professional tone are adopted to email structure between genders, there may be no harm in using the Internet to pass on valuable information. However, individuals should always be careful that their interaction with strangers, via the world wide web, does not go beyond the bounds set by Allah and His Messenger (peace be upon him) who is reported to have said: 'When a man and a woman (who are not bound by the prescribed degrees of family or by marriage) are alone together, Shaitain (evil) makes the third.' Allah says in His glorious Recitation: 'The ear and the eye and the heart shall be called to account' (17:36) and 'He (Allah) knows the traitor of the eyes, and that which the bosoms hide.' (40:19).

… Allah is the best one to take as our 'secret' friend …

… our connections to our Creator is direct – no passwords, no firewalls – faster than high speed and cable and all the other methods one usually uses to 'log on' …[45]

Yusuf Qaradawi has contributed a number of *fatwas* to Islam-Online. These can be quite detailed in nature, with extensive references to the Qur'an, hadith, Islamic scholarship and the Bible.[46] Islam-Online represents a significant channel for this specific perspective on Sunni Islam, one that is not always received with acclaim by other Muslim organisations and individuals (as discussed below). It does represent part of a strategy in which Qaradawi identified the Internet as a significant channel for disseminating a specific worldview.[47] Islam-Online certainly indicates, at the time of writing, that as Internet access increases, if it maintains the daily additions to its Fatwa Bank, Counselling Services and related pages, it will continue to enhance its share of the *fatwa* 'market' (and attendant influence and authority).

Qaradawi has been the subject of criticism from a number of Sunni sources, similar in nature to the criticism of al-Munajjid (Islam Q&A) above. 'Qaradawism' is one derisory term that has been used, the suggestion being that any -ism has negative, 'un-Islamic' connotations. Again, this reflects the Salafi argument (above):

Yusuf Al-Qaradaawee, since we came to know of him and heard about him, was a partisan [*hizbee*] and an innovator. As for saying that he is an enemy of the Sunnah, then we cannot say that he is an enemy of the Sunnah. Nor can we say that he is from the children of the Jews. We must be fair, as Allaah says:

'And do not let your hatred of a people cause you to be unjust. Rather, be just, that is closer to Taqwaa' [Surah Al-Maa'idah: 8]. And He says: 'And when you say something, be just' [Surah Al-An'aam: 152]. And He says: 'O you who believe, stand out firmly for justice as witnesses to Allaah even though it be against your own selves, or your parents or your kin, be he rich or poor.

Allaah is a better Protector to both (than you). So follow not the lusts (of your hearts) lest you avoid justice. And if you distort your testimony or refuse to give it, then verily Allaah is All-Aware of what you do' [Surah An-Nisaa: 135].

… Therefore, I do not advise that his tapes be listened to nor that his lectures be attended nor that his books be read because he is foolish. He has a book in which he makes it permissible to have numerous groups (*jamaa'aat*), even though the Prophet (*sallAllaahu 'alayhi wa sallam*) said: 'The Hand of Allaah is with the *Jama'aah* [Group]' and he did not say 'with the *Jamaa'aat* [Groups]! …

… Therefore the Muslims are one Group, so it is not permissible for Al-Qaradaawee to strive to split the ranks of the Muslims and to divide them. And he only weakens them by splitting them up …

… And what is more despicable than this is what has been reported on him in a newspaper that he said: 'We do not fight the Jews because of Islaam, but rather we fight them because they have occupied our lands.'

I say: How terrible is this rotten *fatwa*!

... So the Religion takes precedence over the land and country, but however it is the *hizbiyyah* (partisanship) that causes one to become deaf and blind. Furthermore, we have written a treatise refuting him which is titled: 'Silencing the Howling Dog Yusuf bin 'Abdillaah Al-Qaradaawee.'[48]

This criticism of Qaradawi accuses him of factionalism, poor *fatwas* in relation to Palestine and for innovation in the name of religion. It appears on the al-Manhaj site, discussed above in relation to al-Munajjid, and is reflected extensively elsewhere on the site in other extracts from Salafi publications. For example, a translation of a book by Ahmad bin Yahyaa al-Najmee accuses Qaradawi of allowing division in Islam; claiming democracy is the equivalent to the Islamic concept of '*shura*' consultation; that jihad should only be defensive; that Sufism and Salafi beliefs should be mixed.

In a note introducing al-Najmee's book, Muqbil bin Haadee al-Waadi'ee also discusses Qaradawi:

And from among the callers to misguidance in our time is this Yoosuf bin 'Abdillaah Al-Qaradaawee, the Muftee of Qatar, for he has become the spokesman for the enemies of Islaam. So he has given his tongue and pen into the services of waging war against the Religion of Islaam.[49]

Allaahuakbar.net's section on Yusuf al-Qaradawi describes him as 'the Muftee who allows the common-folk to persist upon their ignorance, time-wasting and indulgence in vanities and novelties, which are but instruments of the Accursed One, and which but cause them to forget the remembrance of Allaah.'[50]

It is not the purpose of this chapter to analyse these accusations, simply to highlight the existence of this conflict and especially its representation online. It brings into question the ways in which online *fatwa* sites might represent themselves as 'definitive' perspectives on Islam. This could be further highlighted, given that neither of these disputing 'Salafi' perspectives is necessarily going to be endorsed by other Muslim viewpoints from within so-called orthodoxy, as well as from diffuse 'Sufi', 'Shi'a' and other understandings of Islam (these umbrella terms cover a broad range of beliefs, not necessarily always complementary).

The production of *fatwas* is not the preserve of Salafi scholars (however the term is defined). Examples emerge from diverse global contexts relating to forms of decision-making. These are not necessarily defined as *'fatwas'*, given that the term is not always considered appropriate or relevant. Religious 'authority' may be interpreted as being beyond human intervention, advice may be provided through other, less 'legalistic' channels, or there may be different emphases on Islamic sources. It is intended to explore some of those perspectives below.

OTHER INFLUENCES IN SUNNI MAJORITY CYBERSPACE

South East Asia

South East Asia was one area in which online *fatwas* appeared at an early stage, for example through the Majlis Ugama Islam Singapura (MUIS) in Singapore and various Malaysian governmental and political-religious sites.[51] The Jabatan Kemajuan Islam Malaysia (JAKIM) site offered 93 *fatwas* in August 2002, in a searchable format, on aspects of ritual, *zakat*, social relations, medical issues and 'contemporary issues' such as approaches to post-mortems. However, many of these 'e-*fatwas*', in fact, dated back to the 1980s.[52] The main 'e-*fatwa*' page links to some of the sites discussed elsewhere in this chapter, such as Fatwa-Online, Islam Q&A, and Ask-Imam, providing a useful perspective on 'officially sanctioned' Islamic perspectives in Malaysia, given that the first three of these sites are non-governmental ('officially'), Sunni and Wahhabi in orientation. The inclusion of Ask-Imam, the South African site, is perhaps less predictable. The JAKIM page also links to regional 'approved' authorities in the Malaysian Federation: these include *fatwas* produced by the Muftis in Kedah, which are primarily associated with ritualistic practices.[53] There are also links to a basic page produced in Pinang, and link pages to other regional authorities (although these lacked extensive *fatwa* resources).

Two Malaysian Federation states that were missing from this listing were Kelantan and Terengganu, both under the regional governmental control of the Parti Islam SeMalaysia (PAS) Islamic political party at the time of writing. This is reflected in the PAS website, a long-standing resource and a hub for national and regional activities. This makes use of multi-media applications to present its messages, links to local and international media, and also to other sympathetic parties (including those associated with Anwar Ibrahim, the imprisoned former deputy prime minister). The local Kelantan site features links to jihadi organisations in Chechnya, Palestine and Afghanistan. Notions of religious authority permeate the pages of the sites, in both textual and multi-media forms, and the site is worthy of detailed evaluation as a religious-political hub utilising the Internet to develop and propagate its values, and network its members. Substantial investment has gone into the site(s), which are updated on a daily basis.

Discussion on Malaysia should also incorporate reference to Angkatan Belia Islam Malaysia (ABIM), the 'Muslim Youth Movement of Malaysia', which played a pivotal role in Malaysian politics in the 1960s and 1970s, and had close ties with Anwar Ibrahim. The ABIM site incorporates extensive commentaries on the Qur'an (*tafsir*) by the president of the organisation, Siddiq Fadhil, together with articles on aspects of Islam and approaches to interpretation.[54] The site is a hub, linking to other ABIM sites.

MUIS, the Islamic Religious Council or Singapore, was discussed in *Virtually Islamic* as being a substantial governmental online resource for Muslims operating in a minority context.[55] The *fatwa* search engine database has expanded, to include 179 *fatwas* in August 2002, including questions on ritual issues, medical ethics and economics. These responses are in Malay, although the MUIS offers a brochure entitled 'What You Need to Know about Fatwa' in English. This explores the definitions of *fatwas*, the processes for their issue, their intellectual and knowledge basis, and ways of contacting the MUIS Fatwa Committee (including online).[56] The *fatwa* section is linked to an Islamic knowledgebase (requiring registration) and sermons (in English and Malay).

There is considerable work to be undertaken on the online *fatwas* emerging from South East Asia, particularly Indonesia, which has the highest Muslim population in the world, and also a relatively high level of Internet connectivity. The Majelis Ulama Indonesia website contains a listing of 50 *fatwas* in Bahasa Indonesia, but this was not functioning at the time of writing.[57] The Muhammadiyah Network, focused in Indonesia but with branches elsewhere in South East Asia, has developed a website linking communities together and providing ideological and informative content online.[58] They represent a particularly interesting group for future observation, given that they have a focus on the application of science and technology being integrated with their *da'wa* mission work.[59] Their Singaporean branch highlights the work of their Information Technology Unit, offering training in systems and software at Madrasah Al Arabiah. A full study of Indonesian Islamic cyberspace would require another volume, given the profound complexities and diversity in the region in relation to religious and cultural perspectives.[60] Locating religious authority requires consideration of the belief spectrum ranging from Liberal Islam through to al-Madina (an 'Ahl-us-Sunnah' site) through to Laskar Jihad.[61] The former site features an article on Yusuf Qaradawi's work and *fatwas*.[62] Other areas of cyberspace encourage dialogue and discussion on issues of interpretation and understanding, notably MyQuran.com, which has discussion areas on various aspects of Sufism, together with (monitored) discussions on the Qur'an and hadith.[63]

BOSNIA

Bosnia is an area requiring detailed, specialist work on the issue of online authority, especially given that external 'authorities' have influenced more traditional understandings of Islam. There are a number of professionally designed sites on issues associated with Islam and Bosnia, many of which naturally reflect on the crimes of genocide inflicted on the region. A good example of this can be found at IslamBosna.com, based in Sarajevo; at the time of writing, this site was dominated by an image of the Muslim Brotherhood's ideologue Sayyid Qutb, hyperlinked to an article and analysis. The same site hosts the IslamBosna Fatwa Council, which can be e-mailed via the site; the *fatwa* archive contained material (accessed from the index page) incorporating advice and links to external (non-religious) sites.[64]

The Rijaset site also offers advice and interpretative information from religious authorities.[65] What is interesting about this site is that it also focuses on the diaspora Bosnian Muslim community, with a special section hyperlinked to various European cities with Bosnian communities, with photos of religious activities.[66] Other sites, such as Islamski Internet Portal, provide hubs for resources including Qur'an interpretations and translations, commentaries and other forms of religious knowledge. Some of this is about basic ritual practice, for example the appropriate ablutions prior to prayer, which is illustrated in photographs.[67] The opening surah of the Qur'an is transliterated for Bosnian readers.[68] The extent to which this resource is utilised is open to question, as the number of impressions for this section was less than 200 for most categories at the time of writing.

Islamski Informativni Portal, amidst materials on the Qur'an, hadith and political Islam, contained a link to an article by the erstwhile Ku Klux Klan leader David Duke (describing himself as National President, European-American Unity and Rights Organization (EURO)), linking the events of 11 September 2001 with Zionists (the article further links to Duke's website, and articles on 'Jewish Supremacism').[69] Other materials on the same page linked to works by (or about) the academic and writer Noam Chomsky, al-Ghazali, Sayyid Qutb and journalist Robert Fisk. The fusion of materials on such Islamic sites is an area worthy of further consideration and study.

NOTES

1. 'Man Divorces Wife by Phone Message', *Reuters*, 29 June 2001. Muslim religious leaders quickly endorsed this opinion in Singapore and Malaysia. 'Text Message Divorces Approved for Muslims', *Ananova*, 10 July 2001. There is potential, by analogy, for divorce by e-mail.
2. Gary R. Bunt, 'Decision-Making and Idjtihad in Islamic Environments: A Comparative Study of Pakistan, Malaysia, Singapore, and the United Kingdom' (PhD dissertation, Lampeter: University of Wales, 1996).
3. An earlier version of the discussion on Fatwa-Online and As-Sunna Foundation can be found in Gary Bunt, 'Interface Dialogues: Cyber Islamic Environments and the On-line Fatwa', *ISIM Newsletter* 6, November 2000, http://isim.leidenuniv.nl/newsletter/6/media/1.html.
4. Discussed in Gary R. Bunt, *Virtually Islamic* (Cardiff: University of Wales Press, 2000), pp. 115–16. This is a significant resource, but represents a transformation from newspaper to Internet – rather than an Internet-specific and e-mail-centred 'authority'.
5. Islam Q&A, www.islam-qa.com. Click on 'English'; then navigate using the subject tree or the search engine in the top right hand corner of the page.
6. These statistics were derived from the site on 1 August 2002.
7. Islam Q&A, Introduction. There is some inconsistency with the transliteration of al-Munajid's name in the site.
8. Islam Q&A, Introduction.
9. Islam Q&A, question 861: Wants to embrace Islam but there are no Muslims Town.
10. Islam Q&A, Question Reference #: 8504, Posted on 25 July 2000.
11. Islam Q&A, Question Reference #: 820, Posted on 19 January 1998.
12. Islam Q&A, Question Reference #: 6453, Posted on 12 November 1999.
13. Islam Q&A, Question Reference #: 4027, Posted on 7 November 2000.
14. Islam Q&A, Question Reference #: 2105, Posted on 19 May 1998.
15. Islam Q&A, Question Reference #: 1848, Posted on 7 February 1999.

16. Islam Q&A, Question Reference #: 2428, Posted on 26 June 1998.
17. Islam Q&A, Question Reference #: 2467, Posted on 29 December 1999.
18. Islam Q&A, Question Reference #: 12087, Posted on October 2000.
19. Islam Q&A, Question Reference #: 8185, Posted on 9 November 2000.
20. Islam Q&A, 'He wants some statistics on Internet filth in order to convince some of his friends', Question Reference #: 21505, Posted on 18 July 2002.
21. Al-Manhaj (Salafi Society of North America), Shaikh Usaamah Al-Qoosee, Concerning Sayyid Qutb, Saalih Al-Munajjid and Al-Maghraawee, 'Questions that were asked to him by SSNA from his visit to the USA on 4/16/01', (16 April 2001) www.al-manhaj.com/Page1.cfm?ArticleID=66.
22. Allaahuakbar.net, Readings in Elementary Qutubism, 11, www.allaahuakbar.net/downloads/qutubism.zip Also see Readings in Intermediate Qutubism, 16 and passim, www.allaahuakbar.net/downloads/qutubism1.zip.
23. See Scholarly Jewels, Ibn Baz section, 'Where is Shaykh 'Abdul-'Azeez ibn Baaz, and When Will He Arrive?', 'One of the pious people had a dream about Shaykh Ibn Baaz shortly before his death', and 'And from the accuracy of the Shaykh's memorisation.' www.fatwa-online.com/scholarlyjewels/ibnbaaz/index.htm.
24. Fatwa-Online, Downloads, www.fatwa-online.com/downloads/index.htm. This page was down in August 2002, as demand for content had exceeded the 20 gigabytes bandwidth quota.
25. Fatwa-Online, www.fatwa-online.com. Mirror site: www.e-fatwa.com.
26. Shaykh 'Abdul-'Azeez Aal ash-Shaykh: 'Indeed waging war against the weak Muslims in Palestine is (Israeli) terrorism and oppression', 21 February 2002, www.fatwa-online.com/news/0020221.htm.
27. Fatwa-Online, New Muslims, www.fatwa-online.com/newmuslims/index.htm.
28. Edited selection of titles drawn from Fatwa-Online, New Muslims, www.fatwa-online.com/newmuslims/index.htm.
29. Shaykh Ibn 'Uthaymeen, Fataawa Muhimmah lil-Muslim al-Jadeed, 65, cited in Fatwa-Online, 'Continual mixing with non-Muslims extinguishes the attitude of vigilant care for the religion', www.fatwa-online.com/fataawa/newmuslims/0000803_3.htm.
30. Shaykh Ibn 'Uthaymeen, *Riyaadhus-Saaliheen* – Volume 1, 165 – 166, www.fatwa-online.com/fataawa/worship/jihaad/jih004/0010915_1.htm.
31. A biographical page on the Shayk provides a link to Mohammed ibn Othaimeen's 'official site' (in Arabic), although the links on this site were not functioning at the time of writing. www.ibnothaimeen.com.
32. Fatwa-Online, Deviant Groups, Introduction, www.fatwa-online.com/deviantgroups/introduction.htm.
33. The ruling concerning the Braylwiyyah, Fataawa al-Lajnah ad-Daa.imah lil-Buhooth al-'Ilmiyyah wal-Iftaa, Volume 2, Page 396, Fatwa No.3090, www.fatwa-online.com/fataawa/creed/deviants/0010517_5.htm.
34. Discussed in Bunt, *Virtually Islamic*, pp. 24–5.
35. Qaradawi.net, www.qaradawi.net. This contains a number of '*fatwas*', on subjects such as 11 September and Muslims in America. For example, see 'Fatawa and Hakam', 12 October 2001.

36. Daniel J. Wakin, 'Online in Cairo, with News, Views and "Fatwa Corner"', *New York Times*, 28 October 2002, www.newyorktimes.com.
37. Ayub Khan and Aaoufik Founi, Islam-Online, Response to e-mail request, 20 March 2000. 'During the period of 10/99 to 10/00, we received 118286989 hits with 26856884 page views. Starting November 00, we are receiving an average of million hits/day.'
38. Cyber Counsellor, list gathered July 2001. Individual pages and their URLs can be located via inputting the title on the page's search-engine. www.islam-online.net/QuestionApplication/English/searchfatwa.asp.
39. Islam-Online, Cyber Counsellor, 'Melanie, United States', 'Met an Iraqi man at the grocery store, chatted online with him, and now he wants to marry me'. www.islamonline.net/QuestionApplication/english/display. asp?hquestionID=3472 Edited version.
40. Islam-Online, Cyber Counsellor, 'Melanie, United States', 'Met an Iraqi man at the grocery store'. The abbreviation 'swt' stands for *sallallah-hu'alaihe wa sallam*, 'May the Peace and Blessings of God be upon him', and is used by some Muslims when Muhammad's name is mentioned. The writer has added brief interpretations of other Islamic terminology in square brackets.
41. Cyber Counsellor, 'Muslima', 'Uncle abused me, and now I have trouble being around other men', Islam-Online, www.islamonline.net/ QuestionApplication/english/display.asp?hquestionID=3449. Edited version.
42. Ibid.
43. Islam-Online, Ask the Scholar, www.islamonline.net/fatwaapplication/ english/Browse.asp?page=1, 31 July 2002.
44. 'Marriage through the Internet', Fatwa question, response by Islam-Online Fatwa Committee, Islam-Online, 4 February 2001 – link removed at time of writing, August 2002.
45. Fatwa Bank, 'Internet Chatting', response by Islam-Online Fatwa Committee, Islam-Online, edited version, 22 February 2001, www. islamonline.net/completesearch/english/FatwaDisplay.asp?hFatwaID= 27829.
46. Fatwa Bank, 'Swearing, Lying, Joking and Looking at Prohibited Things', response by Yusuf Abdullah al-Qaradawi, Islam-Online, edited version, 12 February 2001, www.islamonline.net/completesearch/english/ FatwaDisplay.asp?hFatwaID=21599.
47. Discussed in Bunt, *Virtually Islamic*, pp. 115–16, in relation to Qaradawi's opinions which appeared on the Islamicity Ask the Imam site, http://islamicity.org/Dialogue/topics.htm. Qaradawi's fatwas have a wide online circulation, in many languages.
48. Al-Manhaj, Salafi Society of North America, 'Shaikh Muqbil on Yusuf Al-Qaradaawee', Shaikh Muqbil bin Haadee Al-Waadi'ee (trans. Abu Maryam), *'Tuhfat-ul-Mujeeb 'an As'ilat-il-Haadir wal-Ghareeb'*, pp. 89–91, www.al-manhaj.com/Page1.cfm?ArticleID=138.
49. Translator's note 1, citing Muqbil bin Haadee al-Waadi'ee. Al-Manhaj, Some of the Vile Errors of Yoosuf Al-Qaradaawee, Shaikh Ahmad bin Yahyaa An-Najmee (trans. Abu Maryam), 'Raf'ul-Lithaam 'an

Mukhaalafat-il-Qaradaawee Li-Sharee'at-il-Islaam' [pp. 5–6, 2nd edition] www.al-manhaj.com/Page1.cfm?ArticleID=132.

50. Allaahuakbar.net, Reading in Qaradawism: Part 2 Arts and Entertainment, Ar-Radd al al-Qaradawi, (salafipublications) www.allaahuakbar.net/jamaat-e-islaami/qaradawism/arts_and_entertainment.htm.

51. Discussed in Bunt, *Virtually Islamic*, pp. 83–9.

52. JAKIM, 'E-Fatwa', http://ii.islam.gov.my/e-fatwa/.

53. Pejabat Mufti Negeri Kedah Darul Aman, SIFAT, Sistem Maklumat Fatwa, http://mufti.islam.gov.my/kedah/.

54. ABIM Online, www.abim.org.my/ilmu/tafsir.html, www.abim.org.my/ilmu/artikel.html.

55. Bunt, *Virtually Islamic*, pp. 88–9.

56. MUIS, 'What You Need to Know About Fatwa', www.muis.gov.sg/oomdb/fatwa/engfatwa1.html.

57. Majelis Ulama Indonesia, www.mui.or.id/index_i.htm.

58. Muhammadiyah Online, www.muhammadiyah-online.or.id/.

59. The Muhammadiya Association, Singapore, 'Guiding Principles of Muhammadiya', www.muhammadiyah.org.sg/organ.htm.

60. For an indication of the depth of the subject, see the listing at Hidayatullah.com, www.hidayatullah.com/info/link.htm.

61. Islam Liberal Indonesia, http://islamlib.com, Al-Madina, www.al-madina.s5.com, Laskar Jihad, www.laskarjihad.or.id.

62. Islam Liberal Indonesia, 'Yusuf Qardhawi, Guru Umat Pada Zamannya', http://islamlib.com/TOKOH/qardhawi.html.

63. MyQuran.com, www.myquran.com.

64. IslamBosna, www.islambosna.com.

65. Rijaset, www.rijaset.net/rijaset/alimi.htm.

66. Rijaset, Bosnjacka dijaspora-galerija fotografija, www.rijaset.net/dijaspora/Dijaspora/index.htm.

67. Islamski Internet Portal, Drugi uvjet za namaz, http://islam.dzemat.org/modules.php?name=Sections&op=viewarticle&artid=588.

68. Islamski Internet Portal, Fatiha i Selam, http://islam.dzemat.org/modules.php?name=Sections&op=viewarticle&artid=573.

69. Islamski Informativni Portal, David Duke, Will Anyone Dare to Ask Why? www.islam.co.ba/english/duke.htm.

9   Sunni Religious Authority on the Internet II: Muslim Minority Contexts

Those seeking knowledge from a minority setting may approach a site that functions in a majority context, or indeed not even be aware of where a site is operating from. Specific religious, cultural, social, linguistic and/or ethnic considerations may also transcend 'majority' and 'minority' contexts – members of a particular Muslim religious affiliation may be more likely to connect and network (on- and off-line) to similar groups in other parts of the world, rather than dialogue with local Muslim groups or interests in their neighbourhood. There is evidence that the Internet is being applied as a means of developing cohesion between and within communities in majority and minority contexts, and that dialogues and notions of authority are transcending traditional boundaries through the electronic media. A combination (and occasionally a synthesis) of new media Islamic operators and traditional holders of authority is playing out in cyberspace. As the medium being more prevalent and accessible, it will be interesting to measure the levels of influence of the following 'authorities'.

ANALYSIS OF SUNNI WEBSITES – MINORITY CONTEXTS

Ask-Imam.com

Ask-Imam.com is an example of a single scholar, operating within a minority context, presenting substantial English-language resources and opinions. The site operates from South Africa, where several fatwa *resources have been produced for local and international audiences.*[1]

Ask-Imam.com's imam is Mufti Ebrahim Desai at Dar ul Ifta, Madrasah In'amiyyah, Campertown, KwaZulu/Natal, South Africa. The Ask-Imam site is hosted and maintained in San Jose, California.[2] Desai studied primarily in India. Desai's qualifications would not necessarily, in the eyes of sites such as Fatwa-Online, equip him for *ijtihad* or the issue of *fatwas*. However, this has not stopped a substantial number of questions being sent to him, and he seems to produce opinions prolifically on a daily basis. Ask-Imam contained nearly 4,686 *fatwas* in August 2002 (an increase from 1,900 in March 2001), on issues ranging from Basic Tenets of Faith through to Worldly Possessions. Desai's opinions were augmented by those of other staff at the Madrasah.

New subjects were added daily, although it should be noted that there is an element of repetition, with standard answers being provided for certain common subjects. The largest sections are on Marriage (494), Prayer (424) and Women (261). The section on Health and Wellness includes 94 *fatwas*, on subjects such as organ transplantation, hair loss, sexual issues, herbal medicine, stammering, praying with backache, 'black magic' and remedies from the Qur'an.[3] This is a well-organised resource, with printable versions of *fatwas*, random *fatwas*, and e-mail alerts (tell a friend about the *fatwa*). The site is fully searchable. Ask-Imam closely reflects the religious and cultural outlook of petitioners, with questions about *istikhara* (guidance through prayer), Barelwi-Deobandi differences and 'signs'. The extent to which this brings a 'local' imam into an internationally prominent position is a key issue. There are also a number of 'contemporary questions', including the following issues related to technology:

- Can I use a spying software to monitor what my daughter (22 yrs) is doing through her navigating and chatting while on the Internet?[4]
- Can women communicate with men over the Internet for *dawah* purposes?[5]
- Is marriage via the Internet permissible? If so, how is it done?[6]
- Is it permissible to have photos and videos taken of the jihad that is being fought in Chechnya and place it on the Internet for keeping the Muslims informed?[7]

The final question sought qualification of the role of qoqaz.net (discussed in Chapter 6). Many of the questions are unique in nature, in that they cover ground that other *fatwa* sites have been unable or unwilling to cover. These questions illustrate diffuse contemporary concerns, some of a very mundane nature on issues that are not pressingly high on the list of Muslim religious obligations. There would seem to be an anxiety to cover every issue in life with a *fatwa*:

- Generally, in summer we use an electronic device (common in butchers) to kill insects like flies and mosquitoes. Is this permissible?[8]
- Are Muslims living in non-Muslim countries bound to obey the traffic laws of that country? Is the speeding fine Islamic?[9]
- Tax evasion ... Is is permissible to show false expenses to get maximum tax refund from a non-Islamic govt? Does this come under lying?[10]

The range of questions on the site naturally includes many themes that have been addressed elsewhere on other sites. The question of suicide bombings and their legitimacy in Islam emerged:

Q: What is your opinion on the suicide bombers in Palestine?

A: If a community is oppressed and denied its basic human rights, it is permissible for them to fight against the oppressors and free themselves from such oppression. It is permissible for them to engage in Jihaad – risking their lives in the hope of saving themselves from oppression. The people of Palestine are the most oppressed people and live in constant fear by the rule of the Jewish oppressors. Their extreme frustration and hardships have led them to behave likewise – to resort to suicide bombings. Assuming the suicide bombing is evil but this evil is opposed by a greater evil for which there is no adequate substitute, therefore, their act will also be justified as lesser of the two evils in terms of the Shari'ah.[11]

This justification is significantly different from the answer provided by Fatwa-Online. It lacks, perhaps, a depth of scholarly interpretation and justification, and there is no textual support for the opinion. No doubt it is possible to discover a multiplicity of approaches to this issue on the Internet. The question of jihad has exercised Ask-Imam on at least 22 occasions, with specific *fatwas* on related issues. One contentious question, from a petitioner in Germany, featured under the banner 'Recently I've been talkin' to "jihadis", who say if Islam brings me peace, I have chosen the wrong religion, they say [the] blood of *kafir* is *halal*, it is permissible to kill any non-Muslim.'

The question itself gives an insight into some grassroots opinion, albeit of a minority nature, from so-called jihadis:

Please could you help me, I am on the verge of losing my *imaan* [faith]. I am a recent convert to islam, I converted to islam because of the peace, as well as being convinced its the truth. Very recently I have been talking to some 'jihadis', who say if Islam brings me peace, I have chosen the wrong religion, they tell me the blood of every *kafir* [non-believer] is *halal*, and that it is permissible to kill any non muslim whether they are oppressing you or not. For example, they say it would be permissible to go to somewhere like Bolivia [*sic*], and kill all the local inhabitants for the sin of not being non-muslim. I have also been told that rape during jihad is permissible. Please save my *imaan*. They also tell me if I feel sorry for any *kafir*, I am a *munafiq*, and I am one of them. Please save my *imaan*. I work with several Americans, how should my relationship be with them? According to these guys, I should kill them, just for the sin of holding an American passport. Look forward to hearing from you shortly.[12]

There are a number of divergent themes worthy of analysis here. For example, the position of converts in a minority context; the role of so-called 'jihadis' in a minority context and their status; the suggestion that rape and murder are appropriate, religiously justified options; the fact that the petitioner must e-mail a South African 'authority' in order to obtain an appropriate response (suggesting that local information is not available). Ask-Imam, itself operating in a minority context where suggestions of murdering 'non-Muslims' would not be well received, provides an answer which strongly suggested that the 'jihadis' were operating under an erroneous principle:

The statement, 'promoted killing of non-Muslims' is vague and sweeping and is very much open to misinterpretation. Yes, Rasulullah (Sallallaahu Alayhi Wasallam) promoted the killing of these non-Muslims who are actively engaged in destroying Islam and the Muslims. This is the command of Allah Ta'ala Himself in the Qur'aan. This type of killing is not simply permissible, but commendable and worthy of reward. This does not mean that Islam teaches to kill all non-Muslims.

If, for example, a Muslim intentionally kills a non-Muslim citizen of the Islamic state, then in retribution the Muslim's life will be taken. This indicates that even the life of a non-Muslim is sanctified, if he does not oppose Islam and the Muslims.[13]

This is specific, in terms of noting 'Rasulullah''s (Muhammad's) justification for killing non-Muslims, and that the Qur'an itself makes statements regarding the killing of Islam's enemies. The answer notes the sanctity of non-Muslim life. However, the first paragraph could also reflect the jihadi's own statements, if they perceive the enemy to be seeking to destroy Islam.

There is an implicit endorsement for jihad activity against Israel, in the response to the question:

> Is it obligatory for Muslim all over the world to go for Jihad against the Jews this time to liberate the Holyland in Palestine?
>   Or are we supposed to wait for Imam Mahdi?
>
> *A*: ... Muslims all around the world should assist the oppressed Palestinians in every possible way.[14]

This would suggest support for militaristic campaigning. The majority of the questions on jihad do not feel the need to define the concept, relating it purely to militaristic activity. At times, Ask-Imam exercises understandable caution when approaching this subject, notably in the response to the question:

> Is it permissible to wage (physical war) Jihad against Israel, U.S. and India (for their role in Gujrat Muslims carnage)?
>
> *A*: Your question is a sensitive one.
>   It does not behove one person to issue a ruling on such a matter. It requires one to exercise precaution and have broad consultation before arriving at a conclusion.
>   And Allah Ta'ala Knows Best.[15]

The questioner's assumptions regarding the perpetrators in the July 2002 attack on Muslims in Gujarat is not challenged in this response.

Ask-Imam represents a Muslim institution/individual in a minority context, which has acquired a broad global audience for its opinions, which are sought from a variety of religious perspectives. Several new '*fatwas*' emerge on the site every day, making this a site likely to receive substantial return visits from interested surfers. The questions themselves indicate some of the challenges facing Muslims today, although it is not possible to quantify the effect or influence that this information has on individuals or communities. This would require monitoring and e-mailing the petitioners; however, their anonymity is guaranteed, which is understandable given the nature of some of the questions sent to the site. Some of the questions clearly have only a curiosity value, whilst others are more substantive, 'life-and-death' issues. Desai and his team treat all with seriousness and sensitivity. They acknowledge the difference between *ijtihad* and *fatwas*, and distinguish between the opinions of the four Sunni schools of jurisprudence, and other religious opinions:

> ... The *Ulama* [scholars] of today do not qualify to be *Mujtahids*, hence they are followers of their respective Imams. Their differences of opinion do not stem from differences of opinion in the 'Principles of *Ijtihaad*'. They are rightly *Muqallideen* [followers] of their respective Imams.[16]

Desai is critical of the traditional Sunni scholars from al-Azhar University in Cairo, indicating that they are 'not in a position to be imams', but implying that they seek to set themselves up with the status to create binding rulings:

> Furthermore, a non-*Aalim* [non-scholar] may follow a learned *Muqallid* [guide] of his *Mazhab* [school] as a guide in order to make proper *Taqleed* [rulings to be adhered to] of his respective Imam.
>
> When following a learned *Muqallid*, it is important to know his source of knowledge. It should be noted that the source of education has an influence on an individual's future and direction in life.
>
> The *Aalim* must also be firmly adhering to and practising on the Noble Qurān and the Sunnah of Rasulullah (Sallallaaahu Ālayhi Wasallam) i.e. The Shariāh.
>
> One should avoid following the Azhari *Ulama* [scholars of al-Azhar] in the belief of making their Taqleed.

This reflects a long-standing dispute on the nature of religious authority in Islam and resentment (in some quarters) at the status of some scholars on the Muslim world, particularly those from traditional institutions. Desai sets out the ways in which he believes knowledge can be acquired and religious authority observed. Thus, the status of a scholar trained in non-Azhari institutions outside of the Arab Muslim world is justified, particularly as he seeks to present his opinions and influence in an English-language *fatwa* website which is more comprehensive, wide-ranging and potentially influential than the combined web resources of al-Azhar and its sympathisers.[17]

Troid.org

TROID represents a 'Salafi' perspective, emerging from a minority context, which is sympathetic to the pronouncements of Fatwa-Online and their ideology/decision-making processes. It contains the opinions of Ibn Baz and the Fatwa Committee in Saudi Arabia. TROID (The Reign of Islamic Da'wah, or 'propagation') is based in Toronto. Their website features sections on the Qur'an, fatwas, and introductory information on Islam. TROID hyperlinks to Allahuakbar and other Salafi *websites, as well as Fatwa-Online. TROID is not as substantial as Islam-Online or Fatwa-Online, with relatively few* fatwas *on the site, with titles that include:*

- The Islaamic ruling regarding standing for the national anthem – Answered by the Committee of Major Scholars. An end to the wicked propaganda of the modernists who say there is nothing wrong in standing up for the national anthem.
- Concerning the Peace Treaty – By Shaykh 'Abdul-'Azeez Ibn Baaz. A clarification from the Shaykh concerning his stance on the Peace Treaty with the Jews, and an elucidation of the position of the Muslims towards those who disbelieve in the Religion of Allaah.
- The Verdict upon Those Who Do Not Rule by What Allaah Revealed.[18]
- Marriage, casts and compatibility – Answered by the Noble Shaykh, 'Abdul-'Azeez Ibn Baaz. A brief article consisting of queries in regards to marrying into the clan of the Prophet (sallallaahu 'alayhi wa sallam), and the reasons for which a person is married.
- Dealing with a Troublesome Husband – By Shaykh Ibn Baaz. A decisive verdict expounding how to deal with an unaffectionate and careless husband.[19]
- Is clinging to the Religion a cause for Affliction – By Shaykh 'Abdul-'Azeez Ibn Baaz (d. 1420H) Answering the question: is it permissible to say that the cause of one's affliction was due to him clinging to the commandments of the Religion? ...
- The Splitting of the Ummah – By Imaam Muhammad Saalih Ibnul-'Uthaymeen. An answer explaining the reason for splitting amongst the Muslim Ummah.[20]

Pakistan Link

Pakistan Link is an example of a commercial site, offering answers to religious questions (not described as 'fatwas') as part of its general newspaper and media services. The site provides what could be described as a 'culturally-specific' question-and-answer service on religious questions primarily for people of Pakistani origin in the USA, although it should be acknowledged that Pakistan incorporates a broad range of cultures, religious perspectives and languages.

Pakistan Link describes itself as 'The First Pakistan Newspaper on the Internet since 1994' [*sic*], 'a daily Internet Version of the Weekly Pakistan Link published in Los Angeles'.[21] Muzammil H. Siddiqi has written a weekly column for Pakistan Link, with archives dating back to 1996, answering questions on a broad range of 'Issues and Questions', seeking to present itself as a 'moderate' interpretation of Islam. Siddiqi was educated in Medina and Harvard, is a former director of the Islamic Society of North America (ISNA), and a member of the Majlis Ash-Shura and the Fiqh Council of North America (see below).[22] Siddiqi also has an archive of nearly 400 'Questions and Answers' in the Fiqh Council section of the ISNA site.[23]

Questions surveyed in the Pakistan Link site include the issue of marriage in Islam and its recognition by visa authorities (with regard to the concepts of Nikah and Rukhsati),[24] the rules of divorce,[25] the forms of 'innovation' in Islam,[26] the 'appropriate' use of contraception,[27] 'is it permissible to pay *zakat* using credit card?', and 'Is cybersex or phone sex considered to be "*zina*" [adultery]?'[28] Not surprisingly, perhaps, this receives an emphatic answer:

> Islam does not only forbid illicit sexual intercourse, but it also forbids anything that leads to this sin and crime. 'Cybersex' or 'phone sex' etc. that you mentioned are those activities that can lead to *zina*. The Prophet – peace and blessings be upon him – said: 'The eyes commit *Zina*, the hands commit *Zina* and feet commit *Zina* and the genitals commit *Zina*' (Musnad Ahmad, hadith no. 4258). In another hadith he is reported to have said that 'the genitals confirm it or deny it'.[29]

The questions clearly tap the nerves on contemporary issues, and Siddiqi attempts to provide a pragmatic line within a minority context, as evidenced in the response to the following situation:

Q: I am writing to you regarding a situation at our mosque. Recently the executive committee decided to stop women from attending the mosque.

What I want to know is, what does the Shari'ah say about this? As far as I know Islam treats both men and women equally.

A: The Prophet – peace be upon him – very clearly told men not to exclude women from the mosques. It is reported that Syedna 'Umar's wife used to attend the Jama'ah prayer in the *Masjid* at Fajr and 'Isha times. It was said to her, 'Why do you leave home, you know that 'Umar does not like that and he feels ashamed (that you leave home at that time)?' She said, 'So what is preventing him from forbidding me?' The person said, 'It is this word of the Prophet – peace be upon him, 'Do not prevent the she-servants of Allah from the mosques of Allah' (al-Bukhari, Hadith no. 489).

... In America especially women go everywhere. They are in the markets, in malls, in restaurants, in offices. It is ironic that some men allow them to go to all the places of temptation but they want to stop them from coming to the places where they can pray to their Lord and learn about their faith. Please ask your executive committee to change this un-Islamic decision. If you do not have a proper place for sisters to pray in the Masjid, raise funds and make proper arrangements for them.[30]

Some of the petitioners are obviously not from Pakistani backgrounds, as evidenced in the question 'Is there anti-Semitism in the Qur'an?' from a Jew who is reading the Qur'an.[31] The response is indicative of the tone of the responses elsewhere on the site:

The Qur'an specifically notes that such criticism is not directed against all Jews. Even when the Qur'an criticizes the Jews it always notes that 'among them there are some...' who are pious and righteous people, who command what is right and forbid what is wrong and try to excel each other in acts of charity and goodness. The Qur'an says that such people are assured that whatever good they will do will not be denied them and they shall receive their reward with God (3:113–15).

Taking a few passages from the Qur'an out of proper historical and textual context will not give a proper understanding of the religious scripture. This is not only true of the Qur'an but also of the Bible.[32]

Muzammil H. Siddiqi has had contact with the Jewish community in the United States, as demonstrated in the article 'Healing our Brokenness', a paper given to a Jewish audience.[33] Elsewhere, he discusses the concepts of 'on the love and care of others' in various world religions, to an audience at a Church of the Latter Day Saints in California.[34] The extent to which Siddiqi represents a *'fatwa-producing'* scholar is open to question and is not clearly elucidated on this site.

The Fiqh Council of North America

The Fiqh Council of North America includes Siddiqi amongst its board's eleven prominent scholars who have earned the trust and confidence of the Muslim community in their ability to understand the unique issues and environment in North America.[35]

The Council's application of the term 'opinions' is possibly an equivalent to *fatwa*: 'They regularly receive numerous inquiries from Muslims all over the continent and respond to them with studied opinions on issues of concern.'[36] Its Q&A page contained 36 topics (August 2002), on issues ranging from adoption to ritual practice; the 'Quick Questions' section also contained 13 questions with brief answers: these include:

- Listening to music.
- Dancing with the opposite sex.
- Making out/kissing, oral sex.
- Smoking weeds [*sic*]/cigarettes.
- Christians, do they all go to hell?

Sheikh Muhammad Hanooti, who is active with Islam-Online (possibly suggesting the influence of al-Qaradawi on this Council), answers the last question:

A. Allah (SWT) does not punish a person before he is provided with guidance. 'We never punish until we have sent a messenger' (17:15).
B. After man has access to guidance he will have no excuse to deny oneness of God. Allah never forgives those who 'Ascribe partners to Allah' (4:48).
C. We think that the majority of people in USA and elsewhere in the world have not had access to guidance yet.

D. Allah, then, is the one who decides who will go to hell or heaven.

E. A Muslim is not guaranteed to go to heaven directly after death.[37]

The site's (and the Council's) perspective is also illustrated in the following response to the question:

Is it *wajib* [obligatory] to adhere completely to a particular *Madhab* [school], instead of picking and choosing from amongst the four schools? And could you please list some recommended books regarding this subject?

The answer comes from Taha Alalwani, President of the Graduate School of Islamic and Social Sciences, Leesburg, Virginia, who has written on concepts associated with *ijtihad*, in publications for the International Institute of Islamic Thought (IIIT) in Herndon, Virginia (which has one course designed to qualify imams for service as chaplains in the US armed forces). IIIT has been prominent in its promotion of *ijtihad*, represented as 'independent reasoning'. IIIT has ideological links with Jamaat-e-Islami Pakistan and related networked organisations – themselves linked to the work of Mawdudi and ideological influences from the Wahhabi 'school' of thought. Alalwani writes elsewhere on the site about Ibn Taymiyya, and uses his work as a source for the following answer:

As a matter of rule, Muslims should follow the legal evidence ['*dalil*'] from the Quran and the Sunna of the Prophet, peace be upon him. However, if a Muslim would like to follow a specific legal school of thought ['*madhab*'] exclusively, this practice should be based on a thorough study of its principles, ruling and opinions, and methods of deriving them. In that case, one will know what one is practicing, and will embrace a specific school of thought in an enlightened way. A person with such knowledge will be following the Quran and the Sunna. Otherwise, it will be a blind following, and Allah Subhanahu Ta'la forbids Muslims to do so. Allah SWT has said: 'And pursue not that of which you have no knowledge; for every act of hearing, or of seeing, or of [feeling in] the heart will be enquired into [on the Day of Reckoning]' [17:36].[38]

The Fiqh Council is discreet in referring to ideological issues and theological perspectives, in a 'Shari'ah-centric' outlook that does not refer specifically to particular schools or sources – outside of the Quran and sunna. It discourages following a particular school of interpretation *alone*, without access to other sources of authority. The extent to which a local or global audience follows such online opinion is difficult to ascertain. The Fiqh Council's site was in a developmental stage at the time of writing and may become more competitive in the field of 'opinion formulation' in the future. There is no emphasis *per se* on the production of *fatwas*, but instead the notion of *fiqh* in approaching contemporary issues could be seen as the central focus on the site. Despite this reactive element, there was no obvious reference in August 2002 to the events of 9-11 or to conflicts in Afghanistan.

As-Sunna Foundation of America

The As-Sunna Foundation of America (ASFA), substantially smaller than the sites discussed above, has a discreet Sufi emphasis (this is only implicitly revealed deep in the site, when clicking the About ASFA Chairman link).[39] *This reveals that Shaykh Muhammad Hisham Kabbani, who also founded the Islamic Supreme Council of America, established the ASFA; such titles have to be qualified, perhaps, given that Kabbani's work has a strong Sufi emphasis. He has written about the Sufi poet Jalal al-Din Rumi, and the Naqshabandi Sufi Order, and is linked to the Haqqani Foundation. His biography notes that he has also founded Naqshabandi and other Islamic websites. Affiliations for ASFA seem broad, but not necessarily complementary, as they include al-Azhar University, MUIS (Islamic Council of Singapore), the Abu Nour Islamic Foundation in Syria and an Ahmadiyya network based in Lahore.*[40] *The ASFA site provides in its pages refutations of 'Wahhabism'.*[41] *There is also a discussion on the nature of* ijtihad, *on the qualifications required in order that it can occur, and a lamentation regarding the perceived decline in the quality of* fatwas:

> the decline in quality of fatawa is only a particular manifestation of the more general decline of Muslims in all fields of learning. Moreover, one can only express astonishment at a people who used to compete with one another in the acquisition of learning, but today lead the world in illiteracy! The lack of respect for learning today in the Muslim world is surely a sign (and cause) of Allah's anger with us. I ask Him to rekindle in our hearts the love of learning and respect for those who pursue it.[42]

The *Fatwa* section contains a list of over 20 *fatwas*, drawn from *Muslim Magazine*, on subjects ranging from fasting and mosque attendance to more controversial topics, including 'Revealing Intimate Marital Details', 'He smokes … is he right for me?' and 'My wife was molested'.[43] There are hyperlinks to over 100 Questions and Answers, based directly on questions sent in by e-mail. These are useful indicators of contemporary concerns, as well as presenting an overview of traditional topics: 'The Veil in Islam', 'About Homosexuality' and 'Assisted Suicide' indicate the breadth of questions received and answered by As-Sunna Foundation staff on their site, which is frequently updated.[44] ASFA links to the Kalimat site for Muslim women (founded by Kabbani), which contains other resources.[45] These include an online version of the 'the official pre-nuptial contract upheld by al-Azhar University' and 'The List – Questions for Potential Marriage Partners', which features 20 questions which are intended to help people, particularly Muslim women, to:

> better negotiate pre-marital discussion and the laying of 'ground rules'. This process is fully supported in Islamic tradition, so don't be shy to use it. It's better to find out NOW if your suitor is unwilling to answer your questions, or if his answers are 180 degrees opposed to your own views on life, marriage and parenting.[46]

The range of questions and resources, which are interlinked with online *fatwas*, offers new approaches to knowledge about Islam, and access to networks and authorities, in particular for 'diaspora', English-speaking communities.

CONCLUSION: SUNNI RELIGIOUS AUTHORITY ON THE INTERNET

The discussion in this and Chapters 6 and 7 has introduced *some* of the phenomena associated with '*fatwas*' and online authority in Sunni cyberspace. At times, it can be seen that the lines between *fatwa*-related concepts and other forms of authority become blurred. In the future it may be possible to analyse other perspectives reflecting Islamic authority on the Internet, such as online pronouncements emerging from South America, sub-Saharan Africa (outside of South Africa) and China. This will be particularly pertinent once areas become better connected with the Internet and access improves. Information databases on Islam already cover a wide range of languages, and each cultural and religious perspective will require detailed, specialist study (beyond the scope of this book).

This is an exciting, and perhaps daunting, area for future researchers – especially given the 'information overload' experienced by this writer when perusing materials (essentially in English, French and Arabic). It is essential now to shift outside the 'Sunni' orthodox paradigm of Islam (which itself is defined in many ways), to explore other regions and perspectives. The rigidity of self-definition provided by many 'authorities' in terms of Muslim identity do not have to be matched by external observers or researchers, especially when exploring the rapidly shifting (some would say chaotic) and unstructured elements of cyberspace – which often defies categorisation and rigid typologies.

The Sunni Internet landscape described in this book will change rapidly, so it is essential at least to observe and report what has occurred, in order that some kind of impact of the medium on Sunni thought can be measured. A critical way of undertaking this task is by studying the pronouncements of scholars through the manifestation of *fatwas*. The next stage would be to focus on particular 'schools' or ideological perspectives to see whether the medium is sustained as part of a formative dissemination process (for those with access to the medium), whether it reverts to earlier models or whether some form of mutation of processes occurs.

In *Virtually Islamic*, it was considered whether the attendant growth of the Internet medium, together with improved access and cheaper technology, would increase the global influence of particular Muslim perspectives. At the time, this consideration focused on activist religious-political Sunni Wahhabi organisations, because of their levels of funding and awareness of the medium. This element of propagation and networking is also shared, however, with smaller organisations and perhaps less influential (in the global context) Muslim worldviews. It could also be said that some of these perspectives may be vocal in cyberspace, but are not necessarily representative of a majority, either in their own branch of Islam and/or in relation to the population in which they are operating. The latter consideration can be redundant in cyberspace, where organisations and individuals have globalising – as well as spiritual – considerations in mind.

NOTES

1. For example, Jamiatul Ulama in KwaZulu/Natal, South Africa, have a *Fatwa* Department linked to the Internet, which responds to e-mail questions. Sixty previous answers have been placed online, going beyond conventional subject-matter and covering issues such as 'Suicide Bombing – Shariah View', cloning, 'the Westernised Muslim Wedding' and 'the *Fitna* of Television'. It had not been updated for at least a year since July 2001. Jamiatul Ulama, KwaZulu/Natal, are discussed in Gary R. Bunt, 'Surfing Islam', in J.K. Hadden and D.E. Cowan (eds.), *Religion on the Internet: Research Prospects and Promises* (New York: Elsevier Science, 2000), p. 142, in relation to their opinions about Shi'ism. Jamiatul Ulama, www.jamiat.org.za/isinfo/isl-fatwa.html.

2. Ask-Imam, www.islam.tc/ask-imam/. Ask-Imam also promotes Desai's *al-Mahmood*, a book of contemporary questions and answers about Islam (Islam.tc's index page also advertised North Beach Detectives in San Francisco!). It links to the Madrasah In'amiyyah's own website and online content (including an Islamic Library), which includes an English translation of al-Thanawi's *Bishiti Zewar*, a traditional work intended for young Muslim women. Madrasah In'amiyyah, www.alinaam.org.za/.

3. These principal sections can be located through the side bar on the front page. www.islam.tc/ask-imam/index.php.

4. Ask-Imam, www.islam.tc/ask-imam/view.php?q=1624. Note: the final numbers of the URL represent the question number, which can be accessed directly via a search box on the front page of the site www.islam.tc/ask-imam/.

5. Ask-Imam, www.islam.tc/ask-imam/view.php?q=847.

6. Ask-Imam, www.islam.tc/ask-imam/view.php?q=122.

7. Ask-Imam, www.islam.tc/ask-imam/view.php?q=1175.

8. Ask-Imam, www.islam.tc/ask-imam/view.php?q=1787.

9. Ask-Imam, www.islam.tc/ask-imam/view.php?q=1197.

10. Ask-Imam, www.islam.tc/ask-imam/view.php?q=6261.

11. Ask-Imam, www.islam.tc/ask-imam/view.php?q=6284.

12. Writer's definitions of terminology in parenthesis. Bolivia may have been intended to read 'Bosnia'. www.islam.tc/ask-imam/view.php?q=6184.

13. Moulana Imraan Vawda, response to question 6184, www.islam.tc/ask-imam/view.php?q=6184.

14. Ask-Imam, www.islam.tc/ask-imam/view.php?q=1306.

15. Ask-Imam, www.islam.tc/ask-imam/view.php?q=6271 (grammar adjusted).

16. Ask-Imam, www.islam.tc/ask-imam/view.php?q=390. Writer's definitions of terms in parenthesis.

17. Al-Azhar's online resources are limited. They are discussed in Gary R. Bunt, *Virtually Islamic* (Cardiff: University of Wales Press, 2000), pp. 127–8.

18. TROID, Comprehensive, www.troid.org/new/fatawa/comprehensive/comprehend.htm.

19. TROID, Niqqa, www.troid.org/new/fatawa/niqqa/niqqa.htm.

20. TROID, Aqeedah, www.troid.org/new/fatawa/aqeedah/aqeedah.htm.

21. Pakistan Link, www.pakistanlink.com.

22. 'Dr. Muzammil H. Siddiqi', ISNA, www.isna.net/majlis/Muzammil_Siddiqi.asp.
23. ISNA Library of Knowledge, Fiqh and Q&A, www.isna.net/Library/fiqhqa/questions.asp, 396 questions 9 August 2002.
24. Muzammil H. Siddiqi, 'Issues and Questions', Pakistan Link, www.pakistanlink.com/religion/2001/0504.html.
25. Muzammil H. Siddiqi, 'Issues and Questions', Pakistan Link, www.pakistanlink.com/religion/2000/12–15.html.
26. Muzammil H. Siddiqi, 'Issues and Questions', Pakistan Link, www.pakistanlink.com/religion/2001/0413.html.
27. Muzammil H. Siddiqi, 'Issues and Questions', Pakistan Link, www.pakistanlink.com/religion/2001/0629.html.
28. Muzammil H. Siddiqi, 'Issues and Questions', Pakistan Link, www.pakistanlink.com/religion/2001/0413.html.
29. Ibid.
30. Muzammil H. Siddiqi, Pakistan Link, www.pakistanlink.com/religion/2000/07–28.html.
31. Muzammil H. Siddiqi, Is there anti-Semitism in the Qur'an?, Pakistan Link, www.pakistanlink.com/religion/2002/0104.html.
32. Ibid.
33. Muzammil H. Siddiqi, Healing our Brokenness, Pakistan Link, www.pakistanlink.com/religion/2002/0208.html.
34. Muzammil H. Siddiqi, Unity and Diversity, Pakistan Link, the speech was delivered at the Annual Banquet of Interfaith council of Westminster, Garden Grove and Stanton on 5 May 2001 at the LDS Church in Westminster, California, www.pakistanlink.com/religion/2001/0518.html.
35. Fiqh Council of North America, About Us, www.fiqhcouncil.org/aboutus.asp.
36. Ibid.
37. Fiqh Council of North America, Christians do they all go to hell? www.fiqhcouncil.org/fiqh.asp.
38. Fiqh Council of North America, Following a Madhab, www.fiqhcouncil.org/fiqh.asp.
39. As-Sunna Foundation of America, As-Sayyid Shaykh Muhammad Hisham Kabbani, www.sunnah.org/about/shaykh_muhammad_hisham_kabbani.htm.
40. The latter is particularly interesting, as it disassociates itself from the claims of other Ahmadiyya organisations that the Ahmadiyya's founder Mirza Ghulam Ahmad (1835–1908) was a 'prophet' or a 'messiah' (mahdi), placing him instead into the position of being a mujaddid or 'renewer' of Islam. The site confronts the stereotypes they perceive as being associated with the Ahmadiyya movement. See The Lahori Ahmadi View, http://tariq.bitshop.com/mga/.
41. Mawlana Shaykhu-l-Islam Ahmad Zayni Dahlan, 'Fitnatul Wahhabiyyah – The Menace of Wahhabism', As-Sunna Foundation of America, www.sunnah.org/aqida/fitnatulWahhabiyyah.htm.

42. Mohammad Fadel, 'On the Validity of Ijtihad from the Viewpoint of Usul (Principles of Islamic jurisprudence)', As-Sunna Foundation of America, www.sunnah.org/fiqh/usul/on_the_validity_of_ijtihad.htm.
43. As-Sunna Foundation of America, www.sunnah.org/fatwa/.
44. As-Sunna Foundation of America, MSA-EC Forum, www.sunnah.org/msaec/.
45. Kalimat, http://kalimat.org.
46. The List, www.kamilat.org.

10 The Online *Mujtahid*: Islamic Diversity and Authority Online

The following section shifts outside the Sunni paradigm altogether towards other perspectives, which are equally 'Islamic', but often subsumed by the academic and media focus on Sunni Islam. Their conceptual framework may draw away from ideas associated with '*fatwas*', or different definitions are applied (whilst the terminology may remain the same). Whilst the terms 'Sufi' and 'Shi'a' are applied here, they too do not necessarily conform to a single definition or perspective. Notions of authority can vary too, and the qualifications enabling the individual to interpret a situation (and a text) can frequently be contextual. In some cases, imitation of prior practice by imams (*taqleed*) is preferred to innovation of new practice, whilst in other cases, scholars are only qualified to issue guidance in their own micro-field of knowledge.

The idea of polarisation between Shi'a and Sunni Islam in this area is perhaps a stereotype, as historically there have been exchanges of opinions and ideas between scholars and practitioners in relation to decision-making concerns. The essential difference would be in the nature of spiritual (and legalistic) authority in Shi'ism resting in the hands of an imam, with attributes of divinity being associated with the individual, and being able to assert that he descends from the House or family of the Prophet (*ahl al-Bayt*).

LOCATING SHI'A RELIGIOUS AUTHORITY ON THE INTERNET

The writer has documented Shi'a cyberspace elsewhere, noting the developments surrounding Shi'a diversity online, with particular reference to sites about Ayatullah Khomeini and materials appearing (but not exclusively) from the Islamic Republic of Iran.[1] Substantial resources appear online in relation to Khomeini and his opinions, which have been extensively recorded in digital form as well as in print (a process that is continuing). There are a number of '*fatwa* services' operating within the parameters of 'Shi'a cyberspace', although such a demarcation between Sunni and Shi'a is not always necessarily indicated on the sites themselves. These sites are frequently multilingual and demonstrate some of the unique perspectives on decision-making issues that originate from Shi'a sources. They also reflect the political and cultural diversity between Sunni and Shi'a Islam, as well as the diversity *within* Shi'a Islam. Generally speaking, the Sunni paradigm of religious authority may not necessarily apply in the Shi'a context, in terms of observing all elements of 'Sunni' scholarship in historical and contemporary contexts, but there is a substantial amount of 'sharing' of *some* conceptual frameworks and understandings. This reflects what is interpreted in some sources as a split between the historical 'factions' after the death of Muhammad, although this split has been interpreted as open to historical revisionism, a subject which itself features on some of the sites discussed below. For some Shi'a societies and individuals, in majority and minority contexts (including minorities in a Sunni setting), the Internet has provided a welcome avenue for obtaining definitive scholarly opinions from expertise that is not available in a local environment, in a framework where individuals may be expected to follow a well-qualified scholar on matters of religious opinion. However, the level of polarity between Sunni and Shi'a *may* be minimal in terms of practice and understanding, and it is interesting to note on the Internet the 'cross-fertilisation' of ideas and concepts between these different Muslim dimensions. Shi'a understanding is not just about Iran, and indeed the Internet is an important indicator of how Shi'a discourse goes way beyond the virtual and real borders of the Islamic Republic of Iran, to incorporate dispersed Shi'a communities worldwide.

For the purposes of this discussion, the various sites are integrated into a single narrative, rather than separated out. This is, to an extent, a reflection of the nature of Shi'a sites and their decision-making content, which is less detailed and extensive than Sunni equivalents. One of the earliest Shi'a *fatwa* services was produced by the Shi'a Ahlul Bayt 'Aalim Network, which operated a Question-and-Answer e-mail service between 1995 and 2001, posted automatically to e-mail subscribers, and partly archived online (up to 1999 at the time of writing).[2] This archive in itself would make an interesting case study, representing a particular range of the contemporary interests of (a section of) a Shi'a online community. The discussion forum has been replaced by Shiachat.com, which contains a lively and regularly accessed Islamic Laws section; in August 2001, there were 43 subjects being discussed, including Temporary Marriage, Homosexuality in

Islam, Praying behind a Sunni, Organ Donation and Viewing a Woman before Marriage.[3] Shi'a discussion areas cover a broad range of topics: 'E-jihad.net', operating under the banner 'The Islamic Resistance for the Liberation of Humanity', contains materials assocated with various campaigns (particularly in relation to Palestine), whilst also providing Spiritual and Human Rights sections. The contributors include 'Hizbulla4Life', whilst the postings (for example, in the 'Brothers Only' section) lacked depth and resembled a conventional chat room in nature: participants were complaining about the lack of content or ideas for discussion, and indicated that the absence of women in the discussion had diluted its effectiveness! The number of posts and threads at the time of writing suggests that this service is undersubscribed.[4]

Similar issues of levels of access emerge in other (not necessarily related) sections of Shi'a cyberspace, including Taliyah al-Mahdi, a Cincinnati-based website: their section on Shi'a–Sunni dialogue, refuting Sunni assertions that Shi'a 'rejected' Muhammad, received a couple of hundred 'views' but only two replies.[5] A similar section attacking 'Wahhabism', discusses the links between Sunni Islam and 'Wahhabi Islam':

> I think the link between Wahhabies and the Sunnites is that the latter have been very complicit in the wake of Wahhabi onslaught, and in fact even took part [in] many of their *fitnah* [civil wars, strife]. This is most evident in the shared hatred of both towards Shi'a and Sufi orders, and their general distortion of True Islam ... though this is true on a higher level with Wahhabies, and there are notable exceptions amongst the Sunnites. Generally speaking though, the complicity of the Sunnites did much to nourish the as-Sufyaniyah, and subsequently stooped themselves in the spiritless quagmire of 'do's' and 'don'ts' the Wahhabies are feeding them in their own mosques.[6]

This argument seems to suggest that the legalistic exactitude of the 'Wahhabis' has in fact encouraged mystical Islamic practices.

The Taliyah site was also indicating, in a separate section of Questions and Answers about the Double Eclipse of Ramadan 2003, that the Mahdi or 'rightly guided figure' (descended from the imams) would appear during that time:

If the prophecies of the 313 Mujahidin of the Mahdi (atfs) strike you as unbelievable, and if you rightly recognize that you will never achieve such mastery of the mystic-warrior arts on your own – if you are asking yourself how to begin this monumental task of training for the coming Jihad against the system of Dajjal – then you should contact the Taliyah Al-Mahdi immediately to begin our 'Path to Perfection' training lessons. You will be trained in every aspect of Din, 'Irfan, Martial Arts, firearms, modern weaponry, tactics, natural healing, dietary purity, exercise, strength and fitness.

'Are you not pleased that your enemies are busy with each other [in conflict], while you are safe in your homes? When our Qa'im arises each one of you will gain the energy of forty men. Your heart will become like pieces of iron, which, if hurled against mountains, will break them through. You will be the leaders of the world and its keepers.' – Imam Baqir (as)

Allah does not Reveal to us signs with no importance or reason. The time of passive acceptance of wickedness, and kufr is passed … Now is the time of our Imam's Rise. Now is the time to throw off the shackles of this world. Now is the time to prepare for battle and move forward to Eden!

'If our Shi'a would be firm on their promises wholeheartedly, our meeting would not be delayed.' – Imam Al-Mahdi[7]

This emphatic Shi'a-oriented statement about the forthcoming appearance of a *mahdi* is a motif which has featured in various eschatological sources. Its linking with contemporary contexts and issues is an interesting one, especially in the format of a response to a question essentially about Ramadan.

It has to be emphasised that there is a variety of forms of Shi'a expression online. In terms of seniority online, Ayatullah Khamene'i *could* be seen as one of the most senior Shi'a scholars, although his status would be challenged in other Shi'a quarters (it is not proposed to enter that debate here). In part, this seniority is linked to his association with Qom Theological Centre and his (apparent) designation as Ayatullah Khomeini's 'spiritual successor' (implied on the website). His personal site's material is available in Arabic, English, Farsi, French, Turkish and Urdu. In terms of resources, the online options are probably greater for speakers of Farsi and Arabic than English or French. The site offers an e-mail service, offering to answer questions outside of Iran:

This site has been established to answer religious questions, to introduce the jurisprudential decrees of Imam Khomeini (may Allah's blessings be upon him) and Ayatullah al Udhma Khamenei (may his high shadow endure), and to quickly accommodate related requests from outside the country (I.R. IRAN).[8]

A substantial collection of *fatwas* by Ayatullah Khamene'i has been published online in the various languages (excluding the Farsi and Arabic sites, which have different interface and contents).[9] These include questions sent to him from across the world:

For several years, the office of the leader of the Muslim ummah, honorable Ayatullah al-Uzma Sayyid Ali Hosseini Khamene'i (d) has been being showered with religious questions sent from all corners of the globe. His Excellency has been answering these inquiries – the number of which has surpassed tens of thousands – either based on his noble opinion or, in some cases, according to the opinion of the unique scholar of his time and the founder of the Islamic Republic of Iran, Imam Ruhollah Musawi Khomeini (q). The religious rulings contained in this huge collection concern all topics of Islamic law – particularly the frequently asked ones – in addition to modern problems originating from the heart of contemporary needs and realities.

This collection represents an indicator of some of these 'tens of thousands' of questions. All questions are anonymous, and there are obvious levels of editorial control in what is incorporated into the text. The main sections are *Taqleed* (imitation, adherence to previous decision), *Taharah* ('purity'), Prayers, Fasting, *Khums* (taxation), Enjoining to Good and Forbidding from Evil, and Jihad. This latter section has five technical questions on (militaristic) jihad's 'permissibility', relating specifically to notions surrounding selected concepts of Shi'a leadership and the imamate. One question was concerned about appropriate behaviour during the 'occultation' (or *ghayba*) of the imam, that being the concealment associated primarily with Twelver Shi'ites.[10] The treatment of *dhimmis* (people who are not Muslims) in war is also discussed. Elsewhere in the collection, there is an extensive discussion of the nature of religious decision-making in Shi'a contexts, focusing on the qualifications of a *mujtahid*, conditions of imitation and the understandings surrounding *ijtihad*.[11] It has to be stressed that this is one version of Shi'ism, linked to a specific worldview associated with Iran; this can be seen in the response to a question about the responsibility of a 'Supreme Jurist':

> Q: 'Is the belief in the principle of the Supreme Jurist Leader [*Waliy al-Faqeeh*], with respect to its concept and exemplification, based on reason or derived from Islamic law?

> A: *Wilayah al-Faqeeh*, which is the rule of a just jurist who is learned in the religion, is a devotional religious precept that is confirmed by reason as well as by the Islamic law. There is a rational method for determining the outer exemplification of this precept, which is elaborated upon in the Constitution of the Islamic Republic of Iran.[12]

It also highlights the parameters under which authority can be exercised within this interpretation:

> Q 62: Could someone who does not believe in the absolute authority of the Supreme Jurist Leader [*Waliy al-Faqeeh*] be considered a true Muslim?

> A: The lack of belief, whether based on juristic expertise [*ijtihad*] or imitation [*taqleed*], in the absolute authority of the Supreme Jurist Leader [*Waliy al-Faqeeh*] during the period of occultation of the Imam al-Hujjah [the 12th Imam] – may our souls be sacrifices for his cause – does not lead to apostasy.[13]

Other religious scholars, such as Ayatollah Hossein Ali Montazeri are asserting themselves online, despite the efforts of the Islamic Republic's government to suppress what they define as 'dissident' views.[14]

Shi'a cyberspace also provides substantial other resources providing exhaustive question-and-answer resources. Ahl ul Bayt Global Information Center (al-Shia.org), registered to the address in Qom (not to be confused with the Ahlul Bayt Digital Islamic Library Project registered in Minnesota), provides a '*fatwa* bank' that is focused, in part, on answering questions from Sunni Muslims. Some of this is quite complex to navigate, but there is also a section of questions from readers, in which responses are provided to a variety of questions. 'Q Bank' provides responses on key themes, but is limited in terms of the number of responses (one response in the 'Islam' category).[15] 'Our Q' is apologetic in nature, with ten 'questions' focused on Sunni Islam, refuting aspects of Sunni beliefs and disputing the roles of (Sunni) Muslim scholars.[16] 'Latest Q' would appear to offer the most recent material, with responses to questions on names, Muhammad in battle, purity of 'Christian food', ablutions, sexual practices and ritualised 'self-beating' in the sacred month of Muharram.[17] The nature of authority is approached in a question on following more than one *mujtahid*:

> Is it permissible to do *taqleed* of more than one *mujtahid* at the same time? For instance, can a person follow the rulings of Ayatullah Seestani regarding prayer but follow the rulings of Ayatullah Khamenei on financial transactions? Or does a person have to choose one *mujtahid* and follow all of his rulings? Assalamun Alaikum

> Dear brother, It is permissible to do *taqleed* of more than one *mujtahid*, and it is when you find the first *mujtahid* most learned for example in questions regarding worship such as praying fasting pilgrimage and so on, and the second *mujtahid* most learned in financial transactions. This is an admired method that every wise man selects in his daily affairs.
> Best regards, Yazdani[18]

Other questions are dealt with in a 'theological library', which seeks to provide access to 'numerous books concerning sectarian differences between Shi'a and Sunni faiths'.[19] It also includes 'converts' stories, and articles on Islam and Christianity, Family in Islam, and other issues deemed significant.

The library links to a page providing 'the user access to the scholars presiding in the Islamic Seminary of Qom'.[20] This is a link page, with a rollover button which – when a scholar is highlighted – provides his photo. At least 47 Shi'a scholars are listed. Links go through to pages containing a biography of individual scholars, primarily those based at Qom, highlighting their religious authority and qualifications. An initial overview suggests that individual scholarly opinion is disseminated online by a variety of scholars. E-mail contact details are provided, and in some cases this reflects the extent of their online presence. Whether this is an indication of their scholarly status is open to question, as some Qom scholars have opposed the Internet, whilst other 'online' scholars are deceased. Those with biographical pages, which link through to their online publications, include

Ayatullah Shaykh Tajleel, Ayatullah Ali Saafi Gulpaaigani and
Ayatullah Makaarim-Shiraazi, although few of these works are
translated. There are also webpage links, where relevant, to individual
scholar's pages, such as Ayatullah Uzma Jawad Tabrizi, Ayatullah Ali
Husayni Khamene'i, Reyshahri and Ayatullah Muhammad Taqi
Misbah Yazdi. The latter notes, in relation to the Internet:

> The plenitude of means and appliances has a twofold character. It
> paves the way for both numinous elevation on the one hand, and
> spiritual decadence on the other. The broad range of opportuni-
> ties opened up by the new communication media, a branch of
> which is Internet, is going to evolve the way people live their lives
> in the near future. We should consider such media as means of
> Divine probation.[21]

As this site evolves, it will surely contain a greater proportion of
content from a wider band of scholarly opinion in Qom, and would
be a useful focus for a study of contemporary opinion (in conjunction
with 'traditional sources').

A translation of *fatwas*, produced under the auspices of the World
Federation of Khoja Shi'a Ithna Asharis, is reproduced online by an
Afghanistan-oriented site, WatanOnline, which claims to have a focus
on Afghan culture and the 'unity' of the Afghan people. It might be
interpreted as contentious by some to have the perspectives of a
religious minority in Afghanistan expressed on the site. These are
the *fatwas* of Ayatullah al Uzama As-Sayyed Ali al-Husayni al-Seestani,
contained in *Taudhihul Masae'l*.[22] This consists of 2,800 *fatwas*,
annotated and compared with the output of Ayatullah al-Khoei. The
Khoja Shi'a represent an important minority within Shi'ism (which
itself has further fragmented), and that this minority has dispersed
worldwide (with substantial communities in India, East Africa, the
UK, US, and Canada).[23] These *fatwas* are exhaustive in nature, from
Following a *Mujtahid* through to Hiring a Person to Offer Prayers,
and cover many aspects of ritual belief. Essentially, this is an online
version of a print publication, which is relatively easy to search via
the index page, and accessible for all interested readers. They do not
represent a collection of 'online *fatwas*' in the sense of responding to
email requests for advice or information.[24]

The page links to a separately hosted Ahlul Bayt Digital Islamic
Library Project site of Seestani rulings, based on 'contemporary
issues', which contains 200 questions on themes such as the use of

credit cards, ritual issues and purity, organ donation, magic, music, lottery and angels.[25] The WatanOnline site also hosts a page entitled 'Wahhabis: The Real Terrorists', including an article 'Enemy of Islam: The Wahhabiyya Cult' by Riza al-Tariq Abdullah Ammari, describing the Ibn Wahhabi as 'the origins of apostasy'. The page lists some of the alleged 'Wahhabi' attacks on Shi'a Muslims and 'Wahhabi' complicity in the destruction of sacred sites.[26] Elsewhere on the site, there is a front page link to an 'analysis' which claims that Shi'a are the 'real' Ahl-i-Sunnah (People of the Sunnah), a title attributed to (and by) many Sunni groups to themselves.[27] This networking between sites is an interesting phenomenon, perhaps more prevalent in this sector of cyberspace as compared with some Sunni areas. Shi'a movements, with a history of 'cloaked' or 'underground' ritual and popular practices of belief, have a strong networking tradition (in certain branches of belief), and in some instances a history of being imaginative in their application of communications tools to spread their message to dispersed communities. It would be a generalisation to suggest that Shi'a communities are more 'wired', and indeed the online percentage of Shi'as online is small in relation to the total population. However, the presence of diaspora communities, especially in westernised contexts, has had a part to play in the relative success of the Internet as a networking tool and means of 'answering questions' about Islam.

Shi'a representation in minority contexts can take many forms: the Islamic Research Association's website, based in California, contains detailed information of Shi'a community activities, education, a prison project and ritual practices (including *hajj*, online prayers and burial). Among the activities was a Commemoration of Ayatollah Khomeini.[28] The Council of Shia Ulama of North America is represented online on the site, with photographs and reproduced letters, but little in the way of decision-making.[29]

The Imam Khoei Islamic Center of New York provides an e-mail question service, which offers answers from Sheikh Fadhel al-Sahlani, US representative of Ayatullah Seestani.[30] The Imam Khoei Islamic Centre, Swansea, offers an Ask the Imam e-mail service, but no online archive of questions and responses in English. However, the Arabic equivalent site contains a series on online *fatwas*: the page on *taqlid*, for example, includes 70 short questions and answers on a variety of concerns, whilst a section on ritual purity contained 145 questions and answers.[31] This application of Arabic within the minority UK context is indicative of the main audience for these opinions. The reliance on e-mails is also important, with individual opinions being provided. The writer's previous fieldwork with Shi'a Muslims in the UK revealed that there was considerable demand for opinions, on a variety of matters, and that these could be time-consuming for those in authority to deal with (and at times 'time-wasting') – although it is not suggested here that these opinions fall into that category. One imam suggested that many people sought a listener to their problems, and that discussing issues 'Islamically' became a cathartic process; e-mail may be an extension of this process, although whether web-pages have a similar cathartic effect is open to question.

Other sites place greater emphasis on their leadership and networking issues, rather than the type of advice that populates other areas of Shi'a cyberspace. A good example of this can be found amongst the Ismaili websites, which contain substantial general Ismaili information and regular news about their spiritual leader, the Aga Khan. These are significant, in that Ismaili communities are globally dispersed and do not represent a majority Shi'a perspective. The Internet is a natural medium for communication, and indeed their central website has been a long-standing and frequently innovative one, making use of multi-media and graphics early in the development of cyberspace.[32]

The Dawoodi Bohra Shi'a have also developed their networking through the Internet.[33] One particular focus is their Mumineen hub, which incorporates a variety of services for the dispersed communities. These include Akhbar, detailing the movements and pronouncements of religious leaders, which is complemented by an Audio archive containing 'messages to the mumineen'. Traditional matrimonial practices for Dawoodi Bohras are provided online, 'designed to help you find your life partner in an unobtrusive way, protecting the anonymity and dignity of all involved'.[34] The Shariat section provides advice on issues from a Dawoodi Bohra perspective, such as the *hajj*, calculation of *qibla* (prayer directions) and prayer times, the giving of *zakat*, the prohibition of *riba* (interest), and the interpretation of Qur'an and sunna. These elements convey the unique elements of Bohra identity in their language, symbolism and practice – distinguishing it from other Shi'a and Sunni understandings of Islam. Particularly striking is the assertion of *bara'at* (the cutting of ties) of those opposing Bohra beliefs:

> *Bara'at* is the other side to the coin of *walayat* – one is not complete without the other. To become *barii* means to make oneself free or

clean of something and bara'at is a dissociation from those people or elements that would corrupt or pollute one's faith and conviction.

Conceptually and practically *bara'at* entails a total and utter cutting of ties, communication and any form of interaction with those persons who harbour an enmity to the subject of our *walayat* ...[35]

Walayat in this sense represents 'faith', 'adherence' or 'belief' in the Dawoodi Bohra religious leaders, as well as in (particular) imams, Ali and the Prophet Muhammad. Criticism is levelled at those who offer to answer religious questions, who are described as 'hypocrites' or *munafiq*. This could be a criticism aimed at a broad range of targets, including those 'authorities' pronouncing on religious issues online:

The words of the *munafiq* come in many garbs and guises but, like all those who are dishonest, the outward appearance will rarely reflect the truth of their intentions. It is not merely poetry to say that they are snakelike – soft on the outside but harbouring the same deadly venom within. One need only to look carefully at the story of Adam *nabi* [prophet] to see how.

They may tell you they are there to help and answer your questions, this mere claim being designed to imply that it is not possible to find those answers within the official realms of D'awat. They have one aim and one aim only – the same aim of *Shaitaan* [Satan] (l.a.) himself as he was being cast out from paradise when he proclaimed he would lead mankind astray.

Many of us want answers to our questions and truly we should go seeking them. But does that mean looking for them in the wrong places? When the only aim is to disprove and slur the truth how is it possible that the innocent will find it there? ...

... *Bara'at* is essential – for the protection of those that still require knowledge for their firmness of conviction and for the continued wellbeing of those who have acquired such conviction. This *bara'at* entails total abstinence from the words and invitations of munafiqeen in whatever form they may take – be it the printed word or electronic media or the rumours that creep in from the fringes of *jamaats* [faith communities].[36]

It would be interesting to assess the impact of the 'electronic media' on decision-making processes in the Dawoodi Bohra communities, which are in many ways 'closed' to academic researchers and external assessment. Exploring a site such as Mumineen.org also offers alternatives to the so-called mainstream understandings of Islam, in relation to interpretative approaches and issues of language. The Bohra communities' focus on religious leadership and spiritual authority is integral to their understanding and interpretation of Islam. Attention is drawn to issues surrounding 'translation' and interpretation of the Qur'an in Arabic, which might contradict some traditional Sunni authorities' perspectives (as represented elsewhere in this book). It is useful to reproduce some of the discussion here, as it contrasts sharply a challenge to conventional knowledge in relation to interpretation and authority, especially in its predominant online manifestation, as this is a (minority) Shi'a perspective originating from outside of the Middle East:

> What's the harm in reading a translation? Surely some understanding is better than none at all. Why be suspicious of translations by well-meaning scholars? What is the best translation? Why not have one approved by Aqa Mawla (TUS) [Bohra spiritual leader]?
>
> These are some of the questions raised recently on the Qur'an.
>
> … It was not by accident that Arabic was chosen for this Final Revelation. The language itself was nurtured in preparation for this task. The word Allah written in Arabic, for example, contains volumes of information that is completely lost if written in any other script. We know how Amirul Mu'mineen (SA) spent an entire night talking of the meaning of the dot (nuqta) under the letter 'be' of *bismillah*, without exhausting the subject.
>
> Now how can anyone think that such knowledge can be preserved in translations? In fact, can it even be understood if one knows Arabic fluently? Let me say that being fluent in Arabic will help very little when it comes to understanding the real revelations or the miraculous nature of the Qur'an. Sure, knowing Arabic will help appreciate its poetry, its eloquence and some of its literal meaning, which is quite an achievement in itself. After all, Qur'anic composition remains unchallenged in its beauty and majesty. However, the real import of the revelation transcribed in the Qur'an can hardly be obtained simply by reading its literal meaning. If this were not true, then all speakers of the Arabic language would be transformed into saints immediately on reading the Qur'an as they would be privy to the revelation

contained therein. We know this is not so simply by looking at the Arab world.[37]

The article, by Shaikh Mustafa Abdulhussein, stresses that full knowledge of Islam is something that can be divinely inspired, rather than 'learnt' in a conventional framework of 'Islamic education', and that there are levels of 'understanding':

> So the real knowledge of the Qur'an can only be taught to us by one who has been allowed by Allah to do so. That person is Allah's Wali [God's representative, the Dawoodi Bohra spiritual leader, the representative of the Imam or the Dai al-Mutlaq] in each age, the Imam (SA). Rasulullah (SAW) tied the Qur'an and its interpreters in his famous words: 'I leave behind two things, the Book of Allah (Qur'an) and my progeny. Whosoever adheres to them both will never go astray.' Amirul Mu'mineen (SA) called himself Qur'an-e-Natiq [voiced], and the book itself Qur'an-e-Samit [silent] to demonstrate this point.
>
> Aqa Mawla (TUS) [the Dawoodi Bohra leader] has said (I have heard this myself, in London) words to this effect: '*Mu'mineen*! [believers] Recite the Qur'an daily. You may not understand much of what you recite, but you should recite it daily nevertheless. An *alim* [scholar] could understand the Qur'an more, and one of higher *ilm* [knowledge] even more and so on until finally, the Imam (SA) – his very being is the Qur'an.[38]

The article stresses that only through listening to sermons, statements and reading books from the Dai al-Mutlaq and other religious leaders is it possible to understand Islam. This has implica-tions on a number of levels, not least of which (in the context of this book) being the approach towards sacred texts and the statements concerning online authority articulated on a number of Islamic websites worldwide. These pages stress that a different paradigm of religious authority is required in the Dawoodi Bohra Cyber Islamic Environment, compared with the mainstream Shi'a or Sunni contexts.

Shi'a cyberspace also contains a number of other channels of authority, including extensive resources in audio format, such as lectures and sermons. Azadari.com, registered in Dubai and Bombay, offers 'salutations to the martyrs of Karbala' (associated with the death of Ali's son, Husayn), and has organised substantial resources of materials into categories, which incorporate sermons, recitations and religious songs.[39] There is also a category relating to *fiqh* jurisprudence, presented in the form of lectures on subjects associated with ritual practice and prayers; the lectures were 'recited' by the 'Late Allama Zeeshan Haider Jawadi', suggesting that authority can operate 'beyond the grave' from cyberspace.[40]

Shi'a cyberspace is not fully 'populated' or represented, at least in terms of decision-making concerns. At the time of writing, it was difficult to track down legitimate, belief-centred sites associated with aspects of Shi'ism. This may be for reasons of web access, particularly for Zaydi Shi'a, whose greatest numbers can be found in the Yemen. The Zaydis, which represent an early 'break' within Shi'ism, have been discussed in other Shi'a forums, in terms of their legitimacy and interpretations. For example, the Aalim Network posted a question on Zaydis, which exemplified their ideological and theological inspiration (Imam Zayd) whilst suggesting that he did not claim the imamate for himself.[41] There appears to be no online Zaydi response to this, suggesting a lack of representation online, compared with the 'wired' communities of Dawoodi Bohras.

Others have a distinctly diaspora identity, such as the American Druze Society's site, which was in development at the time of writing. Druze Islam (in its various forms) represents a distinct, esoteric and at times secretive schism from 'mainstream' Shi'a beliefs. The American Druze Society's opening page stresses the importance of the Internet for their future networking and development:

> The Druze people have been on the move for the past 1000 years as they've populated new and existing communities all over the world. The Druze are no more confined to the Middle East as they have spread their way of life and faith to all the places they have inhabited. With this expansion, a new modern means of knitting the Druze communities is a must so that they can continue to promote their message of *Tawhid* (Unitarianism) in the ever-growing global village of humanity. The advent of the computer age and the information superhighway in the form of the Internet has made such a means possible. The American Druze Society has taken the lead in developing and maintaining this Druze Web page for the benefit of all the Druze people wherever they live.
>
> The combination of the latest technology available and freedom of expression will bring an in-depth understanding of the Druze faith for all to understand and share.[42]

Whilst Druze resources are frequently of an academic nature on the Internet, there are some other pages created by Druze which have content of an 'authoritative' nature. For example, Druze.net claims particular authority from the Lebanon:

> Druzenet is brought to you from Lebanon under the sponsorship of Mashiakhat El-Akel, the highest Druze Spiritual Reference in the Middle East and world wide.[43]

Content is in Arabic and English, with a selection of publications based on 'ancient Druze wisdom', primarily of a theological nature. There is no 'question-and-answer' facility.

CONCLUDING COMMENT: SHI'ISM

Shi'a cyberspace features many aspects of Shi'a beliefs, although there is an imbalance towards the (relatively) technology-rich communities. New resources are starting to emerge in Farsi and other languages, which will require future analysis and observation. They may be Shi'a minorities within a wider Shi'a community, or minorities compared with Sunni and other populations. The historical, theological and cultural notion of dispersal seems to fit with the application of Internet technology, at least in terms of reinforcing identity and authority in diverse global Shi'a settings. Despite the fact that access to the Internet may still be in the hands of the few, there is potential for the pulse of Internet authority to resonate within a wider community, given that it is frequently educated people of influence who are accessing the technology. Whether this model will change, when or if Internet access widens to other literate Shi'a communities, is something worthy of future observation.

LOCATING SUFI RELIGIOUS AUTHORITY ON THE INTERNET

The patterns of mystical Islam cannot be stereotyped or reduced to a single paradigm. The spiritual guide, or *murshid*, may be the most appropriate individual to follow from within the aspects of esoteric Islam associated (by commentators, if not always practitioners) with *tasawwuf*, or Sufism. This is a broad framework, discussed elsewhere by the writer.[44] The following is an overview of the phenonena, with particular relevance to the discussion on online authority and its place in the world today. It is less extensive than the Sunni and Shi'a discussions, because of the nature of the content and the sites, and their approaches towards the Internet: there is less demand for (quasi-) legalistic opinions or tracts from readers.

The role of Sufism in relation to religious authority is a critical one. Different 'orders' may approach the nature of authority in diverse ways, relating to religious knowledge, culture, language, translation and the sense of 'spirituality'. The notion of a '*fatwa*' or *ijtihad* may be familiar to Sufi practitioners, but the format and language of spiritual authority is transmitted in many different ways. Not all can necessarily be articulated, although some have attempted to place the words of the Sufi sages into the web's languages of HTML (and increasingly other formats). Sufism has been stereotyped at times as quietist and meditative, and any talk of 'jihad' has been seen as linked to the greater jihad of 'spiritual striving' rather than militaristic forms of the concept(s).

Perhaps there are examples of militaristic contemplative Sufi warriors online; however, in the following section, the emphasis is on the 'inner struggle', as reflected in the work of Abu Hamid Muhammad al-Ghazali (1059–1111), the Sufi philosopher, academic and ascetic who perceived jihad as part of an approach towards knowledge.[45] Al-Ghazali influenced many saints and scholars after him (not all of whom agreed with him!), whose mystical way is now reflected to a degree in cyberspace. Many Sufi scholars and philosophers are well represented online, particularly in academic-related sites (beyond the scope of this section).[46] For example, many of al-Ghazali's works can be found in Arabic and translations.[47]

Sufism can be integrated into the content of general 'Islam' sites, such as al-Sunnah Foundation (above). Notions of authority can include guidance for those seeking to travel on the spiritual path. The Naqshbandi order, as represented on one site by Mawlana Shaykh Nazim Adil al-Haqqani, offers material on subjects as diverse as:

- Have you worshipped too much?
- Limit your Ego or Don't Worry!
- Look Not to the Faults of Others
- Seek Your Sustenance
- Depression: Cause & Cure
- Knowledge from Divine Presence. [48]

This forms part of a detailed and pro-active Naqshbandi site, containing online prayer, recitation and ritual guidance.[49]

Approaches to religious interpretation can be found on a variety of 'Sufi' sites, some based around individuals rather than particular orders. The writer has discussed elsewhere how Shayke Abdoulaye Dieye, the spiritual head of the Senegal-based Muridiyya brotherhood, networks to branches worldwide and provides spiritual advice through the Tariqat-ul-Muridiyya website.[50] A site devoted to Nawob Gudri Shah Baba (d. 1996) explores *fikr* or 'Concentrated observation of the Divine Nature',[51] as well as providing information and images from a broad range of Sufi influences and shrines; 14 pictures of the shrine of Mui'im al-Din Hasan Chisti (1142–1236) represent a 'virtual pilgrimage' to this site of devotion in India.[52] Chisti is detailed elsewhere on the net, on sites that give indications of the different focus and natures of authority and religious practice amongst his followers: the Hazrat Khwaja Moinudin Hasan Chishti site details teachings, including a full biography of Chisti (linking him closely with Muhammad), whilst also detailing how offerings of free food are made, and observance of prayers (*fateha*) at the tomb should be undertaken.[53] Some orders have integrated with the Internet the concept of online knowledge, notably the Qadiri Rifai Order, which discusses the training of dervishes through introductory Guidance to the Path – backing up this easy-to-navigate resource with further reading (from the order's historical founders Abdul Qadir al Geylani and Ahmed ar Rifai), and links to various branches in the US and elsewhere.[54]

OTHER PERSPECTIVES

Further detailed evaluation of online authority would also have to be undertaken amongst so-called schismatic or syncretic groups, such as the Nation of Islam[55] (and offshoots), and branches of the Ahmadiyya and Qadiani movements. The two distinguish themselves from each other in the way that they view their found Mirza Ghulam Ahmad. Qadiana also describe themselves as 'Ahmadiyya' and see Mirza Ghulam Ahmad as a 'prophet'. The apologetic Lahore Ahmadiyya Movement site aims to counter the image of (their branch of) Ahmadiyya Islam as being a 'deviant sect', and instead represents itself in the mainstream. Ahmadiyya have been accused (especially by some 'Wahhabi' followers) of casting their founder Mirza Ghulam Ahmad in the same light as the Prophet Muhammad.[56]

There are several areas that have not been covered by this discussion. Regions including the Central Asian Republics, where access levels to the Internet remain low, are in a developmental stage in relation to the Internet and online authority. For example, Kazakhstan, whose government defines itself as a 'secular state', appeared to have little in the way of materials in the Kazakh languages about Islam other than a site containing prayers for children to learn.[57] For many regions with substantial Muslim populations, Internet access was in the hands of an elite, being relatively low compared with other global access levels.[58]

A more detailed exploration of Islamic authority online could also encompass other groups, such as the Alawi, who have communities and affiliations in Turkey, Iran, Iraq, Lebanon, Central Asia, the Balkans and Syria – together with substantial diaspora communities elsewhere (particularly Germany). The Alawi's broad and diverse syncretic practices have links with aspects of Sufism and Ismaili beliefs – and have been marginalised from 'mainstream' Sunni Islam. Communities have integrated the Internet into their activities, for example, through Alevi.com (based in Germany), which acts as a hub for community activities, with content in Turkish and German.[59] A significant hub has also been produced in English and Turkish, the former section being aimed at the wide international interest in Sufism: Alevilik-Bektasilik Arastirmalari Sitesi features substantial historical and cultural resources, together with links to music and visual materials. It has taken a quietist online perspective in relation to ritual and the representation of authority, although there are a few pages relating to the Basics of the Faith and Religious Guides.[60] This pragmatic line is probably indicative of the site's Turkish origins; Alawi beliefs have been subsumed by attempts to present Islam as a 'cultural' phenomenon in Turkey and are not recognised as part of 'official Islam' or as a religion in their own right.[61] Such religious views, which may not have a place in traditional maps of Islamic knowledge and understanding, can find a place in cyberspace where they are relatively free to articulate their point of view and propagate their perspectives.

ISLAMIC RELIGIOUS AUTHORITY ONLINE: CONCLUSION

Cyber Islamic Environments have the potential to transform aspects of religious understanding and expression, and the power to enable elements within the population to discuss aspects of religious interpretation and authority with each other, and to consult with authorities both from traditional and non-traditional centres, in some cases subverting what were conventional channels for opinions on religious issues. The question needs to be asked as to whether this enhances or challenges traditional forms of knowledge about Islam. One difficulty is clearly measuring the effect the Internet may have, given the substantial range of sites and contents. As access levels rise, in some contexts websites could develop to become a significant channel of information and a means of reinforcing or developing identity(-ies) for Muslim individuals and organisations. One means for this development – including *fatwas, ijtihad* and other forms of religious and spiritual authority in HTML and other formats – makes it a critical area for research, observation and discussion in the future.

NOTES

1. In particular, see Gary R. Bunt, *Virtually Islamic* (Cardiff: University of Wales Press, 2000), pp. 47–57, and Gary R. Bunt, 'Surfing Islam', in J.K. Hadden and D.E. Cowan (eds.), *Computer-mediated Communication and Cyber Islamic Environments* (New York: Elsevier Science, 2000), pp. 140–2.
2. Discussed in Bunt, *Virtually Islamic*, pp. 110–14.
3. Shiachat, www.shiachat.com.
4. E-Jihad.net, www.islamicdigest.net/ej/.
5. Taliyah al-Mahdi, Forum, Reply to a recent letter from a Sunni Sister, www.taliyah.org/boarddir/viewthread.php?tid=70.
6. Taliyah al-Mahdi, Forum, Relationship between Sunni Islamic Movement and Wahhabiya?, www.taliyah.org/boarddir/viewthread.php?tid=415.
7. Taliyah al-Mahdi, 'Isa Adam Nazir, 'Ayat'ul-Mahdi: Questions and Answers About the Double Eclipse of Ramadan 2003', www.taliyah.org/articles/ayat.shtml.
8. Ali Khamene'i, About, www.wilayah.net/english/about/index.htm.
9. See Ali Khamene'i, 'Practical Laws of Islam' (Ajwibah al-Istifta'at), www.wilayah.net/english/ahkam/index.htm. Khamene'i is discussed in Bunt, *Virtually Islamic*, 53.
10. Ali Khamene'i, www.wilayah.net/english/ahkam/jihad.htm.
11. Ali Khamene'i, Rules of Imitation, www.wilayah.net/english/ahkam/taqlid.htm.
12. Ali Khamene'i, www.wilayah.net/english/ahkam/taqlid.htm#f08.
13. Ibid.
14. Geneive Abdo, 'Cyberspace Frees Iran's Rebel Cleric', *Guardian*, 5 August 2000, www.guardianunlimited.co.uk/Archive/Article/0,4273,4047913,00.html. Also see Ali Montazeri, www.montazeri.com.
15. Q Bank, www.al-shia.org/html/eng/books/q&a/fehrest.htm.
16. Our Q, www.al-shia.org/html/eng/q&a/ourq.htm.
17. Latest Q, www.al-shia.org/html/eng/q&a/last.htm, August 2002.
18. Latest Q, www.al-shia.org/html/eng/q&a/last.htm.
19. Theological Library, www.al-shia.org/html/eng/index.htm.
20. Ibid.

21. Ayatullah Muhammad Taqi Misbah Yazdi, www.mesbahyazdi.com.
22. Shi'a Islamic Laws, www.follower.4t.com/laws.html.
23. Khoja Shi'a Ithna Asharis and their use of the Internet are discussed in Bunt, *Virtually Islamic*, pp. 56–7.
24. Al-Islam also hosts Inquiries About Islam, Imam Mohamad Jawad Chirri, www.al-islam.org/inquiries/index.html and al-Imam 'Abd al-Husayn Sharaf al-Din al-Musawi, Questions on Jurisprudence (Masa'il Fiqhiyya), Translator Liyakatali Takim, Ontario, Hydery Canada, 1996, www.al-islam.org/masail. This work by al-Musawi (1872–1957) is essentially a 'classic' Shi'a text, reproduced online.
25. Al-Islam, 'Contemporary Legal Rulings in Shi'i Law in Accordance with the Rulings (*fatawa*) of Ayatullah al-'Uzma al-Sayyid 'Ali al-Husayni al-Seestani', translated by Hamid Mavani, 1996, Ahlul Bayt (a) Digital Islamic Library Project, www.al-islam.org/laws/contemporary.
26. WatanOnline, Wahhabis: The Real Terrorists, http://follower.4t.com/terrorism.html.
27. Muhammad Tijani al-Samawi, Shi'a are the Real Ahl Al-Sunnah, Translated by Yasin T. al-Jibouri, New Jersey, Pyam-e-Aman, n.d. www.al-shia.com/html/eng/books/shia-real/index.htm.
28. Islamic Research, Anniversary of Imam Khomani, www.islamic research.org/anniversary_of_imam_khomani_r.htm.
29. Islamic Research, Council of Shia Ulama (Scholars), www.islamic research.org/Pages/UlamaCouncil.htm.
30. Al-Khoei, Question, www.al-khoei.org/question.asp.
31. Imam Khoei Islamic Centre, Fatwa, Taqlid, www.alkhoei.org.uk/fatawa/1taghleed.htm, Ghusl, Wudu and Tamammum, www.alkhoei.org.uk/fatawa/5ghasaal4.htm.
32. Ismaili Web, www.amaana.org/ismaili.html.
33. See Jonah Blank's discussion of the role of computers in Bohra networking. *Mullahs on the Mainframe: Islam and Modernity among the Daudi Bohras* (Chicago, London: University of Chicago Press, 2001), pp. 176–9 et passim.
34. Mumineen.org, DBNet Matrimonials, http://matrimonial.mumineen.org.
35. Mumineen.org, Mulla Mustafa Shaikh Dawood, 'Bara'at', http://archive.mumineen.org/deen/mf_baraat.html.
36. Ibid.
37. Mumineen.org, Shaikh Mustafa Abdulhussein, 'On the Use of Translations of the Qur'an', http://archive.mumineen.org/deen/translate.html (edited for grammatical and typographical errors).
38. Ibid.
39. Azadari.com, www.azadari.com.
40. Azadari.com, Late Allama Zeeshan Haider Jawadi, 'Collection of Fiqh Lectures on Different Topics Recited in 1995', www.azadari.com/jawadi/zhjfiqh.htm?.
41. Aalim Network, 'Zaydis – An Ithna'ashari view', 7 August 1997, www.al-islam.org/organizations/AalimNetwork/msg00420.html.
42. American Druze Society, www.druze.com.
43. Druze.net, www.druzenet.org/druzenet/dnenglish.html.
44. Bunt, *Virtually Islamic*, pp. 58–65.

45. See Sunnah.org, Al-Ghazali, 'Ghazali on Jihad', www.sunnah.org/ tasawwuf/jihad002.html.
46. The best example is Islamic Philosophy Online, www.muslimphiloso phy.com.
47. Al-Ghazali's Website, www.muslimphilosophy.com/gz/.
48. Naqshbandi Sufi Way, www.naqshbandi.org/suhba/default.htm.
49. Naqshbandi Sufi Way are discussed in Bunt, *Virtually Islamic*, pp. 59–60.
50. Tariqat-ul-Muridiyya are discussed in Bunt, in Hadden and Cowan (eds.), 'Surfing Islam', pp. 144–5. Tariqat-ul-Muridiyya, http://freespace. virgin.net/ismael.essop/index.htm.
51. Zahuri Sufi Web Site, www.zahuri.dircon.co.uk/fikr.htm.
52. Zahuri Sufi Web Site, www.zahuri.dircon.co.uk/shrines_index.htm.
53. Hazrat Khwaja Moinudin Hasan Chishti, www.gharibnawaz.com.
54. Qadiri Rifai Order, www.qadiri-rifai.org/.
55. Nation of Islam, www.noi.org.
56. The Lahore Ahmadiyya Movement site includes 100 'basic' questions on Islam. www.muslim.org.
57. Salaam Central Asia, 'Islam in Kazakhstan', www.ummah.com/salaam centralasia/islam_in_kazakhstan.htm. The related Salaam Kyrgyzstan contains limited 'religious' content: www.ummah.com/salaamkyrgyz stan.
58. 'Mediterranean Islamic Expression on the World Wide Web', in *Islam and the Shaping of the Current Islamic Reformation*, Barbara Allen Roberson (ed.) (London: Frank Cass & Co., 2003).
59. Alevi.com, www.alevi.com.
60. Alevilik-Bektasilik Arastirmalari Sitesi, www.alevibektasi.com/index1. html.
61. For a useful overview to Alawi beliefs, see Alevilik-Bektasilik Arastirmalari Sitesi, John Shindeldecker, 'Turkish Alevis in the 21st Century', www.ale- vibektasi.com/xalevis_home.htm.

11   Islam in the Digital Age

This book has sought to demonstrate that activism and decision-making are two dominant zones in Cyber Islamic Environments, although there can be a blurring between *fatwas* and forms of e-jihad. Elements of both zones are located in the margins of online Muslim activities: certain religious opinions are safer to articulate in cyberspace than in real space and time, whilst the application of disruptive technologies (whether classified as jihad or not) remains in the hands of informed dislocated groups, networks and individuals, not necessarily formally organised under a single banner or associated with one another. They represent examples of the growing electronic connectivity between Muslims living in minority and majority settings, which in some cases augment or supersede traditional networking. It is recognised that computer technology is not accessible to all, and the 'digital divide' is a prominent factor in many Muslim societies. The polarity exists within communities, and it is likely that the media remains in the hands of an educated elite, particularly in some contexts with Muslim majority populations, where access to technology is expensive and where there are limited channels for public computer usage. If (or when) technology for surfing the World Wide Web becomes cheaper, the availability of alternative interfaces may offer improved access for marginalised individuals and communities. These interfaces could take the form of subsidised Internet cafés and other forms of public access, dedicated e-mail and Internet-only hardware, telephone and television interfaces, wireless technology and cheaper computers (including hardware produced and manufactured in Muslim contexts). The relationship of Internet media with other media channels is also one worthy of analysis, especially given the levels of content provided by newspapers and broadcasters, which competes with 'new' Internet portals and channels.

Technology alone is insufficient: there is also the issue of educating users on the medium, to ensure an equality of access between and within generations. Islamic content populating websites *could* be a persuasive factor in enhancing the appeal of the medium, encouraging the extension and development of new forms of Muslim communities in cyberspace, representing a broader range of class and experience. It has to be said that, in some contexts, the issue of literacy itself is an important one (before individuals acquire computers). However, the presence of the Internet could encourage literacy development, whilst the development of software packages (including Islamic content) for non-literate peoples could also represent an extension of Cyber Islamic Environments. Touch-screen technologies and voice recognition systems are two means through which computers can empower non-literate societies, *if* the technologies are made available. Such provision could be motivated by Muslim propagation (*da'wa*), even encouraging people to explore online *fatwas* (in audio-visual and written forms) or to read or even participate in forms of electronic jihad. However, even the most optimistic advocate of the medium as a means of propagating Islam would identify formidable infrastructure barriers inhibiting such developments in the short term, although they may point to increasing levels of access in some urban settings; beyond these barriers are other constructions preventing access, such as cultural and linguistic constraints. The former category could incorporate gender factors, whilst the latter might include those speakers of languages that are not widely represented at present on the Internet.

The websites and perspectives discussed in this book do not follow rigid nation-state boundaries of interest, and at times associate themselves with more globalised concepts associated with specific understandings of Islam and Muslim identity. These websites are currently read and created primarily by an 'elite' (and for an elite), although this does not necessarily negate them as an influence (given the trickle-down factor).

Despite many within its audience forming a relatively educated elite, Internet technology has had a major role to play in the post 9-11 contexts, which redefined relationships between Islam, Muslims and the West. The term 'the West' is perhaps ambiguous or even redundant when discussing Islam and the Internet, given their circulation and expression in a variety of fora, between and within 'western' contexts and other Muslim environments. There is, of course, no reason why Muslims should not use and apply technology, although some orientalistic stereotyping would suggest otherwise, and some observers have been surprised at the levels of technological sophistication found in Cyber Islamic Environments, and the means through which these have engendered and developed traditional and radical new networking patterns.

A significant number of major Islamic sites have their origins in the 'West', although such identity is not always obvious to the casual visitor to a site. The globalising influence in relation to issues of identity is a prominent one in many areas of cyberspace, but especially in relation to Muslims. In some cases, as has been seen in this book, it can be difficult or impossible to determine the origins of particular statements associated with Islam. Online identities, already cloaked in anonymity, allow the expression of ideas and agendas that may not be possible in other locations (for example, for reasons of censorship, security or local sensitivities). However, given security concerns, it was perhaps surprising to some commentators that proactive, 'militant' statements in support of organisations such as the Taliban and al-Qaeda were emerging from Internet sites hosted, maintained and registered in 'western' contexts. 9-11 and its aftermath certainly highlighted Islamic cyberspace to a wider audience, but it also stimulated the development of new sites and content from a variety of perspectives, debating the issues raised in a way that was impossible in other media. It also emphasised security concerns and issues of freedom of expression. Whilst Islamic cyberspace cannot be reduced to a single paradigm or point of view, this did not stop some individuals and organisations from trying to disrupt or close (through legal and other channels) Muslim websites, a number of which suffered a barrage of abusive e-mail and attacks. This in turn has encouraged a culture of Internet security awareness in Cyber Islamic Environments, and investment (in hours and finance), of firewalls and other barriers to stop infiltration and disruption of websites.

This post 9-11 increase in Internet awareness about Muslim cyberspace (from Muslims and others) was coupled with a natural increase in Islamic online content, which reflected a global pattern during 2001. Whilst not negating the digital divide issue, the expansion of a proliferation of Arabic and other language 'Islamic sites' and Internet content emerging from Muslim majority contexts was very significant. One commentator even suggested that Arabic was now the dominant language for Islamic Internet discourse:

Speaking at the Ninth International Conference on 'Youth and Globalization,' ... Dr. Adnan Khalil Basha, secretary-general of the International Islamic Relief Organization (IIRO), pointed out that 88 percent of the Internet users covered by his survey went online for Dawah purposes.

Further, the survey revealed that the technical supervision of these sites was carried out by individuals and not by organizations. Dr. Basha called upon the ministries concerned with Islamic affairs to pay special attention to this medium in view of its growing popularity in all sections of society, especially the youth.[1]

At the time of writing it was not possible to see the research basis of that statement, although it did highlight the need for more language-specific research. The growth of Islamic materials in languages other than English on the Internet will inevitably increase the amount of this 'personal' material, and perhaps shift the current emphasis away from Muslim sites emerging from 'western' contexts, back to the traditional centres of Islamic learning. It may be that there will be an extension of the ideological and spiritual battle in cyberspace for the attention of those surfers interested in Islam-related websites. The increasing applications and utility of multi-media will contribute to this dialogue, facilitating an increase in online Islamic events and resources, and emphasising the need for systematic and integrating methods of recording, cataloguing and archiving such site content for future research.

Future research might also construct maps of web-browsing patterns, for example to determine the routeing of site content, and the origins of site visitors. Such 'cyber-geography' can produce digital mapping of a complex variety of Islamic sites.[2] For example, a Beta version of Tracemap can produce a graphical depiction of Internet routeing for any domain, allowing the user to 'see' the spatial links between networks and sites.[3] Through application of such software, in the future it will be possible to create new maps of Islamic perspectives and affiliations in cyberspace. This technology is becoming increasingly available through a variety of channels to other interested parties.

Whether all of this has any impact on traditional networks is still open to question and further research, probably benefiting from a distance of time from events (which are changing as the writer types!). If impact is measured in the significant events of an individual or community, then those people influenced by the online pronouncements contained in a sermon or *fatwa* are influenced by the Internet. This may also be true if the sermon is derived from the Internet, but disseminated through traditional channels. Clearly, the originators of authoritative *fatwa* sites are motivated by the numbers of visitors to their pages and the ways in which questions are formulated and sent to them online.

The impact of disruptive online activity 'in the name of Islam' is more difficult to measure: if such disruption has a physical or psychological impact on its 'target', is that a measurement of success? It may form part of 'mission' (*da'wa*) or be described as a 'jihad'; but that could just be a convenient label for commentators to apply, and certainly in some cases the application of the term e-jihad (and its root jihad) has to be challenged or used with caution. Digital swords may be effective on selected targets, but be unnoticed in the non-digital sphere. If such disruptive activities spread to the computers that influence everyday lives in some 'target' communities, then more attention may be paid to e-jihad outside those with technical interests and (some) observers of contemporary Muslim expression.

Observing such politicking in cyberspace is a formidable task in itself, probably requiring a division of labour amongst an academic conglomerate. Such cyber fieldwork could also be coupled with 'real' fieldwork, observing the application of Internet sites at ground level, although this requires substantial investment of time and resources – perhaps coupled with teams of researchers operating under shared methodologies. At this stage, such ideals are not matched with realities, although over time it is anticipated that the Internet will form an integral component of conventional fieldwork on Islamic issues.

The application of forms of electronic media by activist organisations, and by clandestine groups such as al-Qaeda, has yet to be fully proven. In some cases, there is a sensationalistic aspect to the reporting, together with suggestions (or a subtext) that the media should somehow be more regulated and in some contexts censored. This belies a lack of understanding of the nature or possibility of such controls, especially outside of domestic arenas. Opposition groups to the Saudi Arabian regime (and their supporters), for example, have been able to circumvent restrictions on producing and accessing the content of critical sites, despite substantial investment in blocking technology in the Kingdom.

The extent to which the Internet is opening up new channels of communication for marginalised groups remains an area requiring further detailed research, especially in association with gender issues. Questions which still need to be approached include how Muslim women are applying the medium in relation to Islam, and whether typologies of female Cyber Islamic Environments are emerging; alternatively, are women being 'relegated' to sections within sites, or being simply content rather that content originators? Separate but related issues have emerged associated with marginalised Muslim perspectives, in terms of political, interpretative, social and/or cultural affiliations and orientations. The issue of Muslim women on the Internet is a very important one, which the writer hopes will be fully researched by appropriate specialists in the field. For reasons of ethics and gender, the writer did not wish to enter as a researcher or anonymous passive observer into the areas of all-female Muslim cyberspace (for example, mailing lists and chatrooms) that could be defined by some as e-*hijab* (covered) or e-*haram* (forbidden).

The consequences of 9-11 have demonstrated that, despite the web being available only to an educated elite, it has been applied as a means of dialogue and dissemination during the crisis, where its immediacy in terms of publication and circumnavigation of censorship has been particularly relevant. The Cyber Islamic discourse is part of a wider dialogue by Muslims (not necessarily within Islamic websites), and indeed contributes to the global opinion contained on the web after 9-11. Its impact may not be as sustained as the Al-Jazeera satellite channel (which has a well-developed website), but does offer evidence of the 'personal' nature of Internet usage within cyber Islamic environments.

Whether the articulation in cyberspace of jihad and *fatwa* would have been familiar to the Prophet Muhammad in the seventh century is open to question. Certainly some of the conceptual themes are contained in the Qur'an, which is deemed to be a divine source, and in the body of authoritative scholarship surrounding the paradigm of the Prophet (such as his sayings). The development of intellectual themes associated with *fatwa* and jihad were integral to the intellectual, theological and philosophical activities undertaken through Muslim networks in a rapidly expanding arena, during the centuries following Muhammad's death. The themes of jihad and notions of authority integral to the concept of a *fatwa* were developed and refined in Islamic centres and institutions, as well as by individual scholars, politicians and otherwise 'inspired' people. In hadith scholarship, the notion of a train of transmission validates or negates (in a sliding scale) the attributes of knowledge contained in Muhammad's statements and actions, based on the levels of 'authority' of the transmitters. The process of knowledge transmission has now entered a new electronic phase, one that is closely connected to (and perhaps a continuation of) a process, which is idealised in a number of Muslim contexts as dating back to the

Prophet. The speed of transmission has now increased, subject to bandwidth. By seeing it as part of this process, it may be that the technology will become so natural that it is ignored altogether, being seamless with the extracts from the Qur'an that were inscribed on rocks and skins, and memorised in the minds of believers. For an elite, the Internet now forms part of a religious conceptual framework, incorporating symbols, divine utterances, sacred texts and the power to inspire and motivate individuals in both their personal practice and in wider worldly and sacred goals. A fusion of electronic, neural and divine circuits have integrated themselves in the minds of believers, and it is through a digital interface that an increasing number of people will view their religion and their place in the Muslim worlds, affiliated to wider communities in which 'the West' becomes, at least in cyberspace, increasingly redundant.

NOTES

1. Javid Hassan, 'Most Islamic websites are in Arabic: Survey', *Arab News*, http://arabnews.com/Article.asp?ID=20030.
2. Atlas of Cyberspace, www.cybergeography.org/atlas/surf.html.
3. Matrix, http://tracemap.mids.org/test/tracemap/.

Bibliography

THE QUR'AN

Interpretations of the Meaning of the Holy Qur'an in the English Language, Muhammad Taqi-ud-Din al-Hilali and Muhammad Muhsin Khan (Riyadh: Maktba Dar-us-Salam, 1993)

The Message of the Qur'an, Translated and Explained by Muhammad Asad (Gibraltar: Dar al-Andalus, 1980, 1984, 1993)

The Qur'an: Text, Translation and Commentary, trans. Abdullah Yusuf Ali (Jeddah: Islamic Education Centre, 1934, 1946)

HADITH

Anas, Malik ibn, *Al-Muwatta, Imam Malik*, 'A'isha 'Abdarahman at-Tarjumana and Ya'qub Johnson (trans.) (Norwich: Diwan Press, 1982)

Al-Qushayri, Muslim b. al-Hajjaj, *Sahih Muslim*, Abdul Hamid Siddiqui (trans.) (Lahore: Sh. Muhammad Ashraf, 1971–75)/International Islamic University, Malaysia, www.iiu.edu.my/deed/hadith/muslim/

PUBLISHED TEXTS

Ahmed, Akbar S. and Hastings Donnan, 'Islam in the Age of Postmodernity', in *Islam, Globalization and Postmodernity*, Akbar S. Ahmed and Hastings Donnan (eds.), (London: Routledge, 1994)

Alavi, Hamza, 'Ethnicity, Muslim Society, and the Pakistan Ideology', in *Islamic Reassertion in Pakistan: The Application of Islamic Laws in a Modern State*, Anita M. Weiss (ed.) (New York: Syracuse University Press, 1986)

Anderson, Jon W., 'Arabizing the Internet', *Emirates Occasional Papers*, 30 (1998)

Anderson, Jon W. and Dale F. Eickelman (eds.), *New Media in the Muslim World: The Emerging Public Sphere* (Bloomington: Indiana University Press, 1999)

Antrim, Zayle G., 'Renegotiating Islam: the Reception of al-'Ashmawi's *al-Islam al-siyasi* in the Egyptian Press', *Bulletin of the Royal Institute of Inter-Faith Studies*, Vol. 1, No. 1, 1999

Arquilla, John and David Ronfeldt, 'Cyberwar is Coming!', *Comparative Strategy*, Vol. 12, No. 2, Spring 1993, 141-65

Arquilla, John and David Ronfeldt (eds.), *Networks and Netwars: The Future of Terror, Crime and Militancy* (California: RAND, 2001)

al-'Ashmawi, Muhammad Sa'id, *al-Islam al-siyasi* (Cairo: Sinan li al-Nashr, 1992)

Blank, Jonah, *Mullahs on the Mainframe: Islam and Modernity among the Daudi Bohras* (Chicago, London: The University of Chicago Press, 2001)

Brouwer, Lenie, 'Muslimmail in the Netherlands', paper presented at the 'Writing Diasporas' conference, Virtual Diasporas strand, University of Wales, Swansea, 22 September 2000

Brückner, Matthias, *Fatwas zum Alkohol unter dem Einfluss neuer Medien im 20. Jhdt* (Würzburg: Ergon-Verlag, 2000)

Bunt, Gary R., 'Decision-Making and Idjtihad in Islamic Environments: A Comparative Study of Pakistan, Malaysia, Singapore, and the United Kingdom' (PhD thesis, Lampeter: University of Wales, 1996)

Bunt, Gary R., 'Islam in Cyberspace: Islamic Studies Resources on the World Wide Web', *Muslim World Book Review*, Vol. 18, No. 1, 1997, 3-13

Bunt, Gary R., '*islam@britain.net*: "British Muslim" Identities in Cyberspace', *Islam and Christian-Muslim Relations*, Vol. 10, 1999, 353-63

Bunt, Gary R., 'Surfing Islam: Ayatollahs, Shayks and Hajjis on the Superhighway', in *Religion on the Internet: Research Prospects and Promises*, Jeffrey K. Hadden and Douglas E. Cowan (eds.), (New York, Elsevier Science, 2000)

Bunt, Gary R., *Virtually Islamic: Computer-mediated Communication and Cyber Islamic Environments* (Cardiff: University of Wales Press, 2000)

Bunt, Gary R., *The Good Web Guide to World Religions* (London: The Good Web Guide, 2001)

Bunt, Gary R., 'Islam Interactive: Mediterranean Islamic Expression on the World Wide Web', in *Islam and the Shaping of the Current Islamic Reformation*, Barbara Allen Roberson (ed.) (London: Frank Cass, 2003)

Castells, Manuel, *The Rise of the Network Society* (Oxford and Malden: Blackwell, 1996)

cooke, miriam and Bruce B. Lawrence (eds.), *Muslim Networks Across Time* (Chapel Hill: North Carolina Press, forthcoming)

Denning, Dorothy E. 'Activism, Hacktivism and Cyberterrorism', in *Networks and Netwars: The Future of Terror, Crime and Militancy*, John Arquilla and David Ronfeldt (eds.), (California: RAND, 2001)

Duran, Khalid, 'Jihadism in Europe', *The Journal of Counterterrorism & Security International*, Vol. 7, No. 1, n.d., 12-15

Dutton, Yasin, *The Origins of Islamic Law: The Qur'an, the Muwatta' and Madinan 'Amal* (London: RoutledgeCurzon, 2nd edn., 2002)

Eickelman, Dale F. and James Piscatori, *Muslim Politics* (Princeton, NJ: Princeton University Press, 1996)

Fadia, Ankit, *Unofficial Guide to Ethical Hacking* (New York: Macmillan, 2001)

Farruki, Kemal A., *Islamic Jurisprudence* (Karachi: Pakistan Publishing House, 1962)

Gauntlett, David (ed.), *Web.Studies: Rewiring Media Studies for the Digital Age* (London: Arnold, 2000)

Jones, Maggie and Neil Beagrie, *Preservation Management of Digital Materials: A Handbook* (London: British Library, 2002)

Kai Hafez (ed.), *Islam and the West in the Mass Media* (Cresskill, NJ: Hampton Press, 2000)

Khadduri, Majid, *War and Peace in the Law of Islam* (Baltimore: Johns Hopkins Press, 1955, 1962)

Lane, Edward W., *An Account of the Manners and Customs of the Modern Egyptians* (London, 1836)

Lawrence, Bruce, *Shattering the Myth: Islam Beyond Violence* (Princeton, NJ: Princeton University Press, 1998)

Leppard, David, 'Cyber Criminals Cost Companies £10 billion a Year', *The Sunday Times*, 14 April 2002

Lings, Martin, *Muhammad: His Life Based on the Earliest Sources* (London: George Allen and Unwin, 1983)

Mandaville, Peter, 'Reimagining the Ummah? Information Technology and the Changing Boundaries of Political Islam', in *Islam Encountering Globalisation*, Ali Mohammadi (ed.) (London: RoutledgeCurzon, 2002)

Marwani, Rizwan, 'Community, Identity and the Internet: The Case of the Ismaili Muslims'. 'The Ismaili Community and the Internet: Exploring an Encounter', n.d., unpublished papers.

Mawdudi, Sayyid Abul A'la, *Towards Understanding Islam* (Safat, Kuwait: Sahaba Islamic Press)

McLuhan, Marshall and Bruce R. Powers, *The Global Village: Transformations in World Life and Media in the 21st Century* (New York and Oxford: Oxford University Press, 1989)

McLuhan, Marshall and Quentin Fiore, *The Medium is the Massage: An Inventory of Effects* (London: Random House, 1967)

Metcalf, Barbara Daly, *Islamic Revival in British India: Deoband, 1860-1900* (Princeton, NJ: Princeton University Press, 1982)

Norris, Pippa, *Digital Divide: Civic Engagement, Information Poverty, and the Internet* (Cambridge: Cambridge University Press, 2001)

Peters, F.E., *A Reader on Classical Islam* (Princeton, NJ: Princeton University Press, 1994)

Qutb, Sayyid, *This Religion of Islam (hadha 'd-din)* (Damascus: IIFSO, 1977)

Reeve, Simon, *The New Jackals: Ramzi Yousef, Osama bin Laden and the Future of Terrorism* (London: André Deutsch, 1999)

Robinson, Neal, *Islam: A Concise Introduction* (London: Curzon Press, 1999)

Saad-Ghorayeb, Amal, *Hizbu'llah: Politics and Religion* (London and Sterling: Pluto Press, 2002)

Said, Edward W., *Orientalism* (London: Routledge and Kegan Paul, 1978).

Said, Edward W., *Culture and Imperialism* (London: Grafton Books, 1993)

Said, Edward W., *Covering Islam: How the Media and the Experts Determine How We See the Rest of the World* (London: Vintage, revised edn., 1997)

Scambray, Joel, Stuart McClure and George Kurtz, *Hacking Exposed* (Berkeley, California; London: McGraw-Hill Professional, 2nd edn., 2000)

Shariati, Ali, *Reflections of Humanity - Two Views of Civilization and the Plight of Man* (Houston: Free Islamic Literatures, 1984)

Statesman, 'Now, Pak Hackers Wage Cyber Jihad', 22 October 2001

Statesman, 'Enter Al-Qaida Alliance on Cyber Battlefield', 24 October 2001.

The Encyclopedia of Islam: New Edition, H.A.R. Gibb et al. (eds.) (Leiden: E.J. Brill, 1960-)

The Times, '"Holy Wars" Website is Shut Down', 4 October 2001

Wheeler, Debbie, 'New Media, Globalization and Kuwaiti National Identity', *The Middle East Journal*, Vol. 54, No. 3, 2000

Wheeler, Debbie, 'Living At E.Speed: A Look at Egypt's E Readiness', in *Economic Challenges and Opportunities in the MENA Region* (Cairo: Economic Research Forum Publications, AUC Press, 2002)

INTERNET SOURCES

Aalim Network, 'Zaydis - An Ithna'ashari View', 7 August 1997, www.
al-islam.org/organizations/AalimNetwork/msg00420.html

Abdo, Geneive, 'Cyberspace Frees Iran's Rebel Cleric', *Guardian*, 5 August
2000, www.guardianunlimited.co.uk/Archive/Article/0,4273,4047913,00.
html

Abdulhussein, Mumineen.org, Shaikh Mustafa, 'On the Use of Translations
of the Qur'an', http://archive.mumineen.org/deen/translate.html

The Age, 'Al-Qaeda Hackers Hijack Sites', 27 October 2002, www.theage.com.au

Agence France Presse/Mena Report, 'Hizbollah, Israel Fight Cyberwar', 6
November 2000, www.menareport.com

Ahmed, Qari Mansoor, Khurasaan.com, 'Why the Difference?', www.
khurasaan.com/s_content.php?id=2002–04–15–3602

Al Than, Mariam, 'Muslims Discouraged against Hacking Israeli Sites', *Islam-
Online*, 17 January 2001, www.islam-online.net/English/News/2001–01/
17/article6.shtml

Alemahr, 'America in Afghanistan', 30 March 2002, www.alemahr.com

Allaahuakbar.net, 'Readings in Elementary Qutubism', www.allaahuakbar.net/
downloads/qutubism.zip

Alleyne, Richard, 'UK Muslims Disown "Lunatic Fringe"', *Daily Telegraph*, 20
September 2001, http://news.telegraph.co.uk

Ananova, 'Text Message Divorces Approved for Muslims', 10 July 2001

Anderson, Jon, 'New Media in the Muslim World: The Emerging Public
Sphere', *ISIM Newsletter*, 5, www.isim.nl/newsletter/5/media/1.html

Anderson, Jon W., 'Is the Internet Islam's "Third Wave" or the "End of
Civilization"?', *Journal of Electronic Publishing*, 1997, www.press.umich.edu/
jep/archive/Anderson.html

Anderson, Jon W., 'Technology, Media, and the Next Generation in the Middle
East', *New Media and Information Technology Working Papers*, 1999,
http://nmit.georgetown.edu/papers/jwanderson.htm

Anti-Defamation League, 'Jihad Online: Islamic Terrorists and the Internet',
www.adl.org/internet/jiha.asp, 2002

Arif, Mir Adeel, Khurasaan.com, 'My 12-day Visit to Afghanistan', www.
khurasaan.com/s_content.php?id=2002–04–08–2905

Ash-Shuaibi, Hammoud bin Uqlaa', Al-Madina, *Fatwa on the Shariah
Implementation of the Taliban Government in Afghanistan*, 29 November 2000,
www.almadinah.org/DawaLinks/talebanfatwa.htm

Associated Press, 'Talib's Anti-American E-mails', reproduced by *Wired*,
www.wired.com/news/politics/0,1283,50286,00.html, 7 February 2002

Azzam, 'Fatwa of Sheikh Hammoud Al-Uqlaa' on the Taliban', 29 November
2000, www.azzam.com

Al-Bawaba, 'Algeria Hopes to Improve Telecommunications by 2010', 10 April
2001, www.al-bawaba.com/news

Al-Bawaba, 'Egypt to Serve Less Privileged Areas with 100 Youth Centers
Yearly', 27 July 2001, www.al-bawaba.com/news

Al-Bawaba, 'Expert: Rising Mideast PC Demand Bucks Global Trend', 15
August 2001, www.al-bawaba.com/news

BBC News Online, 'British Muslims Join "Holy War"', 26 June 2000, http://news.bbc.co.uk/hi/english/uk/newsid-806000/806422.stm

BBC News Online, 'Hamas Hit by Porn Attack', http://news.bbc.co.uk/hi/english/world/middle_east/newsid_1207000/1207551.stm, 7 March 2001

BBC News Online, 'Tracing the Kidnappers' E-mails', 6 February 2002, http://news.bbc.co.uk/hi/english/sci/tech/newsid_1805000/1805173.stm

Bewley, Aisha (trans.) *The Sahih Collection of al-Bukhari* (Muhammad ibn Ismail Bukhari), http://bewley.virtualave.net/bukhcont.html

Blackhurst, Chris, 'Bin Laden Web Link Registered in Suffolk', *Independent*, 28 October 2001, www.independent.co.uk/story.jsp?story=101895

Bölsche, Jochen, 'Mailing-Liste gehackt', *Spiegel Online*, 19 September 2002, www.spiegel.de

Brückner, Matthias, 'IslamiCity - Creating an Islamic Cybersociety', *ISIM Newsletter*, 8, 2001, www.isim.nl/newsletter/8/bruckner.htm

Brunker, Mike, 'Did "Jihad" Arms Course Visit U.S.?', *MSNBC*, 27 December 2001, www.msnbc.com/news

Bunt, Gary R., 'Interface Dialogues: Cyber Islamic Environments and the On-line Fatwa', *ISIM Newsletter* 6, November 2000, http://isim.leidenuniv.nl/newsletter/6/media/1.html

Canadian Office of Critical Infrastructure Protection and Emergency Services, 'Al-Qaida Cyber Capability', 2 November 2001, www.epc-pcc.gc.ca/emergencies/other/TA01–001_E.html

Centre for Islamic Studies and Research, 'From God's Servant Osama ben Laden to the Peoples of the Countries allied with the American Government', 19 December 2002, www.cambuur.net/cocI/indexe.php?subject=2&rec=8

Channel 4 News, '"Jihad" Chef Cleared', 9 August 2002, www.channel4.com/news

Chaos Computer Club, 'CCC Condemns Attacks against Communication Systems', 13 September 2001, www.ccc.de/CRD/CRD20010913.en.html

Chaudhuri, Pramit Pai, 'What are Islamic Fundamentalists Doing in Porn Sites? The CIA Tells You', *Hindustan Times Online*, 18 February 2001, www.hvk.org/articles/0201/92.html

CNN, 'Egyptian Physician with a $5 million Price on his Head', n.d., www.cnn.com/CNN/Programs/people/shows/zawahiri/profile.html

CNN, 'Authorities Track E-mails Sent by Alleged Shoe Bomber', 21 January 2002, www.cnn.com/2002/WORLD/europe/01/21/inv.reid.emails/

Condrey, David, *Black and White*, Hackerthreads, www.hackerthreads.org/downloads/black_white.pdf25

Council on American-Islamic Relations, 'Muslims Question Choice of Author for Book on Islam', 4 April 2001, www.cair-net.org/asp/article.asp?id=347&page=NR

Cullison, Alan and Andrew Higgins, 'Computer in Kabul Holds Chilling Memories', *Wall Street Journal*, 31 December 2001, reproduced on *MSNBC*, www.msnbc.com/news

Cullison, Alan and Andrew Higgins, 'Spy Trip Log Matches Reid's Travels', *The Wall Street Journal*, 16 January 2002, reproduced on *MSNBC*, www.msnbc.com/news

Daba, Hasan Ali, 'Jihad Unspun, Sheikh Qaradawi's Jumu'ah Khutbah, "I Am a Terrorist"', www.jihadunspun.net/IslamUnderAttack/articles/iaat.cfm

Dahlan, Mawlana Shaykhu-l-Islam Ahmad Zayni, 'Fitnatul Wahhabiyyah - The Menace of Wahhabism', As-Sunna Foundation of America, www.sunnah.org/aqida/fitnatulWahhabiyyah.htm

Daily Star, Lebanon, 'Palestinians are Taking the Intifada Online', 2 November 2001, reproduced on Hizbullah's Moqama website, www.moqawama.org/articles/doc_2001/taking.htm

di Justo, Patrick, 'Does Official Taliban Site Exist?', *Wired*, 30 October 2001, www.wired.com/news/0,1294,47956,00.html

Dibbell, Julian, 'In Gold We Trust', *Wired*, 10.01, January 2002, www.wired.com/wired/archive/10.01/egold.html

Eedle, Paul, 'Terrorism.com', *Guardian*, 17 July 2002, www.guardian.co.uk/g2story/0,3604,756498,00.html

El-Nawawy, Mohamed A., 'Profiling Internet Users in Egypt: Understanding the Primary Deterrent against Their Growth in Number', *Internet Society* (2000) www.isoc.org/inet2000/cdproceedings/8d/s8

Fadel, Mohammad, 'On the Validity of Ijtihad from the Viewpoint of Usul (Principles of Islamic Jurisprudence)', As-Sunna Foundation of America, www.sunnah.org/fiqh/usul/on_the_validity_of_ijtihad.htm

Foreign Broadcast Information Service, 'Al-Qa'ida Affiliated Website Back Online; Taliban Official's Statements Reported', 19 July 2002, trans. from al-Sharq al-Awsat. Source: http://cryptome.org/alneda-up.htm (accessed October 2002)

Front Islamique du Salut, 'Claims of Vindication on the Back of a Tragedy', 18 September 2001, www.ccfis.org

Front Islamique du Salut, 'PR30: The Events in the USA and the Vile Opportunists of Algeria', www.ccfis.org

Gold, Steve, 'Alleged Jihad Internet Terrorist Pleads not Guilty', *Computeruser*, 15 October 2001, www.computeruser.com/mews/01.10/15/news2.html

Gonzalez-Quijano, Yves, 'Essai de Cartographie de l'information sur Internet au Liban', 2001, www.pisweb.net/mmm/3_quijano/3-quijano.html

Goodwin, Bill, 'Cybercrime Crackdown on pan-European Scale', *Computer Weekly*, 22 November 2001, www.cw360.com

Greene, Thomas C., 'Celebrity Hacktivist Joins the Mid-East Cyber-war', *The Register*, 7 November 2000, www.theregister.co.uk

Greene, Thomas C., 'How Carnivore Works', *The Register*, 19 December 2000, www.theregister.co.uk/content/archive/15591.html

Greene, Thomas C., 'Mideast "Cyberwar" Veteran Indicted', *The Register*, 1 November 2001, www.theregister.co.uk

Greene, Thomas C., 'Do-it-Yourself Internet Anonymity', *The Register*, 14 November 2001, www.theregister.co.uk/content/6/22831.html

Hassan, Javid, 'Most Islamic Websites are in Arabic: Survey', *Arab News*, http://arabnews.com/Article.asp?ID=20030

Hezb-e-Mughalstan, 'Join the Cyber-Army of Mughalstan', www.dalitstan.org/mughalstan/azad/joincybr.html

Hezb-e-Mughalstan, www.dalitstan.org/mughalstan/laden/targetin.html, reproducing *India Today*, 'Now We Should Target India', 4 October 1999

Hockstader, Lee, 'Pings and E-Arrows Fly in Mideast Cyber-War', *Washington Post Foreign Service*, 27 October 2000, www.washingonpost.com

Hopper, D. Ian, 'Kashmir-minded Pakistani "Hacktivists" Blitz Web Sites', *CNN*, 8 October 1999, www.cnn.com/TECH/computing/9910/08/pakistani.hack/

Human Rights Watch, 'The Internet in the Mideast and North Africa', 1999, www.hrw.org/advocacy/Internet/mena/

Hussain, Khalid, 'Inside Track on Pak Hackers', *Times Computing Online*, 16 May 2001, www.timescomputing.com/20010516/nws1.html

iDefense, *Israeli-Palestine Cyber Conflict*, Version 2.0PR, 3 January 2001, www.idefense.com/pages/ialertexcl/MidEast_010501.htm

Imam Khoei Islamic Centre, 'Fatwa, Taqlid', www.alkhoei.org.uk/fatawa/1taghleed.htm

'Internet in the Arab World', summarised in *Policywatch*, 356, Washington Institute for Near East Policy, 11 December 1998, www.washingtoninstitute.org/watch/Policywatch/policywatch1998/356.htm

Islahul Muslimeen of North America, 'Mission Statement of Islahul Muslimeen', http://chishti.net/mission_statement.htm

Islahul Muslimeen of North America, 'The Spiritual Foundation of IMNA', http://chishti.net/chishti_lineage.htm

Al-Islam, 'Contemporary Legal Rulings in Shi'i Law in Accordance with the Rulings (Fatawa) of Ayatullah al-'Uzma al-Sayyid 'Ali al-Husayni al-Seestani', translated by Hamid Mavani, 1996, Ahlul Bayt (a) Digital Islamic Library Project, www.al-islam.org/laws/contemporary

Al-Islam, Imam Mohamad Jawad Chirri, 'Inquiries about Islam', www.al-islam.org/inquiries/index.html

Islam for Today, 'Muslims against Terrorism', 25 October 2001, www.islamfortoday.com/terrorism.htm

Islam for Today, 'The Taliban of Afghanistan', 2001, www.islamfortoday.com/taliban.htm

Islam Liberal Indonesia, 'Yusuf Qardhawi, Guru Umat Pada Zamannya', 9 July 2002, http://islamlib.com/TOKOH/qardhawi.html

Islam Online, 'U.S. Muslim Scholars Condemn Attacks', 12 September 2001, www.islam-online.net/English/News/2001–09/13/article1.shtml

Islamic Research, 'Anniversary of Imam Khomani', www.islamicresearch.org/anniversary_of_imam_khomani_r.htm

Islamic Research, Council of Shia Ulama (Scholars), www.islamicresearch.org/Pages/UlamaCouncil.htm

Jamaat-e-Islami Pakistan, 'Qazi Condemns US Attacks', 14 September 2001, www.jamaat.org/news

Jamiat USA, 'History of Jamiat USA', http://jamiatusa.org/historyjusa.html

Jawadi, Allama Zeeshan Haider, 'Collection of Fiqh Lectures on Different Topics Recited in 1995', www.azadari.com/jawadi/zhjfiqh.htm?

Jeewan, Mulla, Dharb-i-Mumin, 'Remembering the Past, A Befitting Reply!', http://abuusman03.tripod.com/abu1.htm

Jenkins, Michael L., 'Hacktivism: Compromise Techniques Used by GFORCE-Pakistan', 24 October 2000, SANS Institute, http://rr.sans.org/infowar/hacktivism2.php

Jihad Unspun, 'Al-Zawahiri on the Invasion of Iraq', www.jihadunspun. net/BinLadensNetwork/statements/azotioi.cfm, 8 October

Jolish, Barak, Salon.com, 'The Encrypted Jihad', 4 February 2002, www. salon.com/tech/feature/2002/02/04/terror_encryption

Kataeb Ezzeldeen, 'Karim Mohammed Abu-Abyad', www.kataeb-ezzeldeen. com/shohda2/shaheed.asp?ShaheedID=340

Kettman, Steve, '1,001 Arabian Nights of Sex', Wired, 24 April 2001, www.wired.com/news/print/0,1294,43243,00.html

Khamene'i, Ali, 'Practical Laws of Islam' (Ajwibah al-Istifta'at), www. wilayah.net/english/ahkam/index.htm

Khamene'i, Ali, 'Rules of Imitation', www.wilayah.net/english/ahkam/ taqlid.htm

Khurasaan.com, 'A Practical Guide to Dealing with Hassle from British Authorities', www.khurasaan.com/s_content.php?id=2002–03–03–2119

Khurasaan.com, 'Afghan Women Find New Freedom', www.khurasaan.com/ s_content.php?id=2002–03–29–2201

Khurasaan.com, 'Angels Fight along with Mujaahideen in Palestine', www.khurasaan.com/s_content.php?id=2002–04–26–5113

Khurasaan.com, 'Somalia Lions', www.khurasaan.com/s_content.php?id= 2002–02–25–5723

Kirchner, Henner, 'Digital Jihad - Islam im Internet', Quartalszeitschrift der Arbeitsgemeinschaft Kirchlicher Entwicklungsdienst, Vol. 32, No. 4 (1996) 19-22, www.henner-kirchner.de/studies/cybermus.htm

Krebs, Brian, 'Hackers Worldwide Fan Flames in Middle East Conflict', Newsbytes, 25 November 2000, www.newsbytes.com

Lahore Ahmadiyya Movement, 'Fatwas against Individual Leaders', http:// tariq.bitshop.com/misconceptions/fatwas/individual.htm

Laskar Jihad, 'Does Laskar Jihad Fight against Neutral Christians?' 22 March 2001, www.laskarjihad.or.id/english/qa/eqa0103/eqa010322.htm

Lemos, Robert, 'Hackers Split over Vigilante Strikes', ZD Net, 18 September 2001, http://news.zdnet.co.uk

Leyden, John, 'Hackers Lash out at Islamic Usenet Group', The Register, 19 September 2001, www.theregister.co.uk/content/55/21752.html

Leyden, John, 'Hacking Activity Plummets', The Register, 10 January 2002, www.theregister.co.uk/content/55/23628.html

Lohlker, Rüdiger, 'Der Koran im Internet', www.sub.uni-goettingen.de/ ebene_1/orient/koran1.htm#Anmerkung_1a

Lynch, Ian, 'Anti-US Hacker Hits World Trade Portal', VNU Net, 21 September 2001, www.vnunet.com/News/1125576

McDonald, Tim, 'Hackers Mobilize for War against Islamic Web Sites', NewsFactor, 17 September 2001, www.ecommercetimes.com

Al-Madina, Fazail-e-Aamaal, 'Muslim Degeneration and Remedy', www. almadinah.org/FazailAamaal/MuslimDeProcedureForTabligh.htm

Al-Manhaj, Salafi Society of North America, 'Shaikh Muqbil on Yusuf Al-Qaradaawee', Shaikh Muqbil bin Haadee al-Waadi'ee (trans. Abu Maryam), 'Tuhfat-ul-Mujeeb 'an As'ilat-il-Haadir wal-Ghareeb', 89-91, www.al-manhaj. com/Page1.cfm?ArticleID=138

McWilliams, Brian, '"Bin Laden" Worm Targets ICQ, Outlook Users', Newsbytes, 24 October 2001, www.newsbytes.com

McWilliams, Brian, 'Pakistani Group Strikes U.S. Military Web Site', *Newsbytes*, 21 October 2001, www.newsbytes.com/news/01/171341.html

McWilliams, Brian, 'Hacker "Doctor Nuker" Claims FBI Fingered Wrong Person', *Newsbytes*, 31 October 2001, www.newsbytes.com

Mena Report, 'Middle East Tension Fuels Hacker Fury', 3 October 2002, www.menareport.com

mi2g, 'Israel suffers escalating hack attacks', 15 April 2002, www.mi2g.com/cgi/mi2g/press/150402.php

MIRA, 'The American Phenomenon and The Bin Laden Phenomenon', www.miraserve.com/pressrev/ARTICLE1.htm

MSNBC, 'E-mail Ties Richard Reid to Pakistan', 19 January 2002, www.msnbc.com/news

Al-Muhajiroun, 'Fatwa or Divine Decree against General Musharraf-USA', 16 September 2001, www.al-muhajiroun.com

Al-Muhajiroun, 'America under Attack', 20 September 2001, www.al-muhajiroun.com,

Al-Muhajiroun, 'Letter from Bin Laden', 30 March 2002, www.al-muhajiroun.com/lnews/29–03–02.php

Muhammadiya Association, Singapore, 'Guiding Principles of Muhammadiya', www.muhammadiyah.org.sg/organ.htm

Muhammah, Hafiz Abdussalam bin, 'The Excuses and Pretexts against Jihad' www.markazdawa.org/englishweb/islami-articles/200204/excuses.htm,

Mujahideen, 'Encrypted Messages Hidden in Images', www.mujahideen.fsnet.co.uk/hidden-messages.htm

Mujahideen, 'Seven of the WTC Hijackers Found Alive!' www.mujahideen.fsnet.co.uk/wtc/wtc-hijackers.htm

Al-Murabit, Abdalqadir as-Sufi, 'The Kuffar Move to the Endgame', Murabitun of the Americas, April 2002, www.geocities.com/Athens/Delphi/6588/endgame.html

Al-Musawi, Al-Imam 'Abd al-Husayn Sharaf al-Din, 'Questions on Jurisprudence (Masa'il Fiqhiyya)', Liyakatali Takim (trans.), Ontario, Hydery Canada, 1996, www.al-islam.org/masail

National Infrastructure Protection Center, 'Middle East E-mail Flooding and Denial of Service (DoS) Attacks', 26 October 2000, www.nipc.gov/warnings/assessments/2000/00–057.htm

Osama bin Laden, Jihad Unspun, 'The Nineteen Martrys', www.jihadunspun.net/BinLadensNetwork/articles/19martyrs.cfm

Osman, Ahmad, 'Mosque Raps Fateha for "Sign up for Jihad" E-mail', *Straits Times*, http://straitstimes.asia1.com.sg/usattack/story/0,1870,98429–1011823140,00.html

Palestine Information Center, Hamas, 'Qassam communique 270302', 27 March 2002, www.palestine-info.com/hamas/communiques

Paz, Reuven, Qaidat al-Jihad, 7 May 2002, reproduced on Free Republic, www.freerepublic.com/focus/news/763378/posts

Perera, Rick, 'Hacker Cracks Islamist Mailing List', *NetworkWorld Fusion/IDG News Service*, 20 September 2001, www.nwfusion.com

Q Bank, www.al-shia.org/html/eng/books/q&a/fehrest.htm

Qaradawi, Yusuf, Islam Online, 'Why Muslim And Christian Scholars Come Together', www.islamonline.org/English/contemporary/qpolitic-17/qpolitic1.shtml

Qaradawi, Yusuf, Islam Online, Ask the Scholar, Response to question from 'Shoukry, Australia', 'Islamic View on the Latest Attacks on America', 12 September 2001, www.islamonline.net/fatwaapplication/english/display.asp?hFatwaID=49349

Qaradawi, Yusuf, Islam Online, Ask the Scholar, Response to question from 'Zainab, Canada', 'Ulama's Fatwas on American Muslim Participating in US Military Campaign', 16 October 2001, www.islamonline.net/fatwa application/english/display.asp?hFatwaID=52014

Al-Qoosee, Shaikh Usaamah, Concerning Sayyid Qutb, Saalih Al-Munajjid and Al-Maghraawee, 'Questions that were asked to him by SSNA from his visit to the USA on 4/16/01', (16 April 2001), Al-Manhaj (Salafi Society of North America), www.al-manhaj.com/Page1.cfm?ArticleID=66

Rasch, Mark, 'US Assumes Global Cyber-police Authority', *The Register*, 27 November 2001, www.theregister.co.uk/content/6/23036.html

Reuters, 'Man Divorces Wife by Phone Message', 29 June 2001, www.reuters.com

Reuters, 'British Security Chiefs Launch Web Terror Hunt', 25 October 2001, www.reuters.com

Rosser, Nigel, 'British Muslims Training Fighters for "Holy War"', *Evening Standard/This is London*, 21 September 2001, www.thisislondon.co.uk

Ruqaiyah, Abu, 'The Islamic Legitimacy of the "Martyrdom Operations"', Hussein El-Chamy (trans.), *Nida'ul Islam magazine*, Vol. 16, 1996, www.islam.org.au/articles/16/martyrdom.htm

Sahib, Mufti Khubaib, Harkat- ul-Mujahideen, 'Attributes of the Mujahideen: Compliance with the Sunnah', www.ummah.net.pk/harkat/jihad/attribut.htm

Sakina Security Services 'Ultimate Jihad Challenge', 20 September 2001, www.sakinasecurity.com URL deleted

Salaam Central Asia, 'Islam in Kazakhstan', www.ummah.com/salaamcentral asia/islam_in_kazakhstan.htm

Al-Samawi, Muhammad Tijani, 'Shi'a are the Real Ahl Al-Sunnah', Yasin T. al-Jibouri (trans.), New Jersey, Pyam-e-Aman, n.d. www.al-shia.com/html/eng/books/shia-real/index.htm

Schwartz, John, 'Cyberspace Seen as Potential Battleground', *New York Times*, 23 November 2001, www.nytimes.com

Security Watch, 'Political Computer Hacking Increases', 1 November 2002, www.isn.ethz.ch

Shindeldecker, John, Alevilik-Bektasilik Arastirmalari Sitesi, 'Turkish Alevis in the 21st Century', www.alevibektasi.com/xalevis_home.htm

Star (Malaysia)/*Associated Press*, 'Muslim Scholars Debate Legitimacy of Suicide Bombings', 17 September 2001, http://thestar.com.my

Straits Times, 'ISD Finds Videotape Linking S'pore Terror Group to Al-Qaeda', http://straitstimes.asia1.com.sg/usattack/story/0,1870,98907,00.html

Sunaynah, Abu, 'Al-Minbar, Islaam, between the Enemies Plans & the Muslims' Betrayal', Khutbah 2284, www.alminbar.com/khutbaheng/2284.htm

Taipei Times, 'Web Hackers Hit US via Taiwan', 11 January 2002, www.taipeitimes.com/news/2002/01/11/story/0000119478

Taliban OnLine, Osama bin Laden, http://muntaqim.web1000.com/text/taliban/911.htm#Osama

Taliban-News, 'Mujahideen Military Command Council Confirms The Martyrdom of Ibn El-Khattab', 28 April 2002, www.taliban-news.com/article.php?sid=278

Taliban-News, Profile, Ameer Ibn Ul-Khattab, 29 April 2002, www.taliban-news.com/article.php?sid=281

Tan, Amy, 'Singapore Tightens Grip on Vocal Muslim Web Site', *Reuters/Singapore Window*, 25 January 2002, www.singapore-window.org/sw02/020125re.htm

Theological Library, www.al-shia.org/html/eng/index.htm

Trendle, Giles, 'The E-jihad against Western Business', *IT-Director*, 5 April 2002, www.it-director.com/article.php?id=2744

Al-Turabi, Hassan, 'On the Position of Women in Islam and in Islamic Society', www.islamfortoday.com/turabi01.htm

UNESCO Webword News, 'Only 4% of Internet Users in the Arab World are Women', 5 June 2000, www.unesco.org/webworld/news/000605_beijing.shtml

United Nations Development Project, *Making New Technologies Work for Human Development* (New York: United Nations Development Project, 2001), www.undp.org/hdr2001

US Department of Justice, Press Release, 'Computer Hacker Intentionally Damages Protected Computer', 22 October 2001, www.usdoj.gov/criminal/cybercrime/khanindict.htm

US Department of State, 'U.S. Internet Watchdogs Warn of Increased Hacking Activity', 17 September 2001, http://usinfo.state.gov/topical/global/ecom/01091701.htm

Wakin, Daniel J., 'Online in Cairo, with News, Views and "Fatwa Corner"', *New York Times,* 28 October 2002, www.newyorktimes.com

Washington Post, 'Man Hijacks Al-Qaida Website', 20 July 2002, www.washingtonpost.com/wp-dyn/articles/A21548-2002Jul30.html

WatanOnline, 'Wahhabis: The Real Terrorists', http://follower.4t.com/terrorism.html

Weisman, Robyn, 'Teen Hackers Crash Hizbollah ISP', *Newsfactor Network*, 22 January 2001, www.newsfactor.com/perl/story/6880.html

Wheeler, Debbie, 'Islam, Community and the Internet: New Possibilities in the Digital Age', *Journal of Education, Community and Values*, 3, 2002, http://bcis.pacificu.edu/journal/2002/03/islam.php

Windrem, Robert, 'How al-Qaida Keeps in Touch', *MSNBC*, 6 March 2002, www.msnbc.com/news

Wolcott, Peter and Seymour Goodman, 'The Internet in Turkey and Pakistan: A Comparative Analysis' (Center for International Security and Co-operation, Stanford University, 2000) xii, http://mosaic.unomaha.edu/TurkPak_2000.pdf

CD-ROM PUBLICATIONS

Brückner, Matthias, 'Der Mufti im Netz', in *Islam im Internet, Neue Formen der Religion im Cyberspace*, Rüdiger Lohlker (ed.), (Hamburg: Deutsches Orient-Institut, 2000)
Encyclopaedia of Islam CD-ROM Edition 1.0, H.A.R. Gibb et al. (eds.) (Leiden: E.J. Brill, 1999)
Lohlker, Rüdiger (ed.), *Islam im Internet, Neue Formen der Religion im Cyberspace*, (Hamburg: Deutsches Orient-Institut, 2000)

INTERNET SITES

This listing excludes reference to hacked sites or related archives, which are listed only in the Endnotes to individual chapters. Where URLs or pages have been deleted, the general URL is provided when available. All URLs were correct at the time of going to press. Where possible, access to restored pages will be made available on www. virtuallyislamic.com

ABIM Online, Angatan Belia Islam Malaysia, www.abim.org.my
Ahlul Bayt Digital Islamic Library Project, www.al-islam.org
AIPAC, American Israel Public Affairs Committee, www.aipac.org
Alemahr, www.alemahr.com
Alevi.com, www.alevi.com
Alevilik-Bektasilik Arastirmalari Sitesi, www.alevibektasi.com/index1.html
Alexa Internet Archive Wayback Machine, http://web.archive.org
Alforatein, www.geocities.com/alindex_2000/
Ali Montazeri, www.montazeri.com
Alldas.de, http://alldas.de
AlMinbar.com, www.alminbar.com
Allwhois, www.allwhois.com
Al-Bawaba, www.albawaba.com
Al-Qaida Exposed, http://johnathangaltfilmscom.powweb.com/movie.html
American Druze Society, www.druze.com
Arab Information Project, www.georgetown.edu/research/arabtech
Ask-Imam, www.islam.tc/ask-imam
As-Sunna Foundation of America, www.sunnah.org
Atlas of Cyberspace, www.cybergeography.org/atlas/surf.html
Attrition.org www.attrition.org/mirror/attrition/
Ayatullah Muhammad Taqi Misbah Yazdi, www.mesbahyazdi.com
Azadari.com, www.azadari.com
Azzam, www.azzam.com
Belfast Mosque and BIC News, www.ummah.net/bicnews
Betterwhois, www.betterwhois.com
Cryptome, http://cryptome.org
'Cyberfatwa: Index zu Fatwas und Muftis im Internet', www.cyberfatwa.de
Darul Uloom, http://darululoom-deoband.com
Deoband Online, www.deobandonline.com
Dharb-i-Mumin, www.dharb-i-mumin.cjb.net

Digital Preservation Coalition, www.dpconline.org
DMOZ Open Directory Project, http://dmoz.org/Computers/Hacking/desc.html
Druze.net, www.druzenet.org/druzenet/dnenglish.html
E-Jihad.net, www.islamicdigest.net/ej
Fateha.com, www.fateha.com
Fatwa-Online, www.fatwa-online.com, www.e-fatwa.com
Fiqh Council of North America, About Us, www.fiqhcouncil.org
Front Islamique du Salut - Conseil de Coordination, www.ccfis.org
Gebal, http://gebal.virtualave.net/
Al-Ghazali's Website, www.muslimphilosophy.com/gz
Hackerthreads, www.hackerthreads.org
Hamas, http://www.palestine-info.co.uk/hamas/
Haq Chaar Yar, www.kr-hcy.com/
Harkat-ul-Mujahideen, www.ummah.net.pk/harkat
Hazrat Khwaja Moinudin Hasan Chishty, www.gharibnawaz.com
Hezb-e-Mughalstan, www.dalitstan.org/mughalstan/
Hidayatullah.com, www.hidayatullah.com/info/link.htm
Hizbullah, www.hizbullah.org
Al-Huda, www.alhudapk.com
Incidents.org, www.incidents.org
Intifadat El-Aqsa, www.islamiccenterforstudies.org
Internet Haganah, http://haganah.org.il
International Policy Institute for Counter-Terrorism, www.ict.org.il,
Al-Islam, www.al-islam.org
IslamBosna, www.islambosna.com
Islamski Internet Portal, http://islam.dzemat.org
Islam Liberal Indonesia, http://islamlib.com
Islam Q&A, www.islam-qa.com
Islamic Foundation, www.islamic-foundation.org.uk
Islamic Observation Committee, www.ummah.net.pk/ioc/egindex.htm
Islam-Online, www.islam-online.net
Islamic Philosophy Online, www.muslimphilosophy.com
Islamic Studies Pathways, www.lamp.ac.uk/cis/pathways
Ismaili Web, www.amaana.org/ismaili.html
ISNA Library of Knowledge, www.isna.net/Library/
JAKIM, 'E-Fatwa', http://ii.islam.gov.my/e-fatwa/
Jamiatul Ulama, www.jamiat.org.za/isinfo/isl-fatwa.html
Al-Jazeera, www.aljazeera.com
Jehad.net, www.jehad.net/
Jewish Internet Association, www.jewishinternetassociation.org
Jihaad ul-Kuffaari wal-Munaafiqeen, http://jihaadulkuffaarin.jeeran.com/
Jihad Online, www.jihad-online.net
Jihad Unspun, www.jihadunspun.net
Jihad WebRing, http://i.webring.com/webring?ring=jihadring;list
Kalimat, http://kalimat.org
Kataeb Ezzeldeen, www.kataebq.com
Kavkaz, www.kavkaz.org
KhanQah Imdadiya Ashrafiya, www.khanqah.org

Al-Khoei, www.al-khoei.org
Khurasaan.com, www.khurasaan.com
Lahore Ahmadiyya Movement, www.muslim.org
Lahori Ahmadi View, http://tariq.bitshop.com/mga/
Laksar Jihad, www.laskarjihad.or.id
Last Flight to Paradise or Hell/Haus des Islam, www.haus-des-islam.de
Al-Madina, www.almadinah.org
Al-Madina, www.al-madina.s5.com
Madrasah In'amiyyah, www.alinaam.org.za
Matrix, http://tracemap.mids.org/test/tracemap
Majelis Ulama Indonesia, www.mui.or.id/index_i.htm
Majlis Ugama Islam Singapura-Islamic Religious Council of Singapore (MUIS),
    www.muis.gov.sg
mi2g, www.mi2g.com
Middle East Media Research Institute (MEMRI), www.memri.org
Moreover, www.moreover.com
Movement for Islamic Reform in Arabia, www.miraserve.com
Al-Muhajiroun, www.al-muhajiroun.com
Muhammad al-Durrah, www.al-sham.net/al_quds.html
Muhammadiyah Online, www.muhammadiyah-online.or.id/
Mumineen.org, DBNet Matrimonials, http://matrimonial.mumineen.org
Muslim Council of Britain, www.mcb.org.uk
Muslim Hackers Club, www.ummah.net/mhc
Muslims against Terrorism, www.islamfortoday.com/terrorism.htm
MyQuran.com, www.myquran.com
Naqshbandi Sufi Way, www.naqshbandi.org
Nation of Islam, www.noi.org
Al-Neda, www.alneda.com
Neda al-Quds, www.qudsway.com
Netakeoff, www.netakeoff.com
NetVision, http://wwwnew.netvision.net.il/cyber/english
News Now, www.newsnow.co.uk
OBM Network, www.obm.clara.net
Pakistan Link, www.pakistanlink.com
Palestine Information Center, www.palestine-info.com
Pejabat Mufti Negeri Kedah Darul Aman, SIFAT, Sistem Maklumat Fatwa,
    http://mufti.islam.gov.my/kedah/
Qadiri Rifai Order, www.qadiri-rifai.org
Qaradawi.net, www.qaradawi.net
The Register, www.theregister.co.uk
Rijaset, www.rijaset.net/rijaset/alimi.htm
Salaam Kyrgyzstan, www.ummah.com/salaamkyrgyzstan
Sam Spade, www.samspade.org
Samidoon, www.samidoon.com
SANS Institute, www.sans.org
Shiachat, www.shiachat.com
Shi'a Islamic Laws, www.follower.4t.com/laws.html
Shyfile, www.shyfile.net
Simoky Fed, www.simokyfed.com

Sipah-e-Sahaba, www.farooqi.com/ssp/
Supporters of Shariah (SOS), http:// www.shareeah.com
Taliyah al-Mahdi, www.taliyah.org
Tariqat-ul-Muridiyya, http://freespace.virgin.net/ismael.essop/index.htm
Theological Library, www.al-shia.org/html/eng/index.htm
Transnational Sufism http://artsWeb.bham.ac.uk/mdraper/transnatsufi/
    projectdesc.htm
TROID, www.troid.org
UK Islamic Mission, www.ukim.org
UXN, http://combat.uxn.com
Whois, www.whois.org
Wired, www.wired.com
Virtually Islamic, www.virtuallyislamic.com
Zahuri Sufi Web Site, www.zahuri1.dircon.co.uk

Glossary of Islamic Terminology

For the purposes of this glossary, basic transliteration is provided of key terms referred to in this book. (See Transliteration section in Introduction.)

adhan	call to prayer
'ayah	verse from the Qur'an, 'sign', pl. *'ayat*. cf. *sura*
ayatullah	literally the 'sign of God', within Shi'a Islam (q.v.) this can denote the rank of a highly qualified interpreter of Islamic jurisprudence
'alim	a scholar, pl. *'ulama'*
Allah	God
al-arkan (al-Islam)	pillars or foundations (of Islam) [marked* in this Glossary]
al-Azhar	university located in Cairo
da'wa	the propagation of Islam
din	'religion'
Eid al-Fitr, 'Id al-Fitr	the concluding feast of *Ramadan* (q.v.)
fatwa	the opinions of specific contemporary imams (q.v.) and *ayatullah* (q.v.), pl. *fatawa*
fiqh, fikh	Islamic 'jurisprudence'
hadith	a traditional saying and/or report of the actions of Muhammad, pl. *ahadith*
hafiz	a title denoting one who had learnt the Qur'an by heart
hajj	the major pilgrimage to Mecca*
halal	a term applied to denote that which is considered appropriate or permitted within the bounds of Islam
hizb Allah	'Party of God', also transliterated as *Hezbollah* or *Hizbollah*
Ibrahim	Abraham
idda	waiting period
ijtihad	independent judgement based on Islamic sources, a striving for the pragmatic interpretation of Islamic primary sources in the light of contemporary conditions, the term can be synonymous with 'renewal' and 'reform'
al-Ikhwan al-Muslimun	the Muslim Brotherhood, a 'reformist' movement originating in Egypt in 1928, which spread elsewhere in the Muslim world
imam	the term imam [pl. *a'imma*] usually refers to one who leads the prayers, not necessarily 'qualified' in the sense of trained clergy. In Shi'a Islam (q.v.) imam has associations with religious leadership *and* continuity of spiritual authority
Islam	'submission' to God

Ismaili	a form of Shi'a Islam (q.v.), which itself fragmented to forming disparate branches including the *Fatimids*, the *Nizaris*, the *Assassins* and *Bohoras*
istrikhara	seeking guidance from God through prayer
Ithna 'Asharis	the 'Twelvers', a form of Shi'a Islam (q.v.) following a line of twelve imams descended from Muhammad
Jama'at-i-Islami	synonymous with a Pakistani political party, the term is applied elsewhere, and infers a 'congregation', 'collective' or 'party' of Islam
jihad	'striving' to attain an Islamic objective, the term has spiritual and/or militaristic connotations
jihad bil-sayf	*jihad* (q.v.) 'with the sword'
jihadi	an advocate of jihad
Ka'ba	the 'holy house' (in Mecca)
kalam	'theology'
khalifah	caliph, 'vice-regent', 'successor' [to Muhammad (q.v.)]
khutbah	sermon, provided by a *khatib*
Koran	cf. Qur'an
madhhab	a 'school' of Islamic interpretation, such as the broad *Hanafi, Hanbali, Maliki,* and *Shafi'i. Madhahib* [pl.].
mahar	holy month
mahram	group of people who are 'forbidden' for a woman to marry
masjid	mosque, place of prayer
Masjid al-Quds	Mosque of Jerusalem, also known as *Masjid al-Aqsa*
mawlid	birthday of Muhammad *and/or* anniversary of 'saints'
minbar	the mosque equivalent of a 'pulpit'
Muhammad	Muhammad ibn 'Abd Allah, the Prophet of Islam c. 570–632 CE (active c. 610–32)
mujtahad	an 'interpreter' (of Islam, especially Islamic jurisprudence), a practitioner of *ijtihad* (q.v.)
mushaf	the definitive recension of the Qur'an
mutajwid	recitors of the Qur'an
nashids	genre ranging from 'sung' *ahadith* to prayers, and popular 'Islamic' music
qibla	direction of Muslim prayer (towards Mecca)
Qur'an	Revelation received by the Prophet Muhammad, via the Angel Gabriel
Ramadan	month of fasting, and the month in which the Qur'an was revealed, cf. *sawm*
riba	capital interest, usury
sawm	fasting in Ramadan (q.v.)*
salafi	(i) 'pious ancestors', applied in terms of Muhammad's companions and the 'early' Muslim community, representing an exemplum to follow; (ii) used by Muslim 'reformist' movement(s), such as *al-Ikhwan al-Muslimun* (q.v.); (iii) applied by a number of platforms, indicating their intention to 'return' to the principles of Muhammad and his community
salah	prayer*

shahada	the principle of proclaiming a belief in a One God whose Final Prophet is Muhammad*
shahid	a 'witness', frequently used in the sense of a 'martyr'
shaykh	religious leader, leader of a *tariqa* (q.v.)
shari'ah	the body of Islamic law based on the 'source' of the Qur'an (and other Islamic sources); divine 'law', as revealed to Muhammad.
Shi'a	'party' or 'sect', the followers of the line of 'Ali ibn Abu Talib (d. 661)
Sufi	Muslim 'mystic' – the term has broad connotations and definitions, within disparate branches of Sufism [*tasawwuf*]
Sunni	'orthodox' Islam, based on the sunna (q.v.)
sunna	the customary practice of Muhammad, cf. *ahadith*
sura	a chapter within the Qur'an, pl. *suwar*, cf. *ayat*
tafsir	commentary on, or exegesis of, the Qur'an
tariqa	a 'path', generally a term associated with *Sufi* (q.v.) Orders
'ulama'	scholars, cf. *'alim*
ummah	Muslim community
zakah	annual alms taxation*

FURTHER READING ON TERMINOLOGY AND TRANSLITERATION

Arab Gateway, *Romanization of Arabic*, http://www.al-bab.com/arab/language/roman1.htm

The Encyclopedia of Islam: New Edition, H.A.R. Gibb et al. (eds.) (Leiden: E.J. Brill, 1960–)

al-Faruqi, Ismail Raji, *Towards Islamic English* (Virginia: International Institute of Islamic Thought, 1986)

Netton, Ian Richard, *A Popular Dictionary of Islam* (London: Curzon Press, 1991)

Newby, Gordon D., *A Concise Encyclopedia of Islam* (Oxford: Oneworld Publications, 2002)

Robinson, Neal, *Islam, a Concise Introduction* (London: Curzon Press, 1999)

Schimmel, Annemarie, *Deciphering the Signs of God: A Phenomenological Approach to Islam* (Edinburgh: Edinburgh University Press, 1994)

Waines, David, *An Introduction to Islam* (Cambridge: Cambridge University Press, 1995)

Index

11; proxies, 60; security, 16;
spying software, 168; World
Wide Web, 6; *see also*
censorship, computer
hardware; hacking; HushMail;
Internet Service Providers;
Microsoft
Internet Archive Wayback Machine,
18
Internet Haganah (Haganah
b'Internet), 24, 93, *see also*
hacking; Israel
Internet Service Providers (ISPs),
105;
liability, 12; in Muslim contexts,
9
Iran, 9, 47, 78, 184–5, 198, 201
Iran-Iraq war, 35
Iraq, 60, 80, 201;
Iran-Iraq war, 35; Gulf War, 35
Iraq Action Coalition, 120
Iron Guards, 48, 60, *see also* hacking
Islahul Muslimeen of North
America (IMNA), 78
Ismaili, 193, *see also* Shi'a
al-Islam.org, 119
Islam
converts, 170; ethical issues, 152-
3; fundamentalism, 130, 141;
hadith, 210; *hajj*, 1, 143;
innovation, 146; media representation, 15; orientalism, 15;
pillars, 35; prayer, 146, 152,
169, 188; propagation (*da'wa*),
13, 26, 105, 112, 118, 122,
206; reform, 127, 128; religious
authority, 13, 31, 125, 131–2,
172; *shari'ah*, 29, 33, 76, 118,
127, 133, 172, 186-7, 193;
sources, 127, *zakah*, 1. *see also*
Muhammad; Qur'an; sermons;
Shi'a; Sufism; Sunni
IslamBosna.com, 162
Islam-Online, 115, 147–60, 176
Islam for Today, 113–5, 118
Islam Q&A, 136, 138–142, 160
Islamic Assembly of North America,
69
Islamic Association for Palestine, 43

Islamic European Fatwa Council, 46
Islamic Foundation, 114
Islamic Jihad, 99
see also Egyptian Islamic Jihad,
Islamic Jihad Movement in
Palestine
Islamic Jihad Movement in
Palestine, 98
Islamic Kuqiat, 105
Islamic Observation Committee, 81
Islamic Research Association, 192
Islamic Society of North America
(ISNA), 174
Islamicity, 136
Islamic Usenet, 61
Islamski Internet Portal, 162
Islamway, 69
see Islamic Assembly of North
America
Islam Online, 46
Israel, 11, 25, 43, 44, 48, 80,
91–103, 120, 17
.il domain, 54; Israeli Defence
Force, 12, 44, 46; Hebrew, 49;
m0sad, 49; software industry,
56; *see also* e-jihad; inter-fada;
Internet Haganah; Palestine
Israeli International Policy Institute
for Counter Terrorism, 18

Jabatan Kemajuan Islam Malaysia
(JAKIM), 160
Jamaat-e-Islami Pakistan, 115, 120,
177
Jamiat Ulama USA, 78
Jammu, *see* Kashmir
Japanese, 138
Jawadi, Zeeshan Haider, 197
al-Jazeera, 18, 95, 105, 210
Jehad.net, 68, 69
Jemaah Islamiah, 86
Jewish Federation of Southern
Illinois, Southeast Missouri
and Western Kentucky (Simoky
Fed), *see* Internet Haganah
Jewish Internet Association, *see*
Internet Haganah
Jihaad ul-Kuffaari wal-Munaafiqeen,
71